*Nurturing the Peacemakers in
Our Students*

Nurturing the Peacemakers in Our Students

A Guide to Writing and Speaking Out About Issues of War and of Peace

Chris Weber

HEINEMANN
Portsmouth, NH

Heinemann
A division of Reed Elsevier Inc.
361 Hanover Street
Portsmouth, NH 03801–3912
www.heinemann.com

Offices and agents throughout the world

© 2006 by Chris Weber

Library of Congress Cataloging-in-Publication Data
Weber, Chris.
 Nurturing the peacemakers in our students : a guide to writing and speaking out about issues of war and of peace / Chris Weber.
  p. cm.
 Includes bibliographical references.
 ISBN-13: 978-0-325-00749-6
 ISBN-10: 0-325-00749-7 (alk. paper)
 1. Peace—Study and teaching (Secondary)—United States.
2. Toleration—Study and teaching (Secondary)—United States.
3. World citizenship—Study and teaching (Secondary)—United
States. 4. War—Study and teaching (Secondary)—United States.
I. Title.
JZ5534.W43 2006
303.6'6071273—dc22   2006014403

Editor: Danny Miller
Production: Abigail M. Heim
Typesetter: Valerie Levy / Drawing Board Studios
Cover photo: Tearfund / Marcus Perkins. Reprinted with permission.
Cover design: Joni Doherty Design
Manufacturing: Louise Richardson

Printed in the United States of America on acid-free paper

10 09 08 07 06 VP 1 2 3 4 5

A World of Peace for All Children

Imagine all children safe in their
    parents' arms
in a world
where we work together for
peace
for all children.

This road to peace for
all of our children
is worth
every fall,
every step,
every tear,
every smile.

Walk down the road to peace
with your children
one step at a time
and

you are building
miles of serenity
for countless others.

Hug your children
like parents around the world.
Kiss them goodnight
like parents around the world.
Love your children
like parents around the world.

Imagine all children safe in their
    parents' arms
in a world
where we work together for
peace
for all children
around the world.

The Home Team (L to R): Mark, Daddy, and Jackson (photograph by Jeff Lee)

Contents

| PART III | EMPOWERING OUR STUDENTS TO MAKE A DIFFERENCE |

Foreword

One of my strongest childhood memories springs from my tenth birthday, when my mother baked a special cake, complete with candles. I made a wish, took a deep breath, blew out all the candles, and burst into tears.

Of course, my mother was alarmed and upset: "What's the matter?"

"There's no way my wish can come true," I sobbed.

"What is it? I'll do my best," she reassured me.

I kept sobbing, "You can't do a thing!" and after persistent prodding told her my wish had been to end the Korean War.

There was a long silence. Understandably, my mother had no words. Where on earth had this come from? And what was she supposed to do about it? It never occurred to her to turn to the school. School was about nouns agreeing with verbs and about Narcissa Whitman's journey to Oregon, not about a war in a far-off land.

I've often reflected on this incident. My mother's mystification was justified. We had neither relatives nor family friends in the war. Nor was the war a topic of conversation in our house. We had no TV, and although there were news snippets on the radio, we were a family who enjoyed *Fibber McGee & Molly, The Green Hornet, The Shadow, You Bet Your Life, The Sixty-Four Dollar Question.* I was particularly devoted to *The Railroad Hour* with Gordon MacRae, and of course, *Grand Central Station.* Decades later, whenever I'm in New York City, I still walk through the terminal and listen to those mesmerizing words in my mind's ear: *Grand Central Station! Crossroads of a million private lives! Gigantic stage on which are played a thousand dramas daily!*

So where did my very real grief about the war come from? Always a literalist, I link my horror to headlines in the *Sacramento Bee*: A front-page picture of wounded and dead soldiers lying in snow is as clear in my mind as if I'd seen it yesterday. For me, those images were—and are—very real.

I was both a sleepwalker and a sleeptalker, and not long after the birthday incident my sister began complaining about my ongoing conversations with General Douglas MacArthur. My entreaties to the general not to use nuclear force rather spooked her. She would complain at breakfast, "She's talking to MacArthur again."

I tell this story to point out that even children who have no visible connection with war can be traumatized by it. My childhood self and MacArthur discussant are very grateful for Chris Weber's book, which acknowledges children as intellectuals and as caring people capable of deep, unspoken grief. If I could be so affected by a newspaper headline and photograph, what does today's media assault do to children? And where do they go for comfort and explanation?

Some would argue that teachers should not inflict lessons about world problems on helpless students. But maintaining silence about the horrifying and grotesque war images that confront children every day leaves these children emotionally and intellectually naked. Alan Paton wrote, "Cry aloud for the man who is dead, for the woman and children bereaved."

Using both historic and contemporary war images, drawing on the wisdom of both students and experienced teachers, *Nurturing the Peacemakers in Our Students* acknowledges bereavement, offering strategies for helping children speak aloud their connection to the world.

Susan Ohanian

Acknowledgments

Engaging schoolchildren in the world around them and helping raise their awareness of war and peace and associated humanitarian issues offers many academic and moral lessons. The curriculum ideas presented in Nurturing the Peacemakers in Our Students *lend themselves to students translating these lessons into action—for themselves, their families, and their communities. This book offers concrete ways for teachers to push the classroom's boundaries and encourage their students' activism and awareness and ultimately help shape the next generation of global citizens.*
—Stacy Bernard Davis, Outreach and Public-Private Partnership
Officer, Office of Weapons Removal and Abatement, Bureau of
Political-Military Affairs, U.S. Department of State

You are reading *Nurturing the Peacemakers in Our Students* thanks to Danny Miller and Lois Bridges, editors at Heinemann. They believed in this book and convinced Heinemann to publish it. Having such allies inspired me in my journey to write this book, which was a poignant but rewarding one. Throughout, they gave me incredible feedback, assistance, and support. I love you both!

I am very grateful to the Heinemann Editorial Board for publishing this book.

Peter Elbow, Carol Jago, Barry Lane, and Nancy Gorrell reviewed my proposal, and all gave me invaluable suggestions and insights. Dr. Doug Downs, Associate Professor of Composition & Rhetoric at Utah Valley State College, made all of the difference for the Introduction. After struggling with it for a couple of months, his feedback and suggestions inspired me and set me on the right path.

Susan Ohanian's foreword is everything that I could have asked and hoped for. In your brilliant blurbs, Jim Burke, Stacy Bernard Davis, Carol Jago, and Barry Lane, you captured the book's essence.

Jean Daigneau, I ran out of ways to say "thank you." As amazing as your thorough proofreading and feedback was, I was impressed at how quickly you responded to my requests no matter what you were doing. Your careful proofreading made my manuscript more polished for the readers.

Writing a book for Heinemann is a pleasure because of its fantastic staff. Abby Heim, production supervisor; Eric Chalek, copywriter; Roberta Lew, permissions supervisor; and Doria Turner, promotions coordinator, have been wonderful.

Joni Doherty, the cover designer, gave this book a face of hope and a first impression that will deeply touch the readers' hearts and souls. Copyeditor Julia Curry made this book a smooth journey for readers, thanks to her keen eyes.

The front cover photo of the Ugandan refugee boy is reprinted with permission from Tearfund/Marcus Perkins 2004. Tearfund organization strives to relieve suffering and offer hope to the lives of some of the world's poorest people. At www.tearfund.org, you can learn more about how this organization tackles the underlying causes of poverty and helps with disaster relief and local community development. Marcus Perkins is one of Tearfund's longest standing freelance photographers, and his website www.marcusperkins.co.uk/ displays some of his brilliant work.

Considering the times in which we live and the subject of my book, I cannot thank enough my friends Jonathan Steinhoff, Cindy Dulcich, Mar y Sol Rodriguez, and Aurelia Wight. Parents at Atkinson School make my teaching rewarding. Moira Keller, Janet Cowal, Melissa Robinett, and Alice Tang make every day seem like Teacher Appreciation Week. My third and fourth grade students, you are the best! Deborah Peterson, former principal, has been most encouraging of my writing.

A friend of mine told me, "you live to travel." Traveling breathes life into me each summer after a year of teaching. My traveling has been enriched thanks to Mingma Dorji Sherpa, Director of Last Frontiers Trekking (P) Limited and Mike Seymour, Director of Heritage Institute. (Seymour has written *Educating for Humanity*.) Recently, I led a group of teachers to Peru, and what a wonderful experience it was. If you're interested in joining me on a summer adventure, go to www.hol.edu and click on "Study Abroad Classes." You can also e-mail me at chriscarlweber@earthlink.net.

Even though your pieces are not included, Liz Dixon and Elizabeth King, I want to thank you for all of the hours and effort that you put into your writing for me.

Onpavi, I am very fortunate to have a loving and dear wife such as you who understands and supports my writing endeavors. Mark and Jackson, a father couldn't have better sons than you two! Onpavi, Mark, and Jackson, I love you very much.

*Nurturing the Peacemakers in
Our Students*

Introduction

On the Road to Peace

The girl with the pixie haircut said, "I feel is privilege born in Hiroshima. Children here are always doing lesson about peace. When I went first time to Peace Museum, I couldn't believe my eyes because it was very terrible and I cried. So born in Hiroshima very great fortune because it is my wish to spread all over the world what I learn here."

Such idealism, coming from a child in Hiroshima, was chastening. I was still reeling from the selflessness of this response when another girl asked, "Please, Swope-*sensei*. How can we teach children peace?"

Swope-*sensei*! "Respected teacher"! But what could I tell her? I had no answer to this question and I couldn't make one up—not here, not with these kids, not in Hiroshima.

"I'm sorry," I said. "I don't know. Perhaps you can tell me?"

"I think," she said, struggling for the English words, "we can teach children peace by teach them about war." (Swope 2005)

What kind of world do you wish for *all* children and young people?

Have you had feelings about war but felt helpless to do anything about it?

Would you like to teach your students so their voices will be heard regardless of where they stand on war-related issues?

Would you like them to have the chance to listen to and learn from young people who have been in war?

What can you do to bring about change in the world?

Teach.

Children Always Are

When the bombs began falling on Baghdad, I looked at my two young sons and wanted to be able to do something to make this a more peaceful world. I felt helpless. My soul sat on me and demanded, "You write a book." With each passing day and more people dying, my desire grew stronger, and my soul implored me to carry on until the idea became reality. I couldn't bear the thought of reading about Iraqi children being hurt or killed and not doing anything.

I hope that *Nurturing the Peacemakers in Our Students* will rouse teachers and their students. My fervent hope is that you use this book to help inspire and nurture these peacemakers. Students need to learn from young people's experiences in war and become advocates for peace. After reading and discussing firsthand narratives by children who experienced war, students will know and better understand the horrible consequences of war, especially on children and young people. When they learn of other children's suffering, students will want to help. After each narrative, there will be a list of online organizations and projects in which students can participate. Activist peers speak about making a difference in the world. As students help others, they will empower and help themselves. Their cooperative efforts will foster hope, tolerance, and peace.

If knowledge, experience, and wisdom acquired from this book are used to prevent just one baby or child from being killed in future wars, then it will be priceless. Children always are.

Why Include Firsthand Accounts of War by Children in This Book?

Children who have been in war know the terrible consequences of war. Armed conflicts are a global scourge with devastating effects on children. Most wars now are being fought not between states but within them. The estimated numbers of child victims of armed conflicts during the past decade are as follows:

- killed: two million
- disabled: four to five million
- left homeless: twelve million
- orphaned or separated from their families: more than one million
- psychologically traumatized: some ten million. (UNICEF 2003)

Even so, why not write a book with essays by adults, instead? Because their work is infused with their agendas and biases, whereas young people just want to tell their story and share their thoughts and feelings about what they have gone through. Only children in war can tell other young people about war. Students will trust their peers' versions of what happened to them. They will more likely believe, listen more attentively to, better understand, and empathize with young authors who have suffered the ravages of war.

Student Writing

The selection process for the student writings consumed tissue boxes of tears. The young authors prove firsthand that war is not a glamorous, "shock and awe" video game. I chose pieces that rang true with the voices of young people but did not stun you with excessive graphic violence and the pain and suffering they endured. Unselected pieces were just too close to the pain—too unbearable for teachers and their students. When I chose them, I wanted pieces that would both touch and move students to action on whatever issues need change. The activism section, which blossomed late, bursts forth with students who are finding their voices and striving to make a difference in the world. As students learn about and discuss what others are doing to make a difference, they will silently say, "If those students can, we can, too."

Using the Book

Nurturing the Peacemakers in Our Students is organized into three sections. In the first section, teachers are provided with lessons that focus on leading class discussions along with ways in which students might respond in writing to the war-related topics addressed in the book. Following the first five chapters are those that deal directly with topics reflecting the ways in which children are affected by war: landmines and becoming refugees or child soldiers. Firsthand accounts by young people are the centerpieces of these chapters. Their voices are rarely, if ever, heard on U.S. media, and our young people need to have the opportunity to listen to them and learn about and consider their viewpoints. Author Barry Lane wrote that *Nurturing the Peacemakers in Our Students* is about the "losers," those innocent victims of war whose faces we do not see. This book will put a face on them and their stories.

The rest of the book deals primarily with ways in which students can respond to war-related topics, such as becoming media literate, speaking out, becoming peace activists, and so on. These topics are not the focus of most middle and high school social studies, language arts, or English curriculums, so they provide students with an opportunity to explore, and more importantly, incorporate activism into their daily lives.

Learning becomes more meaningful when students can experience it. In almost every chapter, I include an array of ongoing projects in which students can participate to make a difference in the world. Those projects are sponsored by well-known nongovernmental organizations, which often have links to other related organizations and their projects. For example, if you want more web links about nuclear weapons, the Nuclear Peace Age Foundation at www.wagingpeace.org has an excellent links page.

Where do you start? Follow your heart and begin with the chapter(s) of most interest and importance to you. That said, I would encourage you to consider involving your class in some of the first five chapters so they will gain skills needed for the rest of the book.

This book is not designed to be followed page-by-page or chapter-by-chapter, or completed within a year. The lessons provide general guidelines but no hard time lines because of the nature of the subjects and students. Once they begin, you do not know how much or little time your students will want to invest in any given topic. Adjust to the momentum in your class and explore any one topic as long or as little as students desire.

The life-and-death nature of the book's issues will probably weigh heavily on the hearts and minds of students. Those chapters containing heartrending accounts by children who suffered in war will surely affect your students. For that reason alone, I suggest that during a school year, you engage students in just one or two of these chapters: child soldiers, refugees, landmines, or war-related trauma. The subject matter in the other chapters might not be quite as heavy, and students could experience as many chapters as time and interest allow.

Background Material

In some of the chapters, I provide background material that precedes the students' firsthand accounts, relevant lessons, and activities. This is to provide teachers with an overview of the subject matter. You can use this information as you teach the lessons and lead activities. There are two reasons why this background material is intended *primarily* for teachers: it might contain information that is too intense for young people to handle, and it is best if students are invited to explore each issue themselves.

Your Role

You may have very strong viewpoints about the issues I've presented. The question is: What role should the teacher take? Do you state your position on the matter or stay as neutral as possible? It is hard *not* to give your opinion on a topic of discussion. I tell my class that they probably will feel more comfortable exploring the issues if I do not weigh in with my personal thoughts. If students press me, I tell them what I think but always let them know this is just my opinion and that everyone's opinions are equally valued, regardless of where they stand. I quickly slip back into my role as discussion facilitator and stay there during the course of examining an issue. However, what I do might not work for you or your students.

They Are Here Among Us

This book has everything to do with students at your school. You do not have to visit a war-torn country to meet traumatized children because they are among us, and as teachers and counselors, we can help them. In the United States, violence has affected more children than ever; a large number of them may be traumatized through witnessing violence. Refugee children here have frequently witnessed or experienced violence (Kinzie et al. 1991; Mollica et al. 1997) and studies have shown that refugees exhibit high rates of post-traumatic stress disorder symptoms (Sack et al. 1999).

An increasing body of anecdotal and survey evidence has documented a high degree of chronic exposure to violence among children and youths residing in areas of concentrated urban poverty (Greene 1996). Based on an international comparison of homicide rates for young males, the United States is the most violent country in the industrialized world (Richters & Martinez 1993). Homicide is the second leading cause of death among young people ages 15–24. Sheley and Wright (1993) found that forty-five percent of inner-city high school students had been threatened with a gun or shot at and that one in three had been beaten up on their way to school. In a 1995 survey of St. Louis teenagers (ages 14–17), seventy-five percent had heard or seen a shooting, fifty percent had seen a killing or serious beating, fifty percent reported that murders occur in their neighborhood, thirty-nine percent had had a friend beaten or killed, and twenty-five percent reported that teachers at their school had been injured by students (Everding 1995). Everding reports that "only 8 percent reported no exposure to violence." Direct and indirect child victims of inner-city violence are affected by isolated episodes of violence, and often they exhibit symptoms of post-traumatic stress disorder (Marans & Cohen 1993).

Parts of this book can help us and our students better understand each other and how we can also begin resolving conflict in our everyday lives, at home, and at school.

The Struggle of Memory Against Forgetting

After the fall of Baghdad in 2003, newspaper articles and TV discussions focused on possible military scenarios in North Korea and Syria to the extent that the unthinkable was being normalized. In 2006, the media reported military scenarios against Iran. John Pilger believed that the underlying reason for government normalizing war was ". . . the conquest of us all: of our minds, our humanity and our self-respect at the very least. If we say and do nothing, victory over us is assured."

If, as Milan Kundera wrote, "the struggle of people against power is the struggle of memory against forgetting," then we must not forget (Pilger 2003). If we forget the pain and misery that warring governments bring upon innocent civilians, we will be responsible for more suffering of innocents in other lands in future wars. Use this book so that your students and you will remember, because governments and their military leaderships want us to forget. If we remember, reflect upon our country's mistakes, and then speak out, we might be better able to take a stand for peace.

Chris Weber

If we are to reach real peace in this world . . . we shall have to begin with the children.
—Mohandas Gandhi, Indian nonviolent civil rights leader
(1869–1948)

1

The Art of Discussing Issues of War and of Peace with Students

Discussing Difficult, Crucial Issues

How do you talk about war when it's hard enough just to think about it? Young people may feel afraid, anxious, and/or threatened, or sense the anxiety in adults around them. Yet it's imperative that students have opportunities to learn, think, and discuss war-related issues and peace. What a wonderful opportunity to offer information and viewpoints about crucial issues (e.g., terrorism, school violence, and so on) so students can discuss and make up their own minds.

Leading discussions with middle and high school students requires skill, to avoid hurt or angry feelings. Well-led discussions are ones in which students are engaged, sharing, and listening to each others' opinions and ideas. War-related issues evoke strong feelings, and we need to learn to accept others' strong emotions, too. Teachers need to encourage students to speak their minds, even if they stand alone. With skill and practice, students will develop the art of civil discourse, and their knowledge of complex, difficult matters will flourish. Students will feel relieved to be able to discuss their thoughts openly.

During war and conflict we all feel powerless, especially young people. "Why are we fighting?" "Will I die or be hurt?" "When will it end?" "What can I do?" By leading discussions and having students read and write about these issues, you will empower them. They will seek answers and increase their understanding. Communications skills will be enhanced as they grow to appreciate divergent thinking and perspectives, as well as to articulate their own positions.

Some Discussion Goals

- Give students a safe place to share and work through difficult, complex issues with one another.
- Help students develop their thinking, listening, and empathy skills.
- Help students be open to and appreciate the power of divergent thinking, feeling, and viewpoints and how much they can learn from others.
- Encourage students to express opinions, even if they are alone.
- Encourage each and every one of them to participate actively in the discussions.
- Help them to learn and develop the art of civil discourse.
- Teach them to participate in nonadversarial dialogues, not debates. Listening to others, learning from them, and understanding the issues more deeply are the goals for any dialogues. Involve your students in dialogue where the topics are explored to reach a clearer and deeper understanding of the issue.

Firm Guidelines

To accomplish those goals, involve your students in developing and setting up firm guidelines for discussion. Your list might contain the following:

- Listen to each other and let the speaker finish.
- Respect others and their views.
- Avoid inflammatory language like put-downs, criticisms, or sarcasm.
- Talk. Do not shout.
- Encourage and allow other people to speak, one at a time.
- If you disagree with someone, speak to ideas and opinions, not the speaker. Don't personalize.
- Encourage as many to speak as possible but allow others just to listen.
- Invite expression of personal feelings and stories.
- Limit the time any student speaks to discourage "speeches." This enables more participation by all students.

In addition, the Constitutional Rights Foundation (2003) has other ground rules in advance of discussing controversial ideas. Students should:

- Represent the opposing positions fairly and accurately.
- Demonstrate an attempt to understand all opposing perspectives.

- Admit doubts and weaknesses in their own position.
- Concentrate on evidence in their arguments.

Useful Language Expressions

Prior to their first discussion, review expressions that may be helpful. Write down the categories below on a blackboard or chartpak and ask students to give appropriate expressions. Your list might include:

Expressing an Opinion or Feeling and Giving Reasons

"In my opinion . . ."
"I feel . . . " "I think . . ." "I believe . . ."

Agreeing

"Yes, I think you're right."
"That's a good point."
"I agree."
"Sure."

Disagreeing

(These forms affirm other viewpoints without making students feel they are wrong.)
"I see things differently."
"I feel differently about it."
"I don't think so."

Showing the Speaker You Are Listening

"Uh-huh."
"I see."
"Okay."

Checking for Understanding

"I don't understand."
"Could you say that in another way?"
"What did you mean?"
"Could you explain that?"

Inviting Others into the Discussion

"What do you have to say about that?"
"What's your opinion?"
"What do you think about this?"

Active Listening

Attentive listening and understanding what someone else is saying is vital for effective communication, especially concerning controversial issues. Remind students they can learn from each other and that different viewpoints will enrich the discussion. Encourage them to see people with different opinions as contributing rather than attacking.

The best way to teach listening is to model it. Smile. Use good posture, head nods, facial expressions. While you want to maintain eye contact with the speaker, *don't expect or demand that* of students from other cultures. In some Asian cultures, children are taught that to look down or away when talking to adults is being respectful. Show them you're listening through verbal cues, too. Model how you want students to listen to you by listening to them.

Validate Their Feelings

"I can sense how anxious you are about the increasing tensions between these countries."
"I hear your concern for refugee children."

Acknowledge and Accept Their Feelings

(While we might not understand why a person feels a certain way, it's important to respect his or her right to feel that way.)

"You're afraid that the Iraqi weapons of mass destruction might be in terrorists' hands."
"You're worried that more American soldiers and Iraqi civilians will continue to die during the occupation."
"You're concerned about the government's desires to build new nuclear weapons."

Maintaining high levels of active listening reduces tension and conflict.

Stella Ting-Toomey (1994) describes one of the highest levels of active listening:

> Practice attentive listening skills and feel the copresence of the other person. In Chinese characters, *hearing* or *wun* means "opening the

door to the ears," while the word *listening* or *ting* means attending to the other person with your "ears, eyes, and heart." Listening means, in the Chinese character, attending to the sounds, movements, and feelings of the other person. Patient and deliberate listening indicates that one person is attending to the other person's needs even if it is an antagonistic conflict situation.

Take a Breath

Before beginning a difficult discussion, take a deep breath. Gather your thoughts, calm yourself, and set the tone for the discussion.

Start off by acknowledging how many different feelings and opinions there are about this issue. Create and set up the framework for each discussion through open-ended, nonconfrontational questions. For each narrative in this book, a set of "Questions to Open Discussions" immediately follows. Feel free to use your own questions instead.

Briefly remind students to stick by the rules. You might even have them displayed so they can be referred to.

There might be times within the discussion when it gets quiet. Don't rush to break the silence. Relish these moments when everyone has time to reflect.

Students with Special Histories

If you're using this book in wartime, a few of your students might have friends or relatives, or might themselves once have been, involved in war (as soldiers, civilians, refugees, and so on) and might be too emotional about an issue to participate in some of the discussions. If you have such students, talk to them beforehand and forewarn them. Give them the choice to be present or not. Since their peers can learn much from them, invite these students to speak to the class about their experiences.

Ways to Encourage Participation

- Give students a chance to talk in discussion pairs or small groups of four to six students.
- Let them write down their thoughts before meeting as a class.
- Have students speak in "rounds" where students speak without interruption. Students can pass if they want. Afterwards the students can respond in a general discussion. (Center for Research on Learning and Teaching 2003)

War in Iraq: Response to War—How Do You Feel? What Do You Think?

("War in Iraq: Response to War," an activity for war and other controversial issues, is reprinted with permission from Constitutional Rights Foundation, Los Angeles, CA, www.crf-usa.org.)

This activity, created by the Constitutional Rights Foundation for use during the Iraq war, gives students the opportunity to express their feelings about the war and discuss their thoughts and perceptions. This activity can easily be adapted for any controversial issue at any time.

Step 1: One-Word Brainstorm—How Do You Feel?

Ask students to take a minute or two to think about one word that best describes their feelings about the issue they're about to discuss. Record all responses on the board. Review the list and point out how strongly many people feel.

If possible, group the various responses under headings such as pride, hope, fear, anger, confusion, or sadness. Point out that many people are feeling the same thing and that people around the world share similar feelings about these issues.

Step 2: Small-Group Work—What Do You Think?

Tell the students that you are interested in what they think and they will have an opportunity to use more than one word to express their views. Divide the class into pairs or triads and distribute the handout, "How Do You Feel? What Do You Think?" (See Step 3.) Each group should discuss the questions and select a person to record their responses.

Remind the class that these are emotional issues. Not everyone needs to agree on the answers to the questions, but they should listen to and discuss their views with each other respectfully.

Step 3: Sharing Perceptions

Conduct a class discussion using the questions below. Allow each group to share its responses. Bring closure to the discussion by explaining that as new developments happen, students may change their views about things, and that you will continue to be interested in their thoughts.

Response to War

[Use these questions for handouts, but adjust spacing as needed.]
    In your opinion . . .

- What are the most important questions Americans should be asking?
- What are the most important things people should be doing?

    American citizens:

- What do you think are the biggest challenges before us?
- What do you hope will happen? Why? What should Americans, including you, do to help bring about change?

Ways to Facilitate Meaningful Discussions

- Use graphic organizers (e.g., KWL charts, Venn diagrams, process charts, time lines) on a chartpak or blackboard to help students organize and visualize the process.
- Engage many students.
- Have students role-play.
- Involve them in simulations.
- Ask your students questions from various perspectives.
- Continually cultivate an atmosphere where opinions are freely voiced and diversity is welcomed.
- Consider viewpoints of people on various sides of the conflict around the world (by researching websites and gathering information to bring to the discussions).
- Stop any oppressive behavior immediately. Challenge expressions of stereotyping and scapegoating. Guard your students against jumping to conclusions about any group of people or generalizing.

When Discussions Boil Over

When volatile issues are discussed, strong emotions might heat up the discussions. Be prepared if the discussion explodes in shouts or stops in uncomfortable silence. Consider questions such as: "What is the basis for contention?" "Why is this so difficult to talk about?" "What is most uncomfortable at this point?"

Teachers can reduce tension by letting students know there are no right or wrong statements or opinions. Inform them that there is no best solution to the subject at hand.

- Tactfully and calmly get to the heart of the matter and determine the issues being disputed.
- If possible, encourage students involved to help each other save face.
- Have students take turns. Use deliberate pauses between statements. Slow down the process.
- Reinforce paraphrasing, especially when discussions heat up. Through paraphrasing, students find they are a lot closer than they think on the issues.
- Think of some questions ahead of time to defuse an eruption or break down prolonged periods of silence, where students are obviously hesitant to speak.
- Allow everyone to take a time-out and cool off. The length of time depends on the situation. During the time-out, you might ask students to write about what went well with the discussion and advice for the next discussion.
- Summarize and discuss common ground. On a chalkboard or chartpak, write down responses to areas of agreement and disagreement. Summarize the session so far. Point out areas of agreement; clarify areas of disagreement.
- "Students should look for a chance to air their own views, hear their opponents' views, and examine both. Be sure students understand that closure of a controversy does not mean one side wins" (Constitutional Rights Foundation 2003). This is not a contest or debate.

Teacher's Role as Tightrope Walker

Leading classroom discussions requires skill and restraint. Ultimately, you want students to arrive at a decision based on evidence that's supportable and reflects their values. Your primary role is to foster and guide productive discussions. Here are some tips that might help.

- Remain calm.
- Listen, listen, listen.
- Be honest. Students read us much better than we want to admit and observe us more closely than we can imagine.

- Request that students support their opinions with facts and logical arguments. You might include a mini-lesson on fact and opinion.
- Say less, not more.
- Start with nonconfrontational, open-ended questions, not lectures.
- Tactfully correct any misinformation.
- Use your judgment in determining what you say.
- Help students to understand questions or concepts either in the discussion or later through research.

Conversations Outside of the Classroom

Project 540, http://www.project540.org/main.cfm, gives students nationwide the opportunity to talk about issues that matter to them and to turn these conversations into real school and community change.

Building Knowledge for Discussion (Optional Activity)

Before discussing the narratives and articles in this book, students can first research the theme of a given chapter. Instruct them to write down viewpoints, facts, and opinions, and then bring this information to the discussions. Invite questions and curiosity. Some websites listed might be places for students to begin gathering information. Or they can always use search engines like Google to find relevant websites. The more they inform themselves, the more comfortable they might feel during the discussions.

Rewarding Journeys

What a priceless gift you give them. These intense discussions might be among the most rewarding and important talks your students have. The issues will be tough, but these are life's real issues. Connect with them every breath of the way. More than techniques, your caring about them matters most, and as they explore controversial issues, gives them hope.

2

The Believing Game

From Opposition to Understanding

The Iraq War. Torture. Terrorism. Every one of us holds an opinion on each issue, but unfortunately, many of us, including myself, sometimes find it difficult to understand a person's belief in an opposing position. However, we could benefit by participating in the believing game more often. In the following essay, Peter Elbow discusses the believing game, which helps you understand someone else's opposing ideas. Moreover, both parties' positions might lead to a more valuable common ground. Picture what our world would be if world leaders played the believing game. Imagine what your home would be like if your family members took part.

THE BELIEVING GAME AND HOW TO MAKE CONFLICTING OPINIONS MORE FRUITFUL

PETER ELBOW

In the chapter before this, Chris Weber suggests ways to help students speak their minds, listen well, and engage in nonadversarial dialogue rather than debate. His suggestions focus on outward behavior. In this essay, I will move inward to the mysterious dimension of thinking and feeling.

Imagine you are looking at one of those inkblot shapes. (For examples of inkblots, ask Google Images for one.) Imagine that you perceive something in it that interests and pleases you—but your colleagues or classmates don't see what you see. In fact they think you are crazy or disturbed for seeing it. What would you do if you wanted to convince them that your interpretation makes sense?

If it were a matter of geometry, you could *prove* you are right (or wrong!). But with inkblots, you don't have logic's leverage. Your only hope is to get them to *enter into your way of seeing*—to have the experience you are having. You need to get them to say the magic words: "Oh *now* I see what you see."

16

This means getting them to exercise the *ability* to see something differently (i.e., seeing the same thing in multiple ways), and also the *willingness* to risk doing so (not knowing where it will lead). In short, you need them to be flexible both cognitively and emotionally. You can't make people enter into a new way of seeing, even if they are capable of it.

From Inkblots to Arguments

Interpreting inkblots is highly subjective, but the process serves to highlight how arguments also have a subjective dimension. Few arguments are settled by logic. Should we invade countries that might attack us? Should we torture prisoners who might know what we need to know? And by the way, what grade is fair for this paper or this student? Should we use grades at all?

I'm not denying the force of logic. Logic can uncover a genuine error in someone's argument. But logic cannot uncover an error in someone's *position*. If we could have proven that Iraq had no weapons of mass destruction, that wouldn't have proven that it was wrong to invade Iraq. "We should invade Iraq" is a claim that is impossible to prove or disprove. We can use logic to strengthen arguments for or against the claim, but we cannot prove or disprove it. Over and over we see illogical arguments for good ideas and logical arguments for bad ideas. No wonder people so seldom change their minds when someone finds bad reasoning in their argument.

This explains a lot about how most people deal with differences of opinion.

- Some people love to argue and disagree, and they do it for fun in a friendly way. They enjoy the disagreement and let criticisms roll right off their backs—even attacks.

- Some people *look* like they enjoy argument. They stay friendly and rational because they've been trained well. But inside they feel hurt when others attack ideas they care about. They hunker down into their ideas behind hidden walls.

- Some people actually get mad, raise their voices, stop listening, and even call each other names. Perhaps they realize that language and logic have no power to *make* their listeners change their minds—so they give in to shouting or anger.

- And some people—seeing that nothing can be proven with words—just give up on argument. They retreat. "Let's just not argue. You see it your way, I'll see it my way. There's no use talking." They sidestep arguments and take a relativist position: any opinion is as good as any other opinion.

But *sometimes,* through listening to someone else's views, people do something amazing: they actually change their thinking. When this happens people demonstrate the two inkblot skills I just described: the ability and the willingness to see something differently—or in this case to *think* or *understand* something differently. These are precious skills, cognitive and psychological. We won't have much luck encouraging them in other people unless we develop them in ourselves.

With inkblots, the risk seems small. If we manage to see a blot the way a classmate or colleague sees it, we don't have to say, "Stupid me. I was wrong." With arguments, however, it feels like win or lose. We often want people not just to *understand* our position; we often want them to *give up* their ("wrong, stupid") position.

I used inkblots earlier to look for the subjective dimension in most arguments (given that logic cannot prove or destroy a position), but they can also teach us that there's actually a "live-and-let-live" dimension in many arguments. We often feel arguments as win/lose situations because we so naturally focus on how our side of an argument *differs* from the other person's side. We assume that one person has to say, "Stupid me. I was wrong."

The believing game will help us understand ideas we disagree with. It can help us see that both sides in an argument are often right; or that both are right *in a sense*; or that both positions are implicitly pointing to some larger, wiser position that both arguers can agree on.

What Is the Believing Game?

In a sense I've already explained it with my analogy between inkblots and arguments. I can summarize it quickly now by contrasting it with the doubting game.

The doubting game represents the kind of thinking most widely honored and taught. It's the disciplined practice of trying to be as *skeptical* and analytic as possible with every idea we encounter. By doubting well, we can discover hidden contradictions, bad reasoning, or other weaknesses in ideas that look true or attractive. We scrutinize with the tool of doubt. This is the tradition that Walter Lippman invokes:

> The opposition is indispensable. A good statesman, like any other sensible human being, always learns more from his opponents than from his fervent supporters. For his supporters will push him to disaster unless his opponents show him where the dangers are. . . . [T]hough it hurts, he ought . . . to pray never to be left without opponents; for they keep him on the path of reason and good sense.

The widespread veneration of "critical thinking" illustrates how our intellectual culture venerates skepticism and doubting. ("Critical thinking" is a fuzzy, fad term, but its various meanings usually appeal to skepticism and analysis for the sake of uncovering bad thinking. When people call a movement "critical linguistics" or "critical legal studies," they are saying that the old linguistics or legal studies are flawed by being insufficiently skeptical or critical—too hospitable to something that's wrong.)

The believing game is the mirror image of the doubting game or critical thinking. It's the disciplined practice of trying to be as welcoming as possible to every idea we encounter: not just listening to views different from our own and holding back from arguing with them, but actually *trying to believe* them. We can use the tool of believing to scrutinize not for flaws but for hidden *virtues* in ideas that are unfashionable or repellent.

"Believing" Is a Scary Word

Many people get nervous when I celebrate believing. They point to an asymmetry between our senses of what "doubting" and "believing" mean. Believing seems to entail *commitment,* where doubting does not. It commonly feels as though we can doubt something without committing ourselves to rejecting it—but that we cannot believe something without committing ourselves to accepting it and even living by it. Thus it feels as though we can doubt and remain unscathed, but believing will scathe us. Indeed believing can feel hopelessly bound up with religion. ("Do you BELIEVE? Yes, Lord, I BELIEVE!")

This contrast in meanings is a fairly valid picture of *natural, individual acts* of doubting and believing. (Though I wonder if doubting leaves us fully unchanged.) But it's not a picture of doubting and believing as *methodological disciplines* or *unnatural games.* Let me explain the distinction.

Natural individual acts of doubting happen when someone tells us something that seems dubious or hard to believe. ("You say the earth is spinning? I doubt it. I feel it steady under my feet.") But our culture has learned to go way beyond natural individual acts of doubting. We humans had to struggle for a long time to learn how to doubt *unnaturally* as a methodological discipline. We now know that for good thinking, we must doubt *everything*, not just what's dubious; indeed the whole point of critical thinking is to try to doubt what we find most obvious or true or right (as Lippman advises).

In order to develop systematic doubting, we had to *overcome believing*: the natural pull to believe what's easy to believe, what we want to believe, or what powerful people tell us to believe. (It's easy to believe that the earth is stationary.) As a culture, we learned systematic doubting through the growth of philosophical thinking (Greek thinkers developing logic, Renaissance thinkers developing science, and Enlightenment thinkers pulling away from established religion). And we each had to learn to be skeptical as individuals, too—for example, learning not to believe that if we are very, very good, Santa Claus/God will bring us everything we want. As children, we begin to notice that naïve belief leads us astray. As adults we begin to notice the dreadful things that belief can lead humans to do—like torturing alleged witches/prisoners till they "confess."

Now that we've finally learned systematic doubting, with its tools of logic and strict reasoning and its attitude of systematic skepticism—critical thinking—we are likely to end up afraid of believing itself. Believing can seem a scary word because our culture has not yet learned to go beyond natural acts of naïve believing to develop *unnatural believing* as a *methodological discipline*. In short, the believing game is not much honored or even known.

When the systematic doubting game asks us to doubt an idea, it doesn't ask us to throw it away forever. We couldn't do that because the game teaches us to doubt all ideas. If we learn well, we find weaknesses even in good ideas. The scrutiny of doubt is *methodological, provisional, conditional*. So when a good doubter finally decides what to do, this involves an additional act of judgment and commitment. The doubting game gives good evidence, but it doesn't do our judging and committing for us.

Similarly, when the believing game asks us to believe *all* ideas—especially those that seem most wrong—it cannot ask us to marry them or commit ourselves to them. Our believing is *methodological, conditional, provisional*—unnatural. And, so too, if we commit ourselves to accepting an idea because the believing game helped us see virtues in it, this involves an additional act of judgment and commitment. The believing game gives us good evidence, but it doesn't do our deciding for us.

In short, we must indeed continue *to resist* the pull to believe what's easy to believe. But believing what's easy to believe is far different from using the disciplined effort to believe as an intellectual methodological tool in order to find hidden strengths in ideas that people want to ignore.

A Surprising Blind Spot for the Doubting Game

The doubting and believing games have symmetrical weaknesses: the doubting game is poor at helping us find hidden virtues; the believing game is poor at helping us find hidden flaws. But many people don't realize that the doubting game is also poor at reaching one of its main goals: helping us find hidden flaws in our own thinking.

The flaws in our own thinking usually come from our assumptions—our ways of thinking that we accept without noticing. But it's hard to doubt what we can't see because we unconsciously take it for granted. The believing game comes to the rescue here. Our best hope for finding invisible flaws in what we can't see in our own thinking is to enter into *different* ideas or points of view—ideas that carry different assumptions.

This blind spot in the doubting game shows up frequently in classrooms and other meetings. When smart people are trained only in critical thinking, they get better and better at doubting and criticizing other people's ideas. They use this skill particularly well when they feel a threat to their own ideas or their unexamined assumptions. Yet they feel justified in fending off what they disagree with because they feel that this doubting activity is "critical thinking." They take refuge in the feeling that they would be "unintellectual" if they said to an opponent what in fact they *ought* to say: "Wow, your idea sounds really wrong to me. It must be alien to how I think. Let me try to enter into it and see if there's something important that I'm missing. Let me see if I can get a better perspective on my own thinking." In short, if we want to be good at finding flaws in our own thinking (a goal that doubters constantly trumpet), we need the believing game.

The Believing Game Is Not Actually New

If we look closely at the behavior of genuinely smart and productive people, we will see that many of them have exactly this skill of entering into views that conflict with their own. Yet this skill of sophisticated unnatural belief is not much understood or celebrated in our culture—and almost never taught.

Let me emphasize that I'm not arguing *against* the doubting game. We *need* the ability to be skeptical and find flaws. Indeed, the doubting game probably deserves the last word in any valid process of trying to work out trustworthy thinking. For even though the scrutiny of belief may lead us to choose a good idea that most people at first wanted to throw away, nevertheless, we mustn't commit ourselves to that idea before applying the scrutiny of doubt to check for hidden problems.

My argument is against the *monopoly* of the doubting game as the *only* kind of good thinking. We need both disciplines. Some of our most needed insights come from opinions that are easy to criticize or dismiss.

Concrete Ways to Learn to Play the Believing Game

As teachers and students we are in a good position to learn the ability to see things differently from how we usually see them, and the willingness to risk doing it. If we want to learn those skills, it helps to notice the *inner stances*—the cognitive and psychological dispositions—we need for doubting and believing:

- If we want to doubt or find flaws in ideas that we are tempted to accept or believe (perhaps they are ideas that "everyone knows are true"), we need to work at *extricating* or *distancing* ourselves from those ideas. There's a kind of language that helps here: clear, impersonal sentences that lay bare the logic or lack of logic in them.

- If, on the other hand, we want to believe ideas that we are tempted to reject ("Anyone can see that's a crazy idea")—if we are trying to *enter in* or *experience* or *dwell in* those ideas—we benefit from the language of imagination, narrative, and the personal experience.

Here are some specific practices to help us experience things from someone else's point of view.

1. If people are stuck in a disagreement, we can invoke Carl Rogers' application of "active listening." John must not try to argue his point till he has restated Mary's point to *her* satisfaction.

2. But what if John has trouble seeing things from Mary's point of view? His lame efforts to restate her view show that "he doesn't get it." He probably needs to stop talking and listen; keep his mouth shut. Thus, in a discussion where someone is trying to advance a view and everyone fights it, there is a simple rule of thumb: the doubters need to stop talking and simply give extended floor time to the minority view. The following three concrete activities give enormous help here:

   - The three-minute or five-minute rule. Any participant who feels he or she is not being heard can make a sign and invoke the rule: no one else can talk for three or five minutes.

   - Allies only—no objections. Others can speak—but only those who are having more success believing or entering into the minority view. No objections allowed. (Most people are familiar with this "no-objections" rule from brainstorming.)

   - "Testimony session." Participants having a hard time being heard or understood are invited to tell stories of the experiences that led them to their point of view and to describe what it's like having or living with this view. Not only must the rest of us not answer or argue or disagree while they are speaking; we must refrain, even afterward, from questioning their stories or experiences or feelings. We may speak only to their ideas. (This process is particularly useful when issues of race, gender, and sexual orientation are being discussed.)

The goal here is safety. Most speakers feel unsafe if they sense we are just waiting to jump in with all our objections. But we listeners need safety, too. We are trying to enter into a view we want to quarrel with or feel threatened by. We're trying to learn the difficult skill of indwelling. It's safer for us if we have permission simply not to talk about it any more for a while. We need time for the words we resist just to sink in for a while with no comment.

3. The language of story and poetry helps us experience alien ideas. Stories, metaphors, and images can often find a path around our resistance. When it's hard to enter into a new point of view, try telling a story of someone who believes it: imagine and describe someone who sees things this way; tell the story of events that might have led people to have this view of the world; what would it be like to be someone who sees things this way? Write a story or poem about the world that this view implies.

4. Step out of language. Language itself can sometimes get in the way of trying to experience or enter into a point of view different from our own. There are various productive ways to set language aside. We can draw or sketch images (rough stick figures are fine). What do you actually *see* when you take this position? It's also powerful to use movement, gesture, dance, sounds, and role-playing. .

5. Silence. For centuries, people have made good use of silence for indwelling. If we're having trouble trying to believe someone's idea, sometimes it's helpful for *no one* to say anything for a couple of minutes. That's not much time out of a meeting or conference or class hour, but it can be surprisingly fertile.

6. Private writing. There's a kind of silence involved when everyone engages in private writing. Stop talking and do seven to ten minutes of writing for no one else's eyes. What's crucial is the invitation to language in conditions of privacy and safety.

7. Use the physical voice. When it's hard to enter into a piece of writing that feels difficult or distant, it helps to try to read it aloud as well and meaningfully as possible. (When I'm teaching a longer text, I choose crucial passages of a few paragraphs or a page.) The goal is not good acting; the goal is simply to say the words so that we feel every meaning in them—so that we fully *mean* every meaning. Get the words to "sound right" or to carry the meanings across—for example, to listeners who don't have a text. After we have three or four different readings of the same passage, we can discuss which ones manage to "sound right"—and usually these readings help us enter in or assent. (It's not fair to put students on the spot by asking them to read with no

preparation time. I ask students to prepare these readings at home or practice them briefly in class in pairs.)

This activity illustrates something interesting about language. It's impossible simply to say words so they "sound right" without *dwelling in* them and thus feeling their meaning. So instead of asking students to "study carefully" this Shakespeare sonnet, I say, "Practice reading it aloud till you can say every word with meaning." This involves giving a kind of *bodily assent*.

8. Nonadversarial argument. Our traditional model of argument is a zero-sum game: "If I'm right, you must be wrong." Essays and dissertations traditionally start off by trying to demolish the views of opponents. "Unless I criticize every other idea," the assumption goes, "I won't have a clear space for my idea." But this approach is usually counterproductive—except with readers who already agree with you and don't need to be persuaded. This traditional argument structure says to readers: "You cannot agree with my ideas—-*or even hear them*—until after you admit that you've been wrong or stupid."

The structure of nonadversarial argument is simple, but it takes practice and discipline: argue only *for your position*, not against other positions. This is easy for me here since I have no criticisms at all of the doubting game or critical thinking in itself. It's much harder if I really hate the idea I'm fighting. It's particularly hard if my essential argument is negative: "Don't invade Iraq." So yes, there are some situations in which we cannot avoid arguing why an idea is wrong. Yet even in my position on Iraq, there is, in fact, some space for nonadversarial argument. I can talk about the *advantages* of not invading Iraq. In this way, I would increase the chances of my opponent actually hearing my arguments.

The general principle is this: if all I have to offer are *negative* reasons why the other person's idea is bad, I'll probably make less progress than if I can give some *positive* reasons for my alternative idea—and even acknowledge why the other person might favor her idea.

I can end by glancing back at the inkblots. Arguments that *look* conflicting *might* both be somehow valid or right. They might need to be articulated better or seen from a larger view—a view the disputants haven't yet figured out. I may be convinced that someone else's idea is dead wrong, but if I'm willing to play the believing game with it, I will not only set a good example, I may even be able to see how we are both on the right track. Nonadversarial argument and the believing game help us work out larger frames of reference and better ideas.

Peter Elbow is Professor of English Emeritus at UMass Amherst. He has taught at M.I.T., Franconia College, and Evergreen State College. He is the author of *Writing Without Teachers* and *Writing with Power*. His recent book, *Everyone Can Write: Essays Toward a Hopeful Theory of Writing and Teaching Writing*, was given the James Britton Award by the Conference on English Education. With a colleague, he has written a pamphlet designed to help students give fellow writers peer response: *Sharing and Responding*. The National Council of Teachers of English (NCTE) recently gave him the James Squire Award "for his transforming influence and lasting intellectual contribution."

3

Reflective Writing

To Pause and Reflect

Gandhi valued taking time to reflect and write. Imagine our world if our leaders took time to do just that. Can you picture a world led by future citizens who had opportunities to learn to write reflective essays in which they shared insights and experiences? Students who develop this skill might live fuller lives.

> When "reflective writing" is assigned, what is suggested is a combination of calm, quiet thinking with a retrospective focus—looking back over a period of time and considering its meaning and significance in connection with your experience. Reflective writing is a route to self-knowledge. (Trupe 2001)

Jim Burke's "Write a Reflective Essay" (Chapter 51 in *Writing Reminders*) provides us with strategies for developing the reflective writer in our students. Read his book for the complete version of this chapter.

WRITE A REFLECTIVE ESSAY

JIM BURKE

Description

To write is to think—or so we hope. Students need time and incentive to pause and reflect. The very act of writing invites reflection by both students and teachers (Hillocks 1995), which can take place in journals, letters, poems, speeches, formal essays, or more informal, personal essays. Whatever the form used, students should see writing as a means of thinking through changes and dilemmas that they and others face. The word *reflect* itself means to look back. However, the larger question is: Why do it? What can they gain? Obvious answers include: insight into themselves and others, an appreciation of how much they have changed or improved, and an understanding of the larger implications of certain events or actions. Reflection is, in short, a "habit of mind" (Costa and Kallick 2000), which writing cultivates most effectively in students.

Some moments demand reflection—as opposed to observation, description, or narration—more than most. Beginning high school [is such a moment], or the wake of a powerful experience whose meaning and importance, students may not fully appreciate yet.

The Reflective Essay at a Glance

The reflective essay:

- considers or responds to a significant event or idea and what that idea means to the writer and the larger world
- answers the questions: Why? So what?
- may be either serious or humorous in tone, though it tends to be serious
- is often anchored in small, even familiar details or occasions that the writer makes more meaningful
- incorporates a variety of forms, including narration and description
- makes it clear not only what the event means to the writer but what it might mean to the reader.

Classroom Connection

Teachers who ask students to reflect, and who take time to think alongside their students, create thoughtful communities within the classroom. They create a place where students have permission—from themselves and those around them—to think, to ponder, and to reflect on who they are, what they are, and what it all means in light of where they are going.

Ashley Arabian's poignant reflective response to the photograph of two soldiers in Figure 3–1 reminds us what a powerful invitation to writing (and reflecting) pictures can provide. She wrote her essay in response to a weekly paper assignment. [See Chapter Four for the essay titled "Teaching Empathy Through Ecphrastic Poetry," which describes the use of photographs in producing poetry.]

Figure 3–1 "A grief stricken American infantryman whose buddy has been killed in action is comforted by another soldier. In the background a corpsman methodically fills out casualty tags, Haktong-ni area Korea." by Sfc. Al Chang, August 28, 1950; National Archives and Records.

WHAT WE LIKE TO THINK

Ashley Arabian

My heart stopped when I saw this picture. You never see a man being comforted by another man like this. I suppose that is what the war does to you. You need comfort from anyone. I sometimes think how it must have been for the men in war. Were they afraid? Were they excited? Nervous? Grim? I can only think that I would be horrified at the sight of others being killed in front of me, let alone having to kill others. What they had to go through was entirely inadequate. None of them had to go to war and kill like that. The world could have gotten along in the first place, but instead we had to put our citizens through this.

Why do we fight? Why did we fight? There are the historical explanations for why we fought the war, but people still wonder why we argued. I speak for almost everyone when I say world peace is extremely important to citizens. What if there was a World War Three involving your country? What if you had to go and fight? Leave your family to kill people. Does that seem right to you? It never seemed right in the first place. Yet we have a Vietnam Memorial wall. There are graveyards filled with soldiers. So many questions come to the mind when we learn about war. Sometimes there are not any answers. When there are no answers to the questions we ask about war, doesn't the fact of someone dying for an unanswered question seem illicit? It is really something to think about.

I have thought about this kind of stuff a lot and peace always is the answer to my questions. If we can keep peace in the world, do you think we will abide? I believe we can survive as a planet, not as humans, if we agree with each other on worldly issues. Is it so hard to believe that one day, even if it is for one day, every country will have peace with each other? I have hope for that day. I have hope that I will live to see that day. I have hope that we all have hope for world peace. Hope is a human need. Can peace be a world need? If we have been surviving without it, maybe not, but many like to think so.

Throughout our study of *All Quiet on the Western Front*, we examined what boys/men lost and how that related to what they *need*. Indy Johal's brainstorm about losses in his own life and the texts we read prepared him to write this opening for the human needs assignment.

Losses are something that everyone has to go through sometime in their life. I have suffered many losses in my life, and I'm not yet sixteen years old. I can't even imagine how many I might go through until I'm gone. Paul Baumer is another individual who had suffered many losses in the novel, *All Quiet on the Western Front*. Paul had losses that will stay in his life forever. There are some losses that when you suffer them you can forget about them easily. Permanent losses are with you every day, from the moment you wake up in the morning until you go to sleep at night. Macbeth's losses are very hard on him as well as others who are affected by his actions. What Macbeth had was a permanent loss which is with him every day until the day he has died. . . .

Overview

We are the result of many influences. People shape our beliefs, our values, and our attitudes, but so do experiences and the eras in which we live. Where we come from, the culture we are born into, our gender and race—these, too, affect us. This conversation suggests you think about these different influences and about those which have made the biggest impact.

1. Generate ideas: brainstorm influences that come to mind. Identify key categories (e.g., people, experiences) and generate examples and details (e.g., who/what influenced you and *how*).

2. Respond to your initial ideas with a 15-minute quick write. Think about how all these factors have influenced you. Whether you write, list, or cluster, *do not stop writing* until the 15 minutes are up.

3. Discuss your quick write with one other person, tell stories, explain what you mean. Don't hesitate to ask questions. Give each person equal time.

4. Write more: with your notes and discussion fresh in your mind, write down any additional stories, details, or examples that come to mind.

5. Draft your introductory paragraph. Read pages 55 and 97 from *Writer's Inc.* about opening paragraphs.

6. Respond and revise opening paragraphs using response groups.

7. Incorporate revisions into your opening paragraphs.

8. Generate details about your most important influence.

9. Draft body paragraphs.

10. Respond to and revise your body paragraphs.

11. Draft your conclusion.

12. Read and respond to essays in writing groups.

13. Revise and print your essay.

14. Adapt essay into a speech.

15. Rehearse.

16. Deliver speech.

Jim Burke teaches at Burlingame High School in Burlingame, California. He has written many books, the most recent of which are *School Smarts: The Four Cs of Academic Success* (2004) and *Writing Reminders: Tools, Tips, and Techniques* (2003), both published by Heinemann. He is also the author of *The English Teacher's Companion: A Complete Guide to Classroom, Curriculum, and the Profession.* Jim Burke created and maintains www.englishcompanion.com, a superb site that includes abundant, creative resources.

"Write a Reflective Essay" is adapted with permission from *Writing Reminders.* Copyright © 2003 by Jim Burke. Published by Heinemann, a division of Reed Elsevier.

4

Living, Teaching, and Learning Empathy

Consider the rights of others before your own feelings, and the feelings of others before your own rights.
                    — John Wooden, legendary UCLA basketball coach

Empathy and Peace

Famous Viennese psychiatrist Alfred Adler noted that to have empathy is "to see with the eyes of another, to hear with the ears of another, to feel with the heart of another" (Bruun 2004). When students act with empathy, they change the quality of their lives and others' near and far. Acts of kindness and compassion, like raising funds for tsunami victims, are felt by many, but possibly help the students themselves the most. Teachers must build opportunities for empathy within curriculum to enable these future citizens to understand and empathize with the Arundhati Roys of the world.

> As a child growing up in the state of Kerala, in South India—where the first democratically elected Communist government in the world came to power in 1959, the year I was born—I worried terribly about being a gook. Kerala was only a few thousand miles west of Vietnam. We had jungles and rivers and rice-fields, and communists, too. I kept imagining my mother, my brother, and myself being blown out of the bushes by a grenade, or mowed down, like the gooks in the movies, by an American marine with muscled arms and chewing gum and a loud background score. In my dreams, I was the burning girl in the famous photograph taken on the road from Trang Bang. . . .
>
> —*Arundhati Roy*, War Talk

If we can nurture a generation of citizens with the ability to empathize, the possibilities for peace are real and meaningful.

31

Tragically, we are living in a world of war, hate, and fear, which might be less so if, as Mary Walworth writes in her heartfelt article "No Child Left Behind . . . *Unscarred*?: Other People's Kids," we would treat all children around the world like our neighbors' children.

> What do you do with other people's kids? Well, you feed them, of course. You figure out what's in your fridge that resembles what they're used to at home. You talk to them. You find out if they would like to make a picture with paints or magic markers (though you secretly hope they say magic markers which are so much easier to deal with). You make them feel safe and loved when they come up to you looking a little scared wondering why mom hasn't picked them up yet, and you say she's almost here, she just called as she was leaving work—you're hoping that accident on the Parkway isn't going to add another hour to this kid's wait—and wouldn't you like to pick out a video: *Magic School Bus? Dora the Explorer*? You find out if they want white milk or chocolate milk, chicken nuggets or meatballs, a Power Puff Girls cup or a Barbie cup.
>
> These are what you do for other people's kids.
>
> One of the things you don't do to other people's kids is bomb them and burn them alive. And blow the limbs off their little sisters and blind their little brothers. And send their mothers (stained with blood and stuck all over with little pieces of broken glass) running away from flames, shrieking with grief. . . .

Walworth's entire article is displayed at www.counterpunch.org.

Nancy Gorrell's article is brilliant and it works. My students have produced poems based on photos of tsunami survivors that were eloquent and poignant. Try out this empathy-invoking strategy with your students.

TEACHING EMPATHY THROUGH ECPHRASTIC POETRY: ENTERING A CURRICULUM OF PEACE

NANCY GORRELL

> The most important thing is . . . I want to help people start to think and to educate themselves and to love each other, so no one ever has to go through what that little Polish boy went through again.
>
> —*Peter L. Fischl, Holocaust survivor*

More than a half century ago, Nazi guns pointed at children. Today, children point guns at children, in our homes, in our schools, and in our communities. In this context, Peter L. Fischl's simple but eloquent words get to the heart of any curriculum of peace. They challenge us to define the teaching of peace as one of the "most important things" we do, and at the same time, they challenge us to reflect: how can we teach for peace? How can we teach our students to feel compassion and kindness towards their fellow human beings? If you believe as I do that the first step in justifying violence against another human being is the objectification of that human being into an "other," then it also follows that any curriculum of peace must have at its core the teaching of empathy, "the power to enter into the feeling and spirit of others."[1]

But the question still remains: how can we teach, not preach, empathy? How can we empower our students to "enter into" the feeling and spirit of others? One answer lies in a remarkable teaching tool—ecphrastic poetry— and one particular ecphrastic poem of address written by Peter L. Fischl, "To the Little Polish Boy Standing with His Arms Up."

Ecphrastic Poetry: The Poetry of Empathy

Ecphrasis, the poetry I like to think of as the poetry of empathy, is a little-known, technical term used by classicists and art historians concerning the long tradition of poetic responses to great works of art. John Hollander, poet and critic, has written a definitive work on the subject, *The Gazer's Spirit: Poems Speaking to Silent Works of Art*, in which he chronicles the history of ecphrasis from ancient to modern times, including ecphrastic poems in response to sculpture, monuments, and photography. By definition, ecphrastic poetry is the poetry of empathy, requiring the viewer/poet to "enter into" the spirit and feeling of the subject through a variety of poetic stances: describing, noting, reflecting, or addressing.

I first became acquainted with Fischl's ecphrastic poem of address when he sent it to me in response to reading my article, "Teaching the Holocaust: Light from the Yellow Star Leads the Way" (*English Journal* 1997). From the moment I first read "To the Little Polish Boy," I knew I had in my hands the companion lesson that would open the door to the teaching of empathy. His poem and personal story, in conjunction with fellow survivor Robert O. Fisch's memoir *Light from the Yellow Star: A Lesson of Love from the Holocaust*, have become the cornerstone of my teaching of peace, prejudice reduction, and Holocaust and genocide literature ever since. Interestingly enough, both survivors, Fischl and Fisch (similarity of names is purely coincidental), grew up in Budapest, Hungary; knew each other at the time; and have remained lifelong friends.

In nearly three decades of teaching English and writing to eleventh and twelfth grade students in a diverse public high school, I have found no introductory lesson more authentic, relevant, and deeply affecting for both myself and my students. In two lessons, one eighty-minute block lesson, and a follow-up lesson, students produce mature, serious, and empathetic poetry, entering our curriculum of peace.

A Lesson in Empathy

Historical Background to the Photograph

I begin by displaying a large poster reproduction of the round-up of Jews in the Warsaw ghetto (1943) with Fischl's poem printed beneath.[2] The photograph immediately captures my students' attention, and a brief discussion naturally follows. I tell them that the photograph of the little Polish boy stands as one of the most powerful photographic images of our century—etched forever in the minds of those who first saw it when it was published in *Life* magazine on November 28, 1960 (106). I mention that the Warsaw ghetto confined nearly a half million Jews and that nearly 45,000 died there in 1941 alone, due to starvation and disease. When, in April 1943, the Nazis attempted to raze the ghetto and deport the remaining 70,000 inhabitants to Treblinka concentration camp, a revolt ensued which lasted five weeks (New Jersey Commission on Holocaust Education 1994). I comment that the photograph we are looking at was taken by Nazi photographers for General Jurgen Stroop, a Nazi official, to document the uprising and the final liquidation of the ghetto.[3] I ask my students if anyone has seen this well-known photograph, as it has been published in many history textbooks and has been reprinted numerous times in popular literature. Despite its historical significance, few of my students can recall seeing it.

Then I ask my students to imagine for a moment a Holocaust survivor seeing this photograph years after the Holocaust. How do you think that survivor might feel? Students speculate that the survivor might be shocked, that the image might bring back painful memories, and that the survivor might not even want to look at the photograph at all. I tell my students that this is what happened to a Holocaust survivor, Peter L. Fischl, whom I have come to know.

Peter Fischl's Personal Story

I share with my students the personal story Peter Fischl related to me. Fischl, like the boy in the photograph, was a child growing up during the Holocaust. At the age of thirteen, he wore the Star of David on his clothes and was subjected to harsh anti-Jewish laws. Soon after, the Nazis invaded Hungary. Separated from his family, he went into hiding in a Catholic school with sixty other boys. A few months later, he received a phone call from his father telling him that he had been discovered by the Gestapo. That was the last contact he had with his father. Fortunately, Fischl managed to survive the last weeks of the war in hiding with his mother and sister. In 1957, during the Hungarian Revolution, he escaped to America, where he settled in southern California.

Years later, in 1965, he saw the photograph of the little Polish boy by accident when he was browsing through old *Life* magazines in a bookstore on Hollywood Boulevard near his home. The effect on him was so powerful that the image of the little boy remained with him every day for four years thereafter, until he woke up one morning at 2 A.M. and, although he was not a poet, wrote a poem to the little Polish boy.

Peter Fischl's Poem of Address

At this point I place on each student's desk a smaller version of the poster with a copy of the photograph and the poem printed beneath. I read the poem aloud as the students follow along[4]:

Figure 4–1   This famous photograph captures the essence of the horrors of Holocaust: Warsaw 1943. (Main Commission for the Investigation of Nazi War Crimes, courtesy of USHMM Photo Archives).

TO THE LITTLE POLISH BOY STANDING WITH HIS ARMS UP

Peter L. Fischl

I would like to be an artist
So I could make a Painting of you
Little Polish Boy

Standing with your Little hat
on your head
The Star of David
on your coat
Standing in the ghetto
with your arms up
as many Nazi machine guns
pointing at you

I would make a monument of you
and the world who said
nothing

I would like to be a composer
so I could write a concerto of
you Little Polish Boy

Standing with your Little hat
on your head
The Star of David
on your coat
Standing in the ghetto
with your arms up
as many Nazi machine guns
pointing at you

I would write a concerto of you
and the world who said
nothing

I am not an artist
But my mind had painted
a painting of you

Ten million Miles High is the Painting
so the whole universe can see you
Now
Little Polish Boy

Standing with your Little hat
on your head
The Star of David
on your coat

Standing in the ghetto
with your arms up
as many Nazi machine guns
pointing at you

And the World who said nothing

I'll make this painting so bright
that it will blind the eyes
of the world who saw nothing

Ten billion miles high will be the
monument
so the whole universe can remember
of you
Little Polish Boy

Standing with your Little hat
on your head
The Star of David
on your coat
Standing in the ghetto
with your arms up
as the many Nazi machine guns
pointing at you

And the monument will tremble
so the blind world
Now
will know
What fear is in the darkness

The world
Who said nothing

I am not a composer
but I will write a composition
for five trillion trumpets
so it will blast the ear drums
of this world

The world
Who heard nothing

I
am
Sorry
that
It was you
and
Not me

After hearing the poem, my students are visibly moved; a sense of awe and silence permeates the room. I ask my students to take out their response journals. I pose the following questions for personal reflection:

- What are you wondering at this moment? Write a list of "wonder" questions.
- What are you feeling? Write about your reactions to the poem.

After a few minutes of writing, I share with my students what happened after Fischl wrote his poem. As he related it to me, until the moment of writing, he had never expressed before his feelings about his Holocaust experience. After writing the poem, he cried "for a long time," and then he put it in his desk drawer where it sat for nearly a quarter of a century. He was not a poet, and he never thought to publish the poem for fear it would be exploiting the memory of the little Polish boy. Then one day he went with his daughter to see the opening of Steven Spielberg's film *Schindler's List*. After seeing the film, he sat frozen to his seat, consumed once again with the image of the little Polish boy. At that moment he knew he had to break his silence, and in 1994, he published his poem in lithograph form, where it is on display in Los Angeles' Museum of Tolerance as well as museums throughout the world.

Student Writing Response: Poems Speaking to the Little Polish Boy Photograph

Without further discussion, I ask my students to turn their attention once again to the photograph before them. I suggest to them to write their own poem to the little Polish boy or to anyone in the photograph. Keeping the instructions open and simple, I pose the following questions:

- If you could speak to the little Polish boy, what would you say?
- If you could speak to anyone in the photograph, what would you say?
- Or, if you could imagine any of the subjects speaking, what do you think they would say?
- On a new page in your journals, write any poem reflecting on your viewing of this photograph. You may re-read your wonder questions and reflections to help you get started.

In the two years I have been teaching this lesson to students of various ability levels and attitudes towards poetry, I never cease to be amazed at how eagerly students respond. After ten minutes of composing I ask, "Who would like to share their poems in progress?" Sitting in our "sharing circle" format, students readily respond with an array of poetic stances: addressing the subjects, letting the subjects speak, reflecting on the subjects.

At this point in the lesson, I want my students to listen to the power of the poems, "to enter into the spirit," and to reflect upon that spirit. As the students do so, they and their poems reveal mature insights into the nature of genocide, the most extreme form of violence, raising the critical questions so vital for our subsequent study. Since I want my students to process those insights, I ask them to go to a blank page in their journals. I tell them we will listen to the poems without commenting, and after hearing each poem, we will reflect in our journals upon that "hearing." I suggest they write what the poem reveals to them about the nature of violence, genocide, or human behavior, or they may write a wonder question. Without further comment, we proceed around the sharing circle, hearing volunteers who are moved to read, reflecting for a few minutes in our journals after each reading.

Karen "enters the spirit" of the little Polish boy in her poem of address, first describing and then ending with her personal reflection. She reads to us:

TO THE LITTLE POLISH BOY

Looking at you little boy
your arms up in the air
thinking of what you may miss
if one of the demons shoots their guns
ending your already scarred life
looking at you little boy
facing the fear that faces you
how brave you really are. . .
looking at you little boy
seeing the star of David staining your clothes
locked up in this ghetto with nowhere to go
looking at you little boy
and seeing only
how precious
life really is.

What more important lesson can we learn in our study of peace than Karen's last lines leading us to the conclusion of the "precious" value of human life?

Lily addresses the little Polish boy by imagining she is his mother. She takes a speculative stance, reading to us:

UNTITLED

What if I were your mother
and held you high in the air
in my tall arms
under the warm sun
exalted and kissed by God
on your rosy cheeks,
And the barbed wire and concrete
grayness and cold were a far off
twister of a storm cloud
soon to be swept to sea
never to rain on us
as I hold you high in the air
no pain of a gun piercing your back.

The hearing of this poem poses for us a most provocative question . . .
what if? . . . prompting us to reflect upon the issue of moral choice: "what if?"
What if we/they choose/chose peace, not violence?

John assumes a different stance, taking on the identity/persona of the
little Polish boy, by letting him speak. John reads to us only four short lines:

UNTITLED

How did I get here?
Why am I here?
What did I do to deserve this?
How will I . . . ?

The sudden break in the poem, indicating either the inability to express
in words the unthinkable, unknowable horror about to come—there are no
answers—or the sudden cliffhanger ending of a vibrant young life—was the
little boy shot at that moment of questioning?—enables us to enter into the
moment with its inexplicable possibilities. In four remarkable lines, John
imaginatively enters the "spirit and feeling" of his subject, "How will I
_____?" leading us to fill in the blank with our own reflections—survive?

Cormisha focuses on the woman in the photograph, letting her address
the little Polish boy:

THE WOMAN'S CRY

Son, whatever you do keep those hands up.
Soon in time, you will be able to put them down
And let them move freely.
You will be able to play with all the children again.
But son, whatever you do, keep those hands up.

Soon in time, you won't have to think about danger or fear.
You will be able to go out at night without crying your heart out.
But son, whatever you do keep those hands up.
Soon in time, they will see how they hurt my little boy...
The gun toward my son is not necessary,
He is just a child.
Son, whatever you do keep those hands up.
Soon in time, the whole world who kept silent
Will come out and help.

Cormisha imagines the mother not thinking of herself, but only how to help her son survive. The mother's assurances affirm the bonds of family and hope for future survival: "Soon in time, the whole world . . . will come out and help." Cormisha's poem reminds us of an important aspect of any curriculum of peace: goodness, love, and bravery must prevail even in the most violent and inhumane circumstances.

Several students address poems to the Nazi soldiers in the photograph. Many of these poems express anger; others struggle to understand. Jessica addresses the Nazi soldier with a litany of questions:

THE KILLING SOLDIER

There you stand with your big bad gun,
There you stand with all the power,
There you stand with your face as a rock.
Don't you care about that boy?
Don't you care about his mother and father?
Don't you care about his other family and friends? . . .
What did this boy do to you?
Did this boy hurt you? . . .
Maybe you should think
before you pull the trigger.

In contrast to Jessica's poem, Amanda struggles to understand the Nazi soldier's behavior:

NUMB

Ignorance
It
        befalls
   you
        like
            rain.
Senses shut down.

No longer can you hear
or feel or see.
SEE the troubled eyes
the little fingers and
the tattered clothes.
They call only to you—
salvation!
Senses shut down.
You cannot cry back
nor do you want to.
This Innocence is your enemy.
Remote controls
    move
        your
    body
With the switch of a button
                     —Your HEART is turned off—

In her poem, Amanda offers an explanation for the Nazi soldier's behavior—"ignorance" and "numbness—" for how could anyone be so inhumane and yet possess the feelings which make us human?

Closing Discussion

As a final exercise, I ask students to speculate what all the poems we have heard in the sharing circle have in common. Students wonder why the world remained silent, what happened to the little Polish boy, and "how can people be so cruel?" We list on the board in brainstorm fashion our collective thoughts, feelings, and insights. As we do so, we frame questions for our subsequent study of peace:

- Why did it happen?
- How can human beings be so cruel?
- What is the nature of violence?
- Why did the "world say nothing"?
- What did America know about the Warsaw ghetto and the little Polish boy?
- What is the nature of good and evil?
- Why do some people choose "good" and others "evil"?

In our discussion I tell my students that the most reliable sources to date contend that we do not know what happened to the little Polish boy; we can only assume that he perished. As far as the question, "Did the world know?" I tell my students about an article recently published in *Newsweek* magazine. In "Word from the Ghetto," *Newsweek* reports that the Polish government-in-exile sent Jan Karski, a courier for the underground resistance, to visit the Warsaw ghetto and other transit camps in Poland. I hold up the March 8, 1999 edition of *Newsweek* with a prominent picture of Karski and the little Polish boy photograph. Karski saw the atrocities and was desperate to tell the world. He did so, but few believed him. When he returned to Washington in June 1943, during the final days of the Warsaw ghetto uprising, he spoke to President Roosevelt. Then I read his words to the class:

> A distinction has to be made. . . . The Germans persecute my people . . . they want to make us a nation of slaves. With the Jews, it is different. They want to exterminate them. . . . Mr. President, I am going back to Poland. . . . Everybody will ask me: What did President Roosevelt tell you? What am I to tell them? (47)

I pause for a moment and then ask my students: What do you think President Roosevelt said? What do you think he should have said? After a few responses, I read Roosevelt's answer:

> You will tell the leaders that we shall win this war! You will tell them that the guilty ones will be punished. Justice and freedom will prevail. You will tell your nation that they have a friend in this house. (47)

As my students reflect on Roosevelt's words, I mention that Karski was awarded by the State of Israel its Honorary Citizenship Award as a distinguished rescuer. At this point I introduce the term "righteous gentile," pointing out the many who made the moral choice to work for peace in the face of genocide. I read Karski's own words in the foreword he wrote for a book of portraits and stories of Holocaust survivors and their messages of hope and compassion:

> I understand the uniqueness of the Holocaust. I saw it. We cannot let history forget it. The Jews were abandoned by governments, by church hierarchies, and by societal structures. But they were not abandoned by humanity. Thousands upon thousands of individuals, priests and nuns, workers and peasants, educated and simpletons— risked their lives or freedom to help . . . we cannot let history forget them. (*The Triumphant Spirit* 10)

As class ends, I distribute to my students the *Newsweek* article and Jan Karski's foreword for further reading that evening. I tell them, "If you are satisfied with the poem in your response journal, write a final, edited draft or, if you are inspired after hearing other students' poems, write a new poem in response to the little Polish boy photograph."

Follow-up Lesson: Expanding Our Circle of Empathy

I open the following class period by asking for examples of new or revised poems written in response to the little Polish boy photograph. Without discussion, we hear a few selections. Then I tell my students that the poems we have been studying and writing are a special kind of poetry, ecphrastic poetry, in which the viewer/poet "speaks to" great works of art, sculpture, and photography. I point out that in that "speaking," the poet "enters into the spirit and feeling of others." I define that "entering" as empathy. At this point, I praise my students' extraordinary poems for helping us enter into the spirit and feeling of the little Polish boy, and by his example, the genocide and Holocaust experience.

Then I tell my students that I want to give them the experience of writing their own poem of address to expand our circle of empathy. In order to do so, I ask them to recall or find a photograph, a work of art or a monument or piece of sculpture which affected them as profoundly as the little Polish boy affected Peter Fischl. In brainstorming fashion, I ask my students to recall any images or photographs that represent for them an important moment or experience they will never forget. Amazingly, Minh-Dang (Mindy), a grandchild of Vietnamese boat refugees, recalls seeing in her history textbook a photograph of a Vietnamese girl running through the streets covered with napalm. I tell her I recall seeing that photograph, too, how it became emblematic of an entire era, and I suggest to her to try to write a poem on viewing that photograph. Other students recall images from the Kennedy assassination they have seen. I tell my students that some images, like the little Polish boy, the napalmed young girl, or JFK Jr. saluting the coffin of his assassinated father, are so profound that they become part of our collective consciousness, reflecting the feelings of an entire community or nation.

Next, I distribute the following instruction sheet.

Ecphrastic Poetry Writing Assignment General Directions

Find a photograph, piece of art, monument, or sculpture which profoundly affects or inspires you. If possible, strive to have this work affect you as the "Little Polish Boy" affected Peter L. Fischl. You may need to search for some time in libraries, photography books, newspapers as well as in your travels to museums, monuments, and memorials. Copy or acquire a copy of the work of art or photograph to display for the class. Your final poetic responses will be due at the completion of the unit. At that time you will present the image/ work and your poetic response(s) to the class.

Step One: Find a Work that Affects You Profoundly

Step Two: Write a Poetic Response to That Work

Choose a Poetic Stance:

1. Describe what you see in detail, step by step.
2. Address a subject in the work.
3. Take on the identity/persona of a subject in the work. Imagine what that subject is thinking or about to do. Or, let the subject speak.
4. Reflect upon what you see; meditate upon the moment of viewing.

Step Three: Copy or Acquire a Picture of the Work for Display

Step Four: Present Your Poem to the Class

After discussing the long-range assignment, I take my students to the library in our school to find images that affect them. Students browse through photography and art books as well as magazines, newspapers, and popular literature. I have placed upon a central table collections of some of the most important photographers and photojournalists of our century: Edward Steichen, Alfred Eisenstaedt, Roman Vishniac, Henri Cartier-Bresson, Dorothea Lange, Robert Capra, Gordon Parks, and Brian Lanker, to name a few available in our high school library. My students consult photographic essays of important eras: photography of the Depression, World War II, the Holocaust, Korea, the Civil Rights Movement, and Vietnam, for example. Particularly popular collections are Roman Vishniac's *A Vanished World*, the Time/Life collections on each decade, *The Family of Man*, and recent Time/ Life books such as *The Meaning of Life: Reflections in Words and Pictures on Why We Are Here*.

I give my students several weeks to search for a work that truly inspires and engages them "to enter into the spirit." The results of this researching and reflecting time prove to be highly productive as students' ecphrastic responses help them to enter, define, and develop a curriculum of peace.

Student Ecphrastic Poems

The poems my students produce from the long-range, follow-up lesson affirm the power of poetry to enable poet and reader alike to "enter the terrain" of human suffering, pain, and grief expanding the circle of empathy connecting us all. Students respond to a wide range of works: art, sculpture, monuments, and photography. I offer here two examples of ecphrastic responses: one connects photojournalism of the past to personal, family history and heritage; the other sees recent photojournalism through the lens of our teaching of empathy.

Minh-Dang (Mindy) Nguyen chooses to "enter that terrain" as she connects personal, family history in her poem of address to the photographic image of a fleeing young Vietnamese girl covered with napalm:

EVERYTHING STANDS STILL

I close my eyes
And I hear your screams
You are running from the Devil
Who has taken your Home
Your Family
Your Clothes
And you are crying for me
For my hands and my help
To take away the hurt
And everything stands still . . .

I open my eyes
And sit in the road
As my Friends, my Family
Run past me
I see you fleeing our home
With your arms outstretched
Trying to fly from the fire
Trying to calm the burning
With the tears running down your face
And everything stands still . . .

This morning you played
You sang the songs of our home
And you tasted the fruits of our land
This morning our mother kissed you
Dressed you for the day
Combed the knots from your black hair
This morning you kissed our father
Before he went to the fields
And lost his life.

This afternoon
The screams came from the sky
Spreading tears of Hell
This afternoon our mother screamed
Somewhere where you could not reach her
And you knew you would never hear her voice again
This afternoon the gods were angry
And they stole your clothes and stung your eyes
Now you run to me.

I open my arms
Ready to embrace you
And shelter you from the pain
Hoping to smooth your hair
Clothe your burning skin
Wipe your tears away
Your screams reach into my heart
How I wish that I could help you
I wish that our hands could meet
And everything stands still . . .

Sister, this morning you kissed the sun
This afternoon it fell from the sky
Your tears haunt me
Your cries echo in time
Just when I almost touch you
When I can almost save you
Everything stands still . . .

You are my nightmare
You are my regret.

Lily Conviser chooses to "enter the terrain" as she views a recent photographic image of a skull buried in dirt in a *Time* magazine article on the war in Kosovo.

MORNING COFFEE, 7:42 A.M.

Today the paper said that
Thousands of bodies were found in
Landfills across Eastern Europe—

This body is half-decayed and blasted,
Hair shot back and half there, exposing
A broken-down skull, lined with cracks and
Footsteps, dirt-stained and parasitic—

I look to see what sex the thing is,
(I smoked too much last night and my lungs
feel tight and raspy, my throat is raw and tastes like
salt, and if I cough real hard I can still taste the
tobacco.) and the caption tells me it's female—

Here a sexless, bloodless body shares the page
With a family on a picnic in central park—

Final Reflections

I am not so naïve as to think that poetry, ecphrastic or any kind, could possibly "solve" all the problems of violence in our society. The underlying causes of one person's inhumanity to another lie in centuries of practice, prejudice, and paradox unimaginable and unknowable. And yet, I am an English teacher, and I must do what I do best—teaching the essence of my discipline. And what is that essence? It has been and always will be for me engagement—imaginatively, aesthetically, and emotionally—with "the text." That engagement, the ability to enter into the spirit and feeling of others, defines what it is to be human, and that, I believe, is the heart of any curriculum of peace.

Lily reveals such engagement when she can no longer drink her morning coffee while turning the pages of horror and tragedy in the magazine before her. I can think of no other weapon more important to combat violence, prejudice, and hatred than the heightened sensitivity of our young people to the plethora of horrific images of inhumanity in the media today.

Without question, the photograph of the little Polish boy and Peter Fischl's response to it have touched the hearts and souls of my students, producing not only mature, serious, and empathetic poetry, but a transformational awareness that is both lifelong and portable.

Hopefully, through the teaching of empathy, our curriculum of peace will take us one step closer to the time when, in Fischl's words, "No one will have to go through what that little Polish boy went through again."

Notes

1. *The New Lexicon Webster's Dictionary of the English Language* (New York: Lexicon Publications, Inc. 1989) offers a definition of empathy particularly useful for our purposes: "The power to enter into emotional harmony with a work of art and so derive aesthetic satisfaction; the power to enter into the feeling and spirit of others."

2. As companion lessons, either one may follow the other. I begin with the *Light from the Yellow Star* lesson followed by the lesson in empathy centering on Fischl's poem of address.

3. The "Little Polish Boy" poster (28" x 18") including the photograph and reprinted poem beneath is available from the Holocaust Resources and Materials catalogue published by the Social Studies School Service, 10200 Jefferson Boulevard, Room J5, P.O. Box 802, Culver City, CA 90232-0802 (1-800-421-4246) (Fax: 1-800-944-5432) catalogue # PFL100-J8; fee $12. Includes a French translation of the poem. The companion resource material, *Light from the Yellow Star: A Lesson of Love,* from the Holocaust by Robert O. Fisch, is also available at $9.95 in the paperback edition. Catalogue # 0P136-J8.

4. The following information, taken from "Glossary of Terms," *The Betrayal of Mankind,* a resource handout from the New Jersey Commission on Holocaust Education, provides historic background:

Warsaw Ghetto: Established in November 1940, the ghetto was surrounded by a wall confining almost 500,000 Jews. Nearly 45,000 Jews died there in 1941 alone due to overcrowding, forced labor, lack of sanitation, starvation and disease. A revolt took place in the ghetto on April 19, 1943, when the Nazis attempted to raze the ghetto and deport the remaining inhabitants to Treblinka. The uprising lasted twenty-eight days and was one of the most important examples of resistance. Unfortunately, the ghetto was liquidated and the heroic resistance fighters perished.

Yellow Badge: The yellow badge is a distinctive sign which Jews were compelled to wear in the Middle Ages. The Nazis adopted the concept, forcing Jews under their control to wear a distinctive badge or arm band with the Star of David.

Nancy Gorrell, poet, writer, and lecturer, has been teaching English and creative writing for more than thirty-five years at Morristown High School, Morristown, New Jersey. Since 1989, she has published articles on the teaching of poetry, writing, and Holocaust literature in *English Journal,* and she has contributed book chapters to several NCTE publications. Her article "Teaching the Holocaust: Light from the Yellow Star Leads the Way" (Gorrell 1997) won the Paul and Kate Farmer Writing Award for most outstanding article of the year. In 1991 she was recognized as New Jersey State Teacher of the Year; in 2001 she received from NJCTE the Outstanding English Language Arts Educator Award; and in 2001 she also received the New Jersey Governor's Award in Arts Education. A lecturer in the areas of poetry, writing, and Holocaust education, Nancy Gorrell has led workshops for over ten years at the following forums and conventions: NJEA, NJCTE, NCTE, TOY (Teachers of the Year) Conventions, NJ Governor's Convocation, Raritan Valley Community College Holocaust Institute, County College of Morris NEA Study Project in Poetry, Geraldine Dodge Poetry Seminar, and Morris School District. As NJ State Teacher of the Year, she wrote a monthly column, "Opinion Shapers," for the *Morristown Daily Record* on pertinent educational issues. Her articles and poetry have been reprinted in several books and anthologies, most recently, Virginia Monseau ed. *A Curriculum of Peace* (NCTE) and *Reflections on the Gift of a Watermelon Pickle* (2nd edition).

"Teaching Empathy Through Ecphrastic Poetry: Entering a Curriculum of Peace" first appeared in *English Journal,* May 2000. Copyright 2000 by the National Council of Teachers of English. Reprinted with permission.

Wars and Disasters Offer Images

"We never see the smoke and the fire, we never smell the blood, we never see the terror in the eyes of the children, whose nightmares will now feature screaming missiles from unseen terrorists, known only as Americans" (Kelley 1998). However, photographers in Afghanistan, Iraq, and elsewhere have given us heartrending photos that portray the suffering of the innocents during war. The deaths and destruction wrought by both the Indian Ocean tsunami and Hurricane Katrina were covered by media around the world. On the Internet, students can locate recent photographs that will affect them and respond with ecphrastic poetry. As they share their poetry with us, our hearts and minds will be touched. As students begin to empathize with the suffering of others around the world, they might work to help those people in need.

5

Helping Our Students Cope

At a Loss

Frankly, I am at a loss for words in introducing Leonore Gordon's article and will let her words do the talking. Her lessons show us a way to help our students cope in these times of fear, hate, and scandal. Her students' poems sing to us and echo their honesty, pain, and hope. Moreover, Gordon shows teachers how they might help heal themselves, too; pick themselves up; and lift their students to the heavens.

EDUCATING WITHOUT TRAUMATIZING: HOW DO WE HELP OUR STUDENTS TO COPE WITH THE TWENTY-FIRST CENTURY? (TRY A DOSE OF POETRY)

LEONORE GORDON

Asking the Questions

As a poetry resident in the New York City public schools, a political activist raised in the spirit of social activism in the 1960s, and the parent of a twelve-year-old son, I confess that in this twenty-first century, I am often at a loss. What can I possibly offer to my son, or to my students, to help them to experience the hope for a better world that I felt in my idealistic youth? The dangers from the world around us seem to grow daily. In the early 1960s, we crouched under our desks for air raid drills during the Cuban missile crisis. The modern world has certainly upped the ante for our children, and with bin Laden still somewhere out there, and a U.S. president who our children know lied to his country as a justification for waging a seemingly interminable war, to whom can they turn in the hope of feeling safe?

Studies show that some children in New York City are still demonstrating post-traumatic stress symptoms years after the 9/11 attacks. Our nation's

51

children who were old enough to watch the news in 2001 remember that day well; many still fear attack. In the late summer of 2005, Hurricane Katrina wreaked havoc upon New Orleans. Our children watched television in disbelief while their fellow Americans begged to be rescued from their rooftops, only to be ignored by their city, state, and federal government. As the week progressed, our children watched as hundreds drowned; starved to death; or languished, homeless, in stadiums and convention centers first assaulted by rain, and then by an unresponsive government. Did this surprise kids from neighborhoods where police officers take their time responding to emergency calls? I wonder.

Many of our children live in low-income neighborhoods where drug traffic and gang violence have instilled fear and helplessness in them at an early age. They don't always believe that the people "in charge" will come to their rescue, because their local police departments somehow can't seem to weed out the criminals. Many have seen their brothers, fathers, and cousins unnecessarily frisked for no other reason than being the "wrong" color. Under such conditions, how do we help them, as parents and educators, to find the voice to express their fears, and then to feel even empowered to try and effect change?

Middle school students, in particular, are losing some of their egocentricity, and observing the adult world around them. They are often outraged by injustice and adult hypocrisy, and insistent on holding us accountable. But they still straddle a line between childhood and adolescence, and at times, they are just scared little kids. The evils of the world can sometimes feel unbearable and, sophisticated as they try to appear, they don't always know how to maintain their balance in the face of those evils. Developmentally, they are not always ready for what they see and hear on the news, in movies, or even in their classrooms.

An example follows: In the first year of teaching the poetry component of a sixth grade jazz strand in Brooklyn, N.Y., I made a terrible mistake. After handing out the lyrics of the song "Strange Fruit," sung by Billie Holiday, a song that spoke of the lynchings that took place in the southern United States in the first half of the twentieth century, I included a video component with little forethought. It included footage from Ken Burns' PBS series on jazz, a spectacular ten-part documentary, narrated by the incomparably poetic jazz trumpeter Wynton Marsalis, and a film that should be seen by anyone who loves jazz. I wanted to show them Holiday actually singing "Strange Fruit" in a New York City jazz club, mesmerizing the audience with her chilling rendition of the song. Interspersed with her performance, however, black and white photos of a lynching flash across the screen—photos that reveal the unspeakable vision of a crowd of white Southern spectators laughing as a black man dangles from a tree. Some townspeople are covered in white Klan hoods.

What was my terrible mistake? My students, mostly African American, knew nothing about lynching, and even less about the Ku Klux Klan. They had not been prepared for this lesson, and certainly didn't need the added visuals of men with their own skin color being hanged from trees. A few were devastated, others, terribly upset. The more I explained, the less they could grasp. Some of them begged to know why the police chiefs and the mayors didn't stop such lynchings, and when their teacher and I explained that some of these policemen and mayors were secretly Klan members, it only made things worse. One girl cried at her seat, and a boy sat with his head laid upon his desk. A state of horror paralyzes and temporarily immobilizes us, which certainly does not inspire the energy to take action against its source. It is unfair to do this to children, who lack the information or resources to explore alternative lenses through which to examine the horror, and thus lift themselves off the floor.

So, how then, as educators, do we help these bewildered, truth-demanding students? How do we discuss the news, or tell the story of racism, without imposing upon them our own politics and values, and without disrespecting their parents' beliefs? Is it educationally sound, or possible, to raise their social consciousness; to teach them that they can have a voice in the world that matters, while remaining even remotely neutral about our own politics? And, if we answer "yes," can we expose the underside of evil; teach them about war, racism, bigotry, and the roles they play in the history of this country; and not frighten them more than they already are as a result of their own experiences living in the midst of such evils? How do we creatively and sensitively transform their fears into empowerment while still allowing them space to first express their fears?

I will try to share my struggle with these questions, along with several of my own solutions in my role as poet-in-residence in the New York City public schools, working out of Teachers & Writers Collaborative. First, some background about the school I will be referencing. For the past seven years, I have taught poetry weekly at P.S. 156, a New York City school in the heart of Brownsville, where primarily low-income residents live either in row houses with apple trees in their yards, or in public housing projects terrorized by drug traffic, drive-by shootings, and gang violence.

My students worry about wearing the "wrong" colors outside and being mistaken for gang members, and consequently shot or knifed. When I have asked them to describe midnight on their blocks, in a "Round

Midnight" exercise accompanied by jazz pianist Thelonius Monk playing the tune of that name, students fill the pages of their poems with the nightly sounds of police helicopters over their roofs, and the cracks of gunshots from drive-by shootings.

Alchemizing Neighborhood Poetry into Civic Empowerment

Kids in the P.S. 156 Brooklyn community know a lot about living with danger, but there are strategies teachers anywhere can employ to address similar problems. I will share one of my own that can be creatively adapted to any classroom. During the course of teaching a strand about American Indians, my fifth grade students exchanged correspondence with students in New Mexico. The Laguna Pueblo teacher and I had each asked our students to describe their homes and neighborhoods in poems and letters to their pen pals, hoping to reciprocally teach our children about a culture other than their own through firsthand contact.

The resulting poems by the classes in Brooklyn left me breathless, and terribly sad. I'd asked my students to list, in poetry form, everything they could see or hear outside their windows. We ended up, instead, with a series of "Living in Brownsville" poems that detailed all of the disturbing scenarios referred to above. *Living in Brownsville is / seeing gangs fight over guns / knives and flags,* wrote fifth grader Edwin Martinez. Yahaira Moore told us, *When I look through / the window, I see people / dying.* Another child asked her pen pal on the pueblo, *The police do their best to get the bad guys, but somehow they end up losing. Do people out there do violence to solve their problems?* This experience led me to a decision to try to get the children's voices heard outside of the school. I could not allow these poems to remain invisible, and believed that there were adults who needed to know what was being written by these young New Yorkers.

Rather quickly, I managed to make contact with a reporter from WNYC, the N.Y.C. affiliate of National Public Radio. Several weeks later, my excited students were interviewed by this same reporter. She and her sound technician recorded numerous students reading their poems and voicing their complaints about their neighborhood—the crime, the filthy housing project elevators, the relentless drug traffic. Following her visit, the reporter spoke to officers from the local precinct about their efforts to stem gang activity.

When a conflict arose between the radio station and the police department regarding the interviews, they were not broadcast. The students, however, undeterred and full of their powers, went on to send their letters and poems to their local assemblyman, who actually came to the school to speak to them, bringing along an officer from the precinct. In addition, a neighbor-hood newspaper printed some of the poems, as did the precinct newspaper.

This lesson in civic awareness, strengthened by the power of verse, added an indispensable lifelong tool to the tool belts of my students. They felt proud and heard, while also learning about the political system and the names of their local representatives. I recommend using this outreach strat-egy for any situation where students share worries about their communities. Let them write petitions and letters and poems, voicing their thoughts and ideas, and make sure they direct them to the decision makers beyond the school grounds.

The Bigger Picture: How to Teach on Your Feet When World Events Threaten to Tip You Over

This lesson can be adapted to help students express their hopes for change during any world crisis. Its purpose is not to teach social activism, but to aid students to feel less helpless through the use of imagination and a poem.

My drums play / soft / sweet / melodies of sugar / that stop / evil / and hate. This poem was written after the March 2003 U.S. invasion of Iraq, by a sixth grade boy, who was trying, through metaphor, to tackle his fears. Shawneil Campbell and his peers wrote their hearts out that day, soothing not only their own worried souls, but mine. Back on September 11, 2001, only eight miles from Ground Zero, my students worried instead if their par-ents working in Manhattan would ever come home. In the days and weeks that followed, we all, from our Brooklyn homes, watched and smelled the smoke from the towers' remains, listened to fighter planes circling our city, and wondered, as we tried to concentrate on lesson plans and schoolwork, if we were going to die.

Now, with the onset of a war, my students had a fresh new set of fears served onto their already overflowing plates. How would they handle it? I was more than aware, as I drove to my poetry residency at P.S. 156, that fear was going to feel, once again, far too familiar to my students. I was enraged with our government for the planned bombing of Baghdad that day, and wept in the car as I listened to my radio, imagining bombs falling on terrified citizens of that far-off city. I worried, too, how to transform my planned po-etry lesson into something relevant to the day's news and wrote a poem in my mind that I would try to use later as a spur to my students.

What I quickly learned was that the fears awakened by this event re-sided close to the children's homes. Many from the neighborhood had family members on active duty in Kuwait, now heading off to Iraq. Parents, aunts, uncles, and siblings of a good number of these fifth and sixth grade students were being called up. As our discussion evolved, students revealed fears about their family members being killed. They were also scared about possible retaliatory terrorism to follow. Some felt fairly sure that they were going to die soon. I choked up as I listened to their concerns, improvising even more the lesson I had begun thinking through in the car, and told them that they would have a chance, if they wanted to, to write about their worries for today's class.

The lesson I'd planned was one that I'd successfully used over the years for the jazz strand. Invented by Teachers & Writers Collaborative's Dave Hollander, it involves a poem written by Michael Fulop, "Imaginary Piano," and asks students to write a poem about an imaginary instrument that plays something other than sound. (See "Writers on Teaching" on T&W's Write-Net website, www.twc.org.) It always evokes spectacular poetry, and so, I decided to adapt it to students' responses to war. It was the perfect way to redirect them into some form of creative hopefulness. It wouldn't stop the war, but might give us all a way to feel less scared.

My classes contained mostly students I'd taught previously and they'd written some staggering poems in the weeks and months following the attacks of 9/11. Their writing skills were awesome. One student, Darnel O'Brien, had written a poem with the personification, *My solitude sobs like the Twin Towers / when the airplanes pierced their souls.* I knew on this March day in 2003, they were going to produce some powerful stuff.

After I handed out the poem "Imaginary Piano," about a piano that plays light instead of sound, students selected their own imaginary instruments. Ideas for expressions of those instruments—such as colors, abstract ideas, emotions, seasons—were written on the board, along with a list of instruments. I improvised and suggested that their instrument might also have the power to somehow help the world. I shared my own car-written poem on the board as a prompt, my saxophone dropping not bombs but strawberries into the mouths of Iraqi children. We wrote a class poem, and then, with some quiet Miles Davis playing, they began to write. Many chose drums as a personal instrument, with their fierce, powerful sound.

Many hung their fears out to dry. In a frightening release of her worries, one girl wrote that when she closed her eyes, she could hear children screaming to the beat of drums. Naquasha Troupe wrote: *Today my / bells / dangle, and make / my heartbeat / loud. / I'm scared. / When the bells ring, / it will be time for war.*

Some poems reflected actively antiwar sentiments. Shawneil's passionate poem also includes *My saxophone / blows / a powerful / protest / to the world: / "Money for Bombs / Not for War, /not / to destroy innocent / lives." / My drums play / soft / sweet / melodies of sugar / that stop / evil / and hate.*

Shamima Salam worried about the children, and was clear who her enemy was.

> My honorable bells, ring as loud
> as you can, so that the small kids
> of Iraq can go to sleep without
> the noise of dark war.
> My honorable bells, tell
> the evil Saddam Hussein to get out
> of Iraq before it is too late,
> before the bombs of fire take the hearts
> of loving people away.

Desean Simon longed on this day for the message of nonviolence he'd learned earlier that year: *I wish my trumpet could go back in time / to stop whoever killed / Martin Luther King, Jr., so he could / be here now to / speak against the war.* Jasmine Cheeves chose to transform weapons into a dessert: *My drums can drum / the bombs into chocolate . . . / . . . and my drumbeat turns Iraq / into a giant house of song.*

I wish I could say this ten-week residency art brought some peace of mind to my students. I simply do not know. They continued to use poetry as a vehicle to discuss the ever-present war. After an assignment using the lyrics of the song "Solitude" to inspire more poems (with Billie Holiday singing as they wrote), Donnell Harris poignantly wrote: *In my solitude, / I wish for non-violence: / no guns, fire, or fighting. / In my solitude, / no more dying. / Lord, please make / the violence stop.*

In the case of P.S. 156, I was, and still am, fortunate enough to have the enormous support of Oswaldo Malave, who was the assistant principal, and who is now principal of the school. This past spring, in a public ceremony, he was given a "Cultural Arts" award by the mayor of New York City, along with internationally known cultural icons. In his acceptance speech, he read aloud an excerpt from a poem written by Nigeria Tate, then a fifth grade student at P.S. 156. It exemplifies so much of what I am trying to help the students I teach to say out loud, and, indeed, what this book is all about.

> My poem has a mind of its own.
> It walks through the streets on its paper feet,
> follows the words that surround it,
> speaks its mind as it buries itself in the moonlight.
> It wants to be heard.
> It wants to be found,
> but it sees no one around.

Summary

There is no way we can guarantee that our lessons will teach our students empathy, or motivate them to believe they have the power to make an impact on the world. Certainly, the more beaten down they are by life's circumstances, the greater our challenge. I have not answered many of the questions posed at the beginning of this article and hopefully, I have posed even more.

Rilke advised a student in his book *Letters to a Young Poet* to try to love the questions themselves. I agree. If we teach our impressionable charges nothing else, it should be to keep challenging and questioning the adults in their lives through poems, letters, and the power of the spoken word. If we are to help them move their dark questions into the light, then we, too, as teachers and parents need to ask ourselves and each other whether we have helped or harmed our students when we raised the painful details of today's or yesterday's news and, of course, how can we do better? We need to be willing to ask the teacher (or parent) next door, "How did your kids handle the news today about . . . ? Do you have any ideas to help them transform the bad news into something they can manage?"

In the aftermath of recent horrific news stories, many students raised money to aid survivors of natural disasters. Ultimately, we have a moral obligation to send them out the door on a "bad news day" with a vision of something better. We need to plant the seeds that will evoke such sentiments as those expressed by fifth grader Sharif Anderson, just one month after 9/11, for a writing exercise designed to teach personification of concepts:

> Hope pulls on our souls.
> Hope screeches for faith.
> Hope leaps from the air into
> our minds.
> Hope is what belongs to us.

Leonore Gordon is a poet, an activist, a writer-in-residence for New York City's Teachers & Writers Collaborative, a family therapist, and a parent of a thirteen-year-old son. Her poetry, nonfiction articles, and translations have appeared in a variety of publications, including *The Council on Interracial Books for Children Bulletin*; *Contemporary Israeli Literature*; *Handbook: Silence 2*; *Rethinking Our Classrooms*; and *Triquarterly Review*. She has been a political activist all of her adult life, and as a result of her diagnosis of Parkinson's disease at age forty-three, is presently a Congressional Coordinator for the Parkinson's Action Network, lobbying nationally and locally for stem cell research. After learning about the long-term health effects of electromagnetic radiation on humans, and about countries and cities that prevent cell towers from going up near schools, she has also recently become deeply involved in a local campaign to prevent wireless cellular base stations from being placed irresponsibly, such as the one weighing sixteen thousand pounds scheduled to be placed on her own residential roof. Her interest in this book's theme began in college when she wrote a thesis about creativity and the unconscious, and later, when she wrote a thesis for her Bank Street College Master's degree about teaching empathy in the classroom.

6

Educating Students About the Scourge of Landmines

The world is too little aware of the waste of life, limb and land which antipersonnel landmines are causing among some of the poorest people on earth.

—Diana, Princess of Wales

Imagine

You wake up this morning in a war-torn country littered with landmines. They lurk everywhere—near paths, in fields, by homes—killing or maiming long after conflict ends. When you say good-bye to your children, do you pray that they will be playing in a field or playground free of landmines? Do you walk or drive to school wondering about the safety of the road? Recess and lunch breaks might require you to follow procedures in case of landmine explosions. If your students walk home for lunch, are they afraid of the unknown dangers that might await them? You cannot help but also worry about your own children, spouse, and relatives. During planning time or after school, you might read a student's narrative like the one that follows.

How I Live with Mines

Zdravko Mitrovic, Grade Six, Knezevo, Bosnia (Reprinted with permission from the Canadian Red Cross)

The war is over. There are feelings of joy and sorrow. Those who have survived and haven't lost anybody are happy, but those who have lost a father, brother, uncle, live with the pain. . . .

There are minefields everywhere with thousands and thousands of mines. Where to go? How to play? "Don't go there my son!" my

59

mother tells me. "Don't go to that meadow!" says my father.

"Don't go to the forest either," my grandma adds. Well, where can I go? It's dangerous wherever I go. There is no safe path. There is no safe game, no happy childhood. I used to be so happy before.

I used to go wherever I wanted to. I used to go to every stream, meadow and forest. However, I can understand everything and I tell my friends that we have to protect ourselves against the mine. I tell them all the mines are the same, be it ours or their mines. They kill, they maim, they make people ugly.

I often ask myself: "Why did the armies do it? Why did they plant those killers? Why did they kill each other? Why do they kill us? Why do they kill my friends and me? Is it really true that I can't go deep in the forest where I used to play before? No, Zdravko, you can't! I really can't!"

Oh, I want to run through all the fields I haven't run through before! I want to go to all these hidden places of my childhood! I want to show all that to my friends who don't come to visit me often! But what can I do? Mines are all around me. They pressure me, they make me feel breathless.

No, don't go there, there are mines over there!

An Excellent Model to Follow

Mark Hyman's piece serves as an excellent model for ways in which to engage your students in learning about the landmine issue. You will be inspired and moved to invite your students to learn about this relevant issue. Moreover, Hyman shows you how to teach your students to educate others. This is a seminal work by a teacher who cares and is impassioned and successful in teaching this topic. I have no doubt you will be eager to put Hyman's ideas and strategies into practice.

NURTURING COMPASSION AND GLOBAL CITIZENSHIP IN YOUTH: AN EDUCATOR'S GUIDE FOR DEVELOPING AND PROMOTING A SUCCESSFUL MINE ACTION SERVICE INITIATIVE

MARK HYMAN

Introduction: The Humanitarian Urgency of Mine Action

Costing as little as three dollars apiece—about the price of a student's lunch at the school cafeteria—they appear in various shapes and sizes, some as seemingly innocuous as a hand-sized toy butterfly. Yet they have one common purpose: to destroy whomever or whatever has the tragic misfortune to step on and detonate them. Approximately thirty million landmines lay in nations encircling much of the globe. Antipersonnel landmines kill or maim approximately 15,000 people annually worldwide, about 85 percent of whom are innocent civilians and 40 percent of whom are children. Animals fall prey to these killing devices at rates significantly above that of humans.

But the real tragedy of landmines cannot be measured or fully understood simply by quantifying the numbers. Landmines terrorize whole communities and regions of countries. Landmines devastate the productive capabilities of mine-affected families, depriving them of access to natural and agricultural resources. They stop children from attending schools or even playing. Landmines frustrate the efforts of refugees to return to their homes and of nongovernmental organizations to supply critical humanitarian aid. They hamper the ability of mine-affected communities and nations to conduct post-conflict reconstruction. Landmines are, in truth, the deadly residue and refuse of war and an affront to civilization.

Since 2000, a small but determined group of middle and high school students from Tenafly, New Jersey, have committed themselves to making a concrete difference in the lives of mine-affected villages and landmine survivors in Bosnia and Cambodia. What follows is drawn from my experience in working with these students.

Organization of This Article

There are three primary components involved in developing a landmine global service learning initiative:

- *curricular unit* on the global landmine problem
- student *landmine presentation*
- *mine action initiative* aimed at providing concrete service.

Beginning the Journey

Symbolically, this chapter is an invitation to begin a transformative educational "journey." The purpose is to familiarize you with some of the paths, obstacles, and terrain associated with this journey. Once you receive this overview, you will have to make your own decision regarding the extent of your interest and/or commitment in pursuing this path. Thus, this chapter should not be used merely to obtain concrete or anecdotal information about landmines; you should also determine the extent to which the prospects of taking this journey may excite you and your students. Whatever amount of classroom time you choose to devote to the topic, you will be performing the critical role of a true educator: that of promoting the expansion and depth of your students' humanity.

Part One: Developing and Introducing a Unit of Study on the Global Landmine Problem

Core Pedagogical Assumptions About Students

As an educator, certain core assumptions inform my practice. I believe students:

- crave opportunities to expand their real-life knowledge about the larger world
- harbor deep humanitarian and moral concerns and seek ways to explore and express them
- yearn for active participation and leadership roles in humanitarian initiatives that have a tangible impact beyond the schoolhouse door.

I believe as educators, we have a *moral and pedagogical imperative* to introduce students to various pathways for discovering and expressing their humanitarian identity and to guide them in charting their own paths of humanitarian service.

Educational Objectives for Landmine Unit

In my view, the educational objectives of an effective landmine curriculum should support student efforts in:

- placing the landmine crisis within the larger *context of human rights and armed conflict*
- recognizing the *broader destructive consequences of landmines* on mine-affected families, villages, and nations, post-conflict
- developing *empathy and compassion* for mine-affected people and communities
- expressing their *moral voices*
- exercising their capacities as *educators and leaders* in a global humanitarian service initiative.

Placing Landmines Within the Context of Human Rights

I highly recommend beginning this journey by introducing and analyzing the United Nations' Universal Declaration of Human Rights. Established in

1948 under the leadership of Eleanor Roosevelt, the U.D.H.R. contains thirty articles of rights, freedoms, and protections promised by nation-states to their citizens. Though it provides no concrete mechanism for implementation, this landmark document has served as a moral beacon for human rights advocates and organizations for decades. (For more, link to: www .udhr.org/index.htm.)

Another seminal human rights reference point is the United Nations' 1989 Convention on the Rights of the Child, which specifies rights deemed especially pertinent to the needs and potentiality of children. (For more, link to: www.unicef.org/crc/).

First Lesson: A Recommendation

Typically, I introduce my first lesson or meeting by providing brief historical context regarding the origin and creation of the U.D.H.R., followed by a brief discussion of the meaning and importance of human rights. Then, I guide the students through a basic understanding of the document's contents. With human rights as the conceptual framework, I show a landmine-related video providing a global overview of, and a visual framework for, the impact of landmines on victims, villages, and whole nations. Following, I encourage students to cite and explain which articles from the U.D.H.R. the presence of landmines violates or compromises.

The ensuing discussion, touching upon the first four educational objectives cited above, will also encourage students to think critically about how the loss or deprivation of one human right leads inevitably to the loss of others. Such a discussion leads to an exploration of how landmines hinder, compromise, or violate virtually all aspects of one's life and identity as an individual and a member of a family, community, and nation. Recognition of this harsh reality nurtures students' natural humanitarian impulses of empathy and compassion.

Suggested Landmine Topics

Certain key topics should be addressed in your unit on the global landmine crisis, including:

- impact of landmines on human rights/children's rights
- stories of landmine survivors
- rehabilitation process for landmine survivors
- impact of landmines on mine-affected communities
- effects of landmines in specific countries and worldwide

- history, types, and uses of landmines
- mine clearance or demining methods and technologies
- Ottawa Convention (Mine Ban Treaty) of 1997.

Recommended Teaching Methods and Strategies

There are many ways to introduce and explore the global landmine problem with youth. Below are educational methods and tools you can use and adapt to your particular style and setting.

Student Journal Writing

Distributing journals to your students and requiring them to record ongoing observations, reflections, and feelings should be imbedded in your educational strategies. Maintaining and modeling the use of your own journal reinforces the use and importance of writing during this process of expanding your students' burgeoning conception of landmines.

Journals can be used to:

- encourage reflection prior to a whole-group activity
- record observations, insights, reflections, and feelings during and after a group activity
- reread and recognize patterns of thought, feeling, and inquiry
- identify "seeds" for developing writing pieces for later use in a group presentation.

Role-Plays

One experience that I will never forget was an exercise that we did in the club. Mr. Hyman had covered the floor with newspapers and had placed disks under them. The disks represented landmines. I remember trying to cross the room without stepping on a disk. To so many people and children this exercise is what they have to go through every day. I ended up stepping on one of the disks. The other members had to help me get to a pretend hospital. I ended up losing my "leg" and not being able to use it the whole day. By first period I couldn't make it and I had to cheat.

Emily Gallagher

Role-plays can be powerful tools to help students identify with and more fully appreciate life in a mine-affected village. They also expose students to questions and dilemmas that they are not faced with in a mine-free country such as the United States.

Ingredients of an Effective Role-Play

There are three conditions necessary for creating and facilitating a successful role-play experience. Teachers must:

- create an interesting and age-appropriate role-play requiring students to have experiences that are interpersonal (interaction with others) and intrapersonal (identifying inner feelings and thoughts)
- insist upon a serious attitude toward the role-play
- facilitate post–role-play student processing.

Sample Middle School/High School Role-Play:
Entering a "Mine-Affected Village"

This role-play, alluded to by Emily, involves creating a mock mine-affected village. Areas for a school, a hospital, a town center, and agricultural areas are designated. Newspapers are strewn across the floor with index cards placed beneath certain pieces of paper to signify landmines. Students are then assigned a purpose to achieve and a destination to reach—such as attending school or planting in the fields—that requires them to walk over the mock minefield. (Students are required to bring journals to record their actions, thoughts, feelings, questions, decisions, and observations *during* the role-play.) As students move on the paper, they must check under it to see if they have "stepped on a mine." If so, the consequence—the loss of a limb or of sight—will be described on the index card and the victim will be required to safely reach the hospital with the aid of another villager. Once there, the victim may be confronted by a shortage of medical supplies that may hamper his/her ability to "survive." As part of the consequence of "stepping" on a landmine, students are asked not to use a designated limb for a specified period of the day.

This role-play provides students with an interactive experience that forces them to ponder and address concerns and questions pertinent only to residents in mine-affected villages. This interactive approach will *encourage identification with and empathy for* residents in real-life villages, as well as a heightened appreciation for the indirect consequences of landmines on all facets of life.

Post–Role-Play Activities

It is critically important to lead and facilitate a post–role-play discussion or exercise. This offers the *greatest opportunity to encourage students to expand and deepen their understanding* about the impact of landmines.

For the role-play just described, students should review and extend their journal responses, then share them with peers, and finally with the whole class. During subsequent whole-class sharing and discussion, you should encourage students to critically examine their role-play decisions and their experiences as "residents" in a mine-affected village. Students should be encouraged to identify ways the role-play may have transformed or deepened their thoughts and feelings about life in a mine-affected village.

Videos

Informational videos are a necessary educational tool to help students form a basic mental picture of:

- different types of landmines
- the explosive and lethal power of mines
- the physical, psychological, and societal consequences of stepping on a mine
- the consequences of landmines on a mine-affected village.

Videos can be used *early and often* as one of the most efficient means of providing a general concept and understanding of the global landmine crisis. Here are two suggested videos:

- "What's Going On?: Landmines in Cambodia" (Produced by the UN Works Programme in collaboration with Showtime Networks and RCN Entertainment. Length: 30 minutes.) Laurence Fishburne hosts this powerful, poignant television report featuring two Cambodian children who survived landmine explosions. Ordering information, along with other materials, is available at: www.un.org/works/goingon /mines/goingon_mines.html.
- "Healing the Wounds of War: Global Care Unlimited and the Youth Coalition for Mine Action" (Produced by Global Care Unlimited, Inc. Length: 34 minutes.) This video uses excerpts from our 2002 Youth Coalition Landmine Conference plus footage from Mark Hyman's trip to Nicaragua to introduce the global landmine problem. Ordering information available at: www.globalcareunlimited.org.

Print Articles

It is imperative to provide students with access to written material about landmines. Two basic types of print resources are useful: *newspapers and periodicals/online articles*. Such articles may be devoted to a particular subtopic such as demining, or a feature article on a landmine survivor, activist, or organization. The most comprehensive periodical devoted to landmines is the *Journal of Mine Action*, published quarterly by James Madison University. While the reading level is geared for high school and college level students, middle school students can certainly benefit from it.

Finding and introducing at least one or two articles that focus on a personal story of a landmine survivor will facilitate your students' ability to empathize with the plight of the featured individual, and the plight of tens of thousands of persons whose stories have not been publicized.

Dialogue

It is essential to provide regular opportunities for students to articulate their thoughts and feelings about the topic of landmines. It is especially important in the beginning to conduct a healthy portion of whole-group discussions, which serve as the means through which the *culture* of your group is created. The way students think, feel, and talk about the topic of landmines will be an outgrowth of the type of interaction and conversation that occurs during these meetings. The teacher must model the type of conversational tone he/she wants reflected in his/her students.

Internet Research

The Internet is a vital educational tool for landmine research and student empowerment. Student discovery, evaluation, and retrieval of landmine-related information and articles give students a tremendous sense of ownership over their landmine education.

It is appropriate at any stage to encourage your students to begin exploring the Web as a supplement to the topics you are working on. Students might begin to accumulate "favorite" websites for later research or to peruse and print informational pages or articles deemed helpful or meaningful. Thus, students begin to take ownership, both individually and collectively, of the accumulation and development of a working and growing landmine curriculum.

Recommended Landmine Websites for Information

- www.mineaction.org/index.asp (United Nations Mine Action Information Network): Information on all aspects of mine action.
- www.landmines.org/crisis (Adopt-A-Minefield): Comprehensive readable overview of the global landmine problem.
- www.icbl.org/lm (Landmine Monitor): Up-to-date profiles about the landmine problem in every mine-affected country.
- http://members.iinet.net.au/~pictim/mines/photos/mines.html (Tim Grant Photos): Riveting landmine images.
  www.howstuffworks.com/landmine.htm (How Stuff Works): Explanation of the technology of landmines.

Online Educational Resources

- www.maic.jmu.edu/journal/index/index.htm (Journal of Mine Action): Articles on every aspect of mine action.
- www.state.gov/t/pm/wra/partners/c14759.htm (Landmine Action Smart Book: A Primer on Mine Action).
- www.newsweekeducation.com/index.php> (Newsweek Education Program): Interactive Map: "Land Mines: Eliminating the Threat."
- www.state.gov/r/pa/prs/ps/2005/57253.htm. Newsweek landmine wall map.

Part Two: Developing a Student Landmine Presentation

At this stage, you and your students may be preparing to take a significant step forward: developing a landmine awareness initiative. Such a step forward involves a serious level of commitment on the part of all participants but the intrinsic rewards are immense. In this section, I provide specific strategies and guidelines for encouraging, guiding, and facilitating the development of student "products"—items created to foster the education of others—as well as for organizing them into a cohesive and powerful landmine awareness presentation.

Facilitating Student Independent Research

The Changing Role of the Teacher

After introducing the major topics that encompass the global landmine problem, it is time to promote student independent research on topics of interest. This focus on student research, ownership, and independence will affect the nature of your meetings as well as your role as advisor-facilitator. Instead of whole-group meetings, the bulk of your time will now be spent conducting teacher-student conferences. During these conferences, you will assist each of your students in:

- identifying and refining their selected topics of inquiry
- locating sufficient and appropriate sources of information
- understanding or clarifying areas of confusion about topics
- organizing information in a logical and concise manner.

Evolving Role of Whole-Group Meetings

The focus and purpose of whole-class meetings shift in accordance with the altered focus on independent student research. The purpose of group meetings at this stage includes:

- sharing student discoveries and enthusiasm regarding their research findings
- negotiating timetables for completion of research tasks
- introducing pertinent or newsworthy articles, videos, or information about landmines
- brainstorming nature and format of student presentations.

Identifying Landmine-Related Research Topics

With your help, students should identify a wide spectrum of potential topics for landmine research. Your role is to ensure that key topics are included in the master list. (See "Suggested Landmine Topics.")

Developing Student Products for Presentations

The research phase involves discussing and establishing a vision for the types of educational products the students will create for use in group presentations. In broad terms, student products can be categorized as "creative" or "informational." *Creative products* refer to the students' exploration and expression of their personal reactions to the topic of landmines. Poetry, essays, stories, paintings, or drawings embody this category. *Informational products* are aimed primarily at providing concise, easily understandable information about some specific aspect of the global landmine problem.

Informational Student Products

Given the importance of presenting both substantial information and vivid visuals, the primary method chosen by my students has been to:

- utilize Microsoft PowerPoint to organize information and visuals into sequential slides
- print the slides and paste onto self-standing three-sided presentation boards.

Creative Student Products

If you have previously used student journal writing, your students will have "seeds" for the creation of poetry, stories, or other creative, reflective, or artistic responses to the landmine problem. Your role is to encourage your students to identify and express their deepest feelings and insights in a heartfelt form.

Transforming Products into a Group Presentation

After accumulating enough student products, it is necessary to coalesce them into a group presentation that will educate your school and surrounding community about the landmine crisis. The first step in this dramatic and exciting transition is for your students to decide upon the type of educational presentation to create. My students have used two basic formats effectively. Each can easily be transported and used in almost any setting and ideally, both should be incorporated into your presentation:

- multimedia *dramatic reading* of student creative writing products
- interactive *gallery tour* of student presentation boards about aspects of the global landmine issue.

Multimedia Dramatic Reading

During its inauguration, the Tenafly Middle School Landmine Awareness Club developed a fifteen-minute multimedia presentation based on dramatic readings of student writings, accompanied by video projections of images of landmines, survivors, mine-affected villages, and other pertinent visuals. Poignant selections of music were used to reinforce the somber and reflective mood. The writing consisted of the following:

- facts about the global landmine crisis
- original student writing
- stories and quotes from landmine survivors
- pertinent articles from the United Nations' Universal Declaration of Human Rights.

These various strands of writing were interwoven into a cohesive and extraordinarily moving presentation. Below is a masterful example of student writing.

METAL

Max Rosmarin

It is a round piece of cold metal.
It lies in the ground, in wait.
It has no mind.
It has no soul.
It has no purpose.
Except to injure.
To kill.
And it does so.
Relentlessly.
Quickly.
It is placed by an army.
It is not always placed to kill another army.
It is often placed to kill civilians.
To stop them from working.
To use up doctors, hospital and medicine.
It creates a pile of amputated limbs.
It creates a mountain of amputated souls.
It is deadly.
It is uncaring.
It is hidden from view.
Until it destroys.
It is a round piece of cold metal.
It is a landmine.

Evaluation of the Multimedia Dramatic Oral Presentation

The advantages of this method for presenting are numerous. This presentation:

- inspires an *affective reaction* from one's audience
- provides students with an opportunity to *passionately* voice their thoughts and feelings
- places the topic of landmines within the framework of *human rights*
- vividly displays a sense of *cohesion and teamwork* among the student-presenters.

Interactive Gallery Tour

In a gallery tour format, student presentation boards are arranged so that people may circulate around them while students provide oral presentations about their areas of expertise.

Evaluation of Gallery Tours

The gallery method of presenting is an effective educational tool as it:

- promotes student *mastery* regarding a particular aspect of landmines
- allows the audience to focus on landmine *topics of particular interest*
- provides a *significant amount of information* about a wide range of topics in an *efficient and interactive* manner.

Student Professionalism

Your audience must perceive your students as professional, serious, and highly competent presenters. Therefore, I urge you to require your student-presenters to maintain an appropriate outward decorum and to wear professional and formal attire.

Part Three

Transforming Local Action into Global Consequence: Developing and Implementing a School-Based Mine-Action Initiative

At eleven years old I hardly knew what I was getting into joining the Landmines Awareness Club at Tenafly Middle School. At most, I expected to learn about the global landmines problem and to write creatively in response to what I studied. I had the opportunity to do those things, but I soon discovered that I was involved in something much greater. Indeed, now in my seventh year with the group, I have come to understand the local and international scope and significance of our work.

My experiences with Global Care Unlimited are not easily summarized or interpreted. Yet they have wrought one result that I consider to be especially important. In a small, affluent community such as Tenafly, it is easy to turn a deaf ear to world crises and to never learn altruism. The work of Mark Hyman and the organization he helped to found drove me far from that tendency and taught me to be a citizen of the world in the purest sense of the phrase. From giving presentations to schools in the area to speaking with landmine survivors like Julio Perez and Ken Rutherford to visiting a landmine survivors' vocational training class in Cambodia, my experiences with Global Care Unlimited have opened my eyes to humanitarian issues and have instilled in me a global conscience which will never leave me. For this I am eternally grateful.

Ben Gallagher

A Touchstone Moment

I watched with pride as tenth grader Ben Gallagher stood before the classroom of Cambodian electronics students to deliver a short statement of appreciation and encouragement. In February 2005, Ben, along with five other middle and high school student-ambassadors, traveled halfway around the world to Kompong Cham along the Mekong River, in large part for this moment. Ben was addressing a classroom of Cambodian landmine survivors who were being given a chance to reclaim their lives through vocational rehabilitation funded, to a significant degree, by Global Care Unlimited, Inc., a youth-led humanitarian organization inspired by students from Tenafly, New Jersey. With this visit our humanitarian mission had come full circle; the students and I were able to meet, speak with, and touch some of the 105 mine-affected Cambodians whom we had worked so long and so hard to assist.

In this section I will retrace—in broad strokes—the humanitarian pathways my students and I blazed, while suggesting ways to assist you in forging a homegrown service pathway of your own. The overall purpose of this section is to help you proceed with confidence with the crucial final step of service learning: from recognition of a problem to making a tangible difference to alleviate it. I will outline *an eight-step process* to ensure a successful mine action campaign in your local school and community.

Step One: Visualizing the Outcome/Defining the Objectives

All your students' efforts will be guided and motivated by the desire to make a tangible difference in the field of mine action. Consequently, it is important to determine as early as possible—even during your formal teaching unit—what concrete service your class hopes to provide.

Guide your students in imagining themselves making a tangible difference in some mine-affected community and encourage them to make this vision concrete: have them articulate it, draw it, and "see" it in their mind's eye. Let their moral imagination expand into a vision of service; whatever image most inspires and compels your students to action should be one of the main guideposts by which you select an objective for mine action.

Possible Objectives for Your Mine Action Initiative

Basically, there are four types of objectives your students can establish for this landmine service initiative.

- support for *landmine removal*
- support for *landmine survivor rehabilitation*
- *community awareness* about the global landmine issue
- advocacy for the United States to sign the *Mine Ban Treaty*.

  Note: I have confined my advice to the first three objectives, since my students did not tackle advocacy as their focus. For more information on this issue, go to the following websites:

  www.icbl.org (International Campaign to Ban Landmines): Nobel-Peace-Prize–winning coalition of nongovernmental organizations advocating universal support of the Mine Ban Treaty.

  www.state.gov/t/pm/wra/c11735.htm: U.S. Department of State Landmine Policy (as of 2/27/04).

The first two objectives require raising funds for a selected implementing organization; they will be my primary focus for the remainder of this article. The third objective—aimed exclusively at educational awareness for school and community—will be embedded in a number of the steps discussed below. The final objective involves your students in the political realm of the issue: American policy and the Mine Ban Treaty.

Factors to Consider in Determining Your Objective for Mine Action

To translate your vision into concrete reality, your students will need to address the following questions:

- What type of assistance do we want to provide?
- If the assistance is monetary, what realistic goal can we set for fundraising?
- What region of the world and beneficiaries do we want to assist?
- What level of commitment in terms of time and energy are we willing to invest?
- What organization will we select to provide direct services to our beneficiaries?

In the ensuing sections, I offer some guidelines to help you make choices, as well as provide brief case studies drawn from my own experiences with students to help clarify my points.

Landmine Removal: Pathways for Peace

Support for landmine removal can take the following forms

- "adoption" of an *entire specified minefield*
- support for some *part* of a larger minefield
- support for the *equipment* used by a demining team
- support for part or all of a *demining dog's training.*

Of those methods of support listed above, the most daunting is adoption of an entire minefield. This is true simply because the price tag for that level of support can be in the tens of thousands of dollars. However, each of the other options can be pursued without this level of responsibility; student funding will simply be pooled with the contributions of other groups.

Whatever your monetary contribution may be, your students can take pride in saving or safeguarding the lives and limbs of persons in a mine-affected village, as well as securing a level of safety necessary for reestablishing humane living conditions.

Landmine Survivor Rehabilitation: Restoring Hope

Another noble path for service involves assisting in the rehabilitation of landmine survivors. A survivor rehabilitation initiative should be seen as restoring hope to the lives of innocent people, families, and communities. Helping to enable even one survivor to regain a sense of purpose and belonging will have an untold positive effect on the survivor's family and local community. It is, in truth, a lifesaving endeavor.

Types of Rehabilitation: Physical and Vocational

The process of rehabilitating a landmine survivor involves a number of stages. Following initial medical intervention, a survivor should ideally undergo an extensive process of physical, psychological, social, and vocational rehabilitation. For our purposes, it is best to divide this process into the following two parts:

- *physical rehabilitation* (fitting prosthetic or artificial limbs and learning their use)

- *vocational rehabilitation and reintegration* (training survivors with vocational skills and assisting in their reintegration into their communities).

The Power of Visualization: Adopting a Mine-Affected Village

In spring 2000, Global Care Unlimited conducted extensive research before "adopting" the mine-affected village of Podzvizd in Bosnia-Herzegovina. This decision was greatly influenced by the ability of our Bosnian demining partners to provide the following items:

- a site survey of Podzvizd and its minefield
- photographs of the town and minefield
- photos of a local youth landmine survivor.

Armed by this information and these visuals, students were gripped by their dream to help remove landmines and restore safety to Podzvizd.

Step Two: Identifying and Selecting Your Implementing Mine Action Partner(s)

In order to make a tangible difference in a global humanitarian initiative, your students must identify and establish a relationship with an organization responsible for implementation of the service initiative you are supporting. Select your implementing partner based on the following factors:

- whether you wish to support demining or landmine survivor rehabilitation
- the geographic location of your focus
- the organization's track record (request official reports documenting their work) and willingness to provide you with specific information about the mine-affected village or landmine survivors your students hope to sponsor.

A Case Study: Finding an Implementing Organization for Our Cambodian Survivor Initiative

In the winter of 2004, my student-leaders decided to focus on assisting Cambodian landmine survivors. Among the organizations conducting rehabilitation in Cambodia, we contacted Clear Path International. After receiving an extensive email report regarding their work, I arranged a school visit and presentation from one of its founders. She delivered separate presentations to our sixth and seventh grade students explaining the purpose of vocational training and citing profiles of survivors who had benefited from their program. This personal contact and clear documentation greatly enhanced our ability to visualize the life conditions of our prospective target population as well as the specific ways in which Clear Path's program helps to restore hope to these people. Consequently, we decided to select CPI as our implementing partner in Cambodia.

Nongovernmental Organizations Involved in Landmine Removal and/or Survivor Assistance Projects

There are dozens of reputable organizations conducting demining and/or survivor assistance projects worldwide. Your best strategy for identifying these organizations is to conduct an online search using "demining" or "landmine rehabilitation" and your country of interest.

Step Three: Building a Network of School-Based Support

The introduction of a mine action initiative will need the support of colleagues, parents, and administration to reach its potential for success. Colleagues can provide assistance in organizing and scheduling events and presentations as well as in suggesting interdisciplinary classroom connections. You should be able to identify and nurture at least one or two like-minded colleagues willing to go the extra mile to assist you. If possible, offer a brief student presentation at a faculty meeting to establish a basic ground of awareness about your initiative among your colleagues.

Parents can provide critical practical support (planning, organizing, and volunteering) related to events and presentations, especially those geared for the larger community. Parent support should be nurtured by holding periodic evening meetings in which you promote their landmine "literacy" while nurturing a corps of committed volunteers.

Of course, it is essential to gain the confidence and support of your building principal or administrator. You need your principal to approve any changes your initiative might require in scheduling and staffing, in particular, regarding the delivery of your students' presentation in classrooms, assemblies, and off-site. To justify such disruptions, you must demonstrate that your initiative will benefit the student body, as well as the reputation of your school.

Step Four: Identifying Target Audiences and Venues for Your Presentation and Fundraising Appeal

Your students should reach out to the following types of audiences for support.

- the school student body

- the student body in other in-district schools
- parents
- local citizens.

Depending on the needs and availability of these population groups, your students may need to deliver presentations in a variety of settings and formats. For students, you should seek to deliver *classroom presentations* to combined classes, when possible, to assure the greatest level of interaction and intimacy between the student presenters and their peers. For parents and the general community, you should try to arrange a school-based *evening presentation* to accommodate the scheduling needs of working adults. For more targeted community outreach, you should try to schedule presentations for *houses of worship* and *local service clubs* (Rotary, Lions).

Step Five: Developing a Fundraising Philosophy and Strategy

Linking Education and Fundraising

Whenever possible, *fundraising should be linked to education via your student presentation*. Such a linkage highlights the role of your students as educators and leaders as well as their genuine concern about the landmine issue. Your students' evident commitment to help mine-affected people should inspire your audience to provide direct support for your initiative and promote a burgeoning "community of concern," as students, colleagues, parents, and citizens become empowered to share their learning with others.

A Powerful Mine Action Symbol: Reclaiming the Butterfly

During Global Care's demining initiative for Podzvizd, we adopted the butterfly as a powerful symbol in response to the reality of the "butterfly landmine" that can attract the attention of small children. Our use of the butterfly was intended as both a protest against the horrific consequence of this landmine and a means of "reclaiming" the butterfly as a form that connotes beauty, gentleness, and innocence.

To this end, our students and parents developed butterfly landmine packets for distribution upon completion of each of our landmine presentations. These packets contained the following:

- fact sheet about the global landmine problem
- description of Podzvizd
- ten small butterfly shapes
- symbolic "butterfly" landmine.

Students were asked to seek donations of at least \$3—the cost of a cheap landmine—for each of their butterflies; these butterflies—with the names of the donors printed on them—were affixed to the surface of the larger butterfly-shaped "landmine." In this way, students symbolically transformed their landmine into a string of butterflies, creating a remarkable public testament to our community's effort to demine Podzvizd one landmine at a time.

Step Six: Promoting Public Awareness and Support

Public Displays

A public display accessible to students, parents, and local residents is an excellent way of promoting awareness about landmines and your initiative. Suggestions include:

- creating a mock minefield
- painting a landmine mural
- displaying samples of student writing and informational panels
- hosting a booth display about landmines at a townwide event.

A Powerful Visual: Creating and Displaying a Mock Minefield

An outstanding way of garnering public awareness about the global landmine problem is to have your students create a mock minefield, consisting of:

- styrofoam balls cut and painted to resemble different types of landmines
- "Danger Landmines" signs printed in different languages and posted *within* your minefield
- "caution tape" *encircling* your minefield
- an explanatory note regarding landmines and your initiative.

Strategically placed on school grounds, your mock minefield will promote significant attention and conversation among your entire school community.

Other Publicity Vehicles

There are a number of other outstanding publicity strategies to utilize. These include:

- a mayor's proclamation
- a kickoff event

- an evening public presentation
- a project website
- a print or television story about your initiative.

Kickoff Event for Podzvizd: Unforeseen Benefits

On April 17, 2000, Global Care Unlimited dramatically launched its Landmine Removal Initiative for Podzvizd by using a number of the suggestions listed above. The ensuing newspaper article inspired outreach from Dave Rabadan of the U.S. Department of State Office of Global Humanitarian Demining (currently known as the Office of Weapons Removal and Abatement). This connection, in turn, produced a remarkable chain of unforeseen benefits:

- a student presentation at the State Department to Ambassador Donald Steinberg, Special Representative of the President and Secretary of State for Global Humanitarian Demining
- a meeting with the then Director of the Department of State's Bureau of Political-Military Affairs' Office of Humanitarian Demining Programs, Pat Patierno, who informed us of a method by which the U.S. government would match our funding for Podzvizd
- an invitation for Global Care Unlimited to become an official "Public-Private Partner" with the U.S. Department of State.

Step Seven: Documenting Your Initiative

It is extremely important to obtain documentation to demonstrate the efforts of your students as well as the actual work conducted by your implementing organization.

Documenting Your Initiative as Narrative

Encourage students to perceive their efforts in terms of an unfolding narrative of compassion. As such, it is essential to document every significant event or presentation of your ongoing initiative through photographs, videotape footage, and, when possible, media coverage. Such documentation builds momentum and credibility as students, colleagues, parents, and community members monitor the progress of your initiative. Documentation can also be used to:

- enhance your website
- create a promotional video.

*Documentation and Verification of the Work of Your
Implementing Organization*

It is critical to receive evidence and verification of your implementing partner's compliance in providing direct services via:

- a written report, complete with any pertinent data (for example, number of landmines detected and removed)
- photographs documenting their work and its benefits.

Such documentation certifies the proper use of your donors' funds and confirms the humanitarian impact of your initiative.

Step Eight: Celebrating Your Accomplishments

Celebrating your group's achievements is an important final phase of any student-led service initiative. You should organize a school-based public event in which you:

- invite a representative of your implementing organization to publicly receive your donation and provide a presentation of the direct services provided to your "adopted" village or landmine survivors
- retell the "story" of your initiative
- acknowledge significant supporters (colleagues, principal, parents, donors)
- honor your student-leaders.

Such a celebration will also build a supportive school culture for compassion and moral leadership, as well as inspire non-participating students to join your student-leaders in future school-based humanitarian endeavors.

"Demining with Partners": Reaching the Summit

On February 8, 2001, Global Care Unlimited culminated its multi-year Landmine Removal Initiative on behalf of Podzvizd with an official signing ceremony with Department of State Department official Pat Patierno—witnessed by the entire student body—that affirmed the successful completion of our demining project by guaranteeing that the Department of State would match our $15,000 donation. The success of this initiative and the resultant media attention that followed inspired my students to continue their commitment to humanitarian service to this day.

Closing Thoughts: The Journey of Compassion

This chapter is an invitation and a conceptual and moral compass to assist you in initiating a challenging but extraordinary journey, one of compassion and transformation with your students, as you attempt to create an educational and humanitarian mine action initiative. It can seem like an overwhelming journey to begin and a demanding one in which to persevere. But, in my experience, the hardest step is the first, the one that places you on the path. Once there, you and your students will likely gain your bearings and build momentum, desire, and passion as you educate yourselves and prepare to educate others about the global landmine problem. You may encounter detours or roadblocks along the way, just as so many children and civilians encounter the danger of landmines on their daily paths. If so, make use of this article, this "compass," and the resources it offers for orienting, navigating, and constructing your own trail. Take advantage of these lessons, then build upon them, refining and updating the path as you go.

A Closing Appeal: Imagine What We Can Do Together

The destruction of innocent life is, everywhere and at all times, a violation of fundamental human rights. It creates a kind of "moral fissure" in our collective human tissue and an accompanying need for some act of compassion to close that gap. By educating our local community and beyond about the global landmine crisis, and by raising funds sufficient to demine a village in Bosnia and rehabilitate landmine survivors in Cambodia, the youth involved in our mine action initiatives have made a profound and unmistakable moral assertion: they have affirmed their conviction that it is both possible and necessary to seek opportunities to heal, to salvage, to affirm life. They have offered, and continue to offer, their most heartfelt responses to this urgent human need for healing the wounds of conflict. In the process, they have demonstrated that youth can play a pivotal role as peacemakers and healers of humanity.

The Talmud says, "He who saves one life, it is as if he has saved the world entire." Please join us in seeking ways to heal, preserve, and make tangible differences in the lives of those halfway around the globe. Please join our Global Care Youth Coalition. Imagine what we can do together.

Mark Hyman is a middle school reading teacher in Tenafly, New Jersey, as well as founder and president of Global Care Unlimited, Inc. Since 2000, Global Care Unlimited has conducted youth-led demining and survivor rehabilitation initiatives in Bosnia and Cambodia. Mark's current project with Global Care Unlimited is the Cambodian Humanitarian Initiative, which focuses on a range of humanitarian needs.

Mark hopes this article will inspire educator and youth participation in a nationwide Youth Coalition for Mine Action spearheaded by Global Care Unlimited. For more information about Mark Hyman, the Youth Coalition, and Global Care Unlimited, Inc., go to: www.globalcareunlimited.org.

7

Child Soldiers: Living in a World of War

We must not close our eyes to the fact that child soldiers are both victims and perpetrators. They sometimes carry out the most barbaric acts of violence. But no matter what the child is guilty of, the main responsibility lies within us, the adults. It is immoral that adults should want children to fight their wars for them. . . . There is simply no excuse, no acceptable argument for arming children.

—Archbishop Desmond M. Tutu

Instead of Going to School, They Go to War

I've seen people get their hands cut off, a ten-year-old girl raped and then die, and so many men and women burned alive. . . . So many times I just cried inside my heart because I didn't dare cry out loud.

Fourteen-year-old girl, abducted in January 1999 by the Revolutionary United Front, a rebel group in Sierra Leone. (www.hrw.org 2004)

While your students attend class, approximately 300,000 child soldiers (Deen 2005) throughout the world might be carrying supplies, acting as spies, charging in human-wave attacks, and performing other duties. While our children might not be able to conceive of life on the battlefield, child soldiers know of little else. Students talk about school, friends, and family. Child soldiers converse about strategies, roles, and responsibilities, attacks, ambush, and surrender.

Abducted, purchased, even handed over by their own families, fighters as young as five have become a vital part of the world's separatist factions. They have emerged as the new warriors in the 21st century on battlefields not only throughout South Asia, but wherever wars rage. They have confronted U.S. forces in Iraq and Afghanistan, carried out suicide missions in Israel, butchered families in Africa, and fought with rebels in Colombia and Peru.

84

A world in which ten-year-olds carry Kalashnikovs and teenagers strap themselves with explosives is nearly unimaginable if you live where war is distant—where children get no closer to battle than a video game. But the figures are staggering in many parts of the world. Sixty percent of the nonstate armed forces today use child soldiers; 23 percent use child soldiers fifteen and younger; as many as 300,000 children "are currently fighting in wars or have recently been demobilized." (Farrell 2005)

While American teenage boys and girls work part-time and participate in school clubs and team sports, children as young as nine years old in war-ravaged countries run the risk of being forcibly recruited through intimidation, abduction, beatings, coercion, death threats, and drugging (UNICEF 2003). Child soldiers may be raped or become sexual slaves to military commanders (Dusauchoit 2003).

Child soldiers might well grow up in a world alien to the childhood described by the preamble to the UN Convention on the Rights of the Child—in a family environment of happiness, love, and understanding.

> One day, my friends and I were forced by our commanders to kill a family . . . I decided I had to flee and I ran away to the forest . . . but some soldiers found me and brought me back to a military camp. They imprisoned me and beat me every day . . . Today I am afraid. I don't know how to read, I don't know where my family is. I have no future . . . My life is lost . . . At night I can no longer sleep, I keep thinking of those horrible things I have seen and done as a soldier.
>
> *"Kalami," fifteen-year-old boy from the Democratic Republic of Congo who fought with various armed forces from the age of nine. (© Human Rights Watch 2004)*

> Even though I was pregnant, I had to fight the enemy . . . I had confrontations with the enemy with the baby on my chest . . . to have my baby there with me and thinking my baby might die too was very, very hard for me—the baby is the most precious thing in the world to me.
>
> *Maria, a twelve-year-old fighting in Colombia's fifty-year-old guerilla war. (Save the Children 2003)*

In this chapter, your students will learn how child soldiers live and about an effort to end the arming of children for conflict. As your students explore this issue, have them keep in mind that the practice of using seventeen-year-old Americans in conflicts in Iraq and Afghanistan has been eliminated (Human Rights Watch 2004).

Who Are the Child Soldiers? (Class Activity)

Give students the definition of a child soldier and discuss the question, "How big a problem is the use of child soldiers today and why should we be concerned about it?"

The CSC (Coalition to Stop the Use of Child Soldiers) defines a "child soldier" as "any person under eighteen years of age who is a member of or attached to the armed forces or an armed group, whether or not there is an armed conflict." Child soldiers perform tasks ranging from direct participation in combat and military activities such as scouting, spying, sabotage, acting as decoys, couriers, or guards, to that of sex slaves and forced labor (CSC 2002).

Teaching Empathy About Child Soldiers Through Ecphrastic Poetry

Before students can begin to understand and help put an end to the use of child soldiers, they need to empathize with them. One of the best ways I know of is through ecphrastic poetry lessons. For a more comprehensive description, read Nancy Gorrell's article in Chapter Four. Here are guidelines for this activity, which I took from Gorrell's piece.

- Display a photo of a child soldier.
- Ask the class, "How do you think that child soldier might feel?"
- Once they have discussed the photo, you may take a photo for which you have written an ecphrastic poem and share both with students. The power of such modeling for the class and its effects cannot be underestimated.
- Display copies of child soldier photos and let students choose which photo to use.
- Have them study the photos for a few quiet minutes. Then have students write questions or reactions they have to their photos.
- Keeping instructions open and simple, pose the following questions:
    1. If you could speak to the child soldier, what would you say?
    2. If you could speak to anyone in the photograph, what would you say?
    3. If you could imagine any of the subjects speaking, what do you think they would say?
    4. In your journals, write any poem reflecting on your viewing of this photograph. You may re-read your wonder questions and reflections to help you get started.
- Sitting in a circle, have students share and discuss each other's poems.

- Encourage students to continue revising their poems.
- Ask students to make an artistic display with both photos and poems.

  Great sources of child soldiers photos are:

  Google images

  www.childsoldiers.org/ourimages/

  www.spur.asn.au/photos.html

  http://hrw.org/photos/2003/colombia/

Rachel Klein, a student of Nancy Gorrell's (see Chapter Four for more information about her) at Morristown High School, Morristown, New Jersey, wrote the following poem in response to viewing a photo of a child soldier.

CHILD SOLDIER

Rachel Klein, seventeen, Morristown High School, Morristown, New Jersey

They say I have no use
I am wounded, battered, broken
And have service no more,
Yet now I am more useful than
Ever before.
My story
My song
Shall be sung across the hill tops
I am what the world has become
My struggle is the tool
To our change
And never
In my life
Have I been
More
Useful.

Discussing Facts About Child Soldiers

Have students read the following fact sheet and discuss the information it contains.

FACTS ABOUT CHILD SOLDIERS

© Human Rights Watch 2006. Reprinted with permission.

- Today, as many as 300,000 children under the age of eighteen—and some as young as eight—serve in government forces or armed rebel groups.

- Participation of child soldiers has been reported in 33 ongoing or recent armed conflicts in almost every region of the world.

- Child soldiers are used by armed opposition forces; many are used by government armies.

- Children are uniquely vulnerable to recruitment because of their emotional and physical immaturity. Easily manipulated, they can be drawn into violence they are too young to resist or understand.

- Technological advances in weaponry and the proliferation of small arms have contributed to the increased use of child soldiers. Light-weight automatic weapons—simple to operate, often easily accessible—can be easily used by children.

- Child soldiers usually are poor, separated from their families, displaced from their homes, living in a combat zone, or have limited access to education. Orphans and refugees are particularly vulnerable.

- Many children join armed groups because of economic or social pressure, or because they believe the group will offer food or security. Others are forcibly recruited, "press-ganged," or abducted by armed groups.

- Both girls and boys are used as child soldiers. In case studies in El Salvador, Ethiopia, and Uganda, almost a third were reported to be girls. Girls may be raped or given to military commanders as "wives."

- Once recruited, child soldiers may serve as porters or cooks, guards, messengers, or spies. Pressed into combat, many are forced to the front lines or sent into minefields ahead of older troops. Children have been used for suicide missions.

- Children are sometimes forced to commit atrocities against their family or neighbors. Such practices ensure that the child is "stigmatized" and unable to return home.

- Approximately one out of 10 soldiers fighting today is a child (Zelinski 2005).

- Child soldiers participate in 75 percent of the current wars (Zelinski 2005).

Children at War (Lesson)

The following lesson was developed by Doug DuBrin, an English and history teacher as well as a professional writer. (His news- and culture-based work can be found on the Online NewsHour, www.newshour.org, and Busted Halo.com, www.bustedhalo.com. DuBrin also writes Chicago-oriented pieces for the travel site NFT: Not for Tourists, www.notfortourists.com. His Children at War lesson is excerpted from Online NewsHour Extra, copyright MacNeil-Lehrer Productions. Reprinted with permission.)

DOUG DUBRIN

Objective

This lesson will familiarize students with the extensive use of children in combat so they can begin to examine both causes and consequences of the practice.

Procedure

1. Have students read the following materials accessed via the Internet either beforehand or as a class:

   - Copy of NewsHour Extra article: "Disarming Liberian Child Soldiers," www.pbs.org/newshour/extra/features/july-dec03 /liberia_8-27.html

   - Copy of Human Rights Watch overview, www.hrw.org/campaigns /crp/index.htm

   - In-depth investigation of impact titled "Children at Both Ends of the Gun," www.unicef.org/graca/

2. As the students refer to the readings, have them answer the following questions (either in small groups or individually). Possible answers are provided in the teacher key which follows, but the link www.unicef.org/graca/ to UNICEF will significantly deepen your (their) knowledge.

   - What are some reasons that children, as opposed to adults, are chosen for combat?

   - What circumstances in a society might lead children into combat situations?

   - What do you imagine are some of the consequences to children who take part in war?

   - In most U.S. states, 16-years-olds can legally work, drive, or leave school, although they may not vote until 18 or drink alcohol until 21. If the U.S. were to adopt an official policy of children at 16 serving in combat, while maintaining the current voting and drinking age, how would you respond? If the voting and drinking ages were also lowered to 16, would you be more likely to support the policy of children in combat?

3. Discuss the responses as a class.

Teacher Key for Questions

- *What are some reasons that children, as opposed to adults, are chosen for combat?*

  Children tend to have boundless energy that can be helpful in physically exhausting combat situations; are typically more aggressive and quicker to react than adults, which can be useful in battle; usually defer to authority and take orders easily; do not have as well developed consciences as most adults, and therefore are less inclined to feel guilt or remorse about injuring or killing another; personalities are not yet fully formed, so they can be molded in a way that military leaders find valuable.

- *What circumstances in a society might lead children into combat situations?*

  The breakdown of family structures due to war, violence, or poverty can lead children to find sustenance and a sense of belonging in the armed forces; military leaders sometimes use force or coercion to "recruit" children from schools and their families; and ongoing and deeply rooted hostilities, such as those in Northern Ireland or Palestine, can cause children to feel obligated to exact revenge against an enemy or honor one's religion or family in battle.

- *What do you imagine are some of the consequences to children who take part in war?*

  Like adults, children can suffer acute psychological problems as a result of the trauma of combat. Children's minds, though (like their bodies), can be more resilient than those of adults, so once in a stable and supportive environment, the child can heal. Yet children can experience profound damage to their fragile psyches, and as they search for ways outside the battlefield to cope with the physical and mental pain from combat, they can lash out violently, experience deep depression, or fall prey to substance abuse.

Why Fight When So Young? (Lesson)

Prior to class, have students think about the questions below and be prepared for discussion. The questions are from www.epals.com/waraffected children/chap2, where students can participate in an online discussion related to these questions and more.

- Have you ever been forced to do something you didn't want to do? How did that make you feel?

- Have you ever felt pressured by an entire group of people to do something you knew was wrong? How did you handle it?
- Would you leave school to find a job if it meant your family could eat?
- Would you take a job that challenged your ethics in order to feed your family?

Following discussion, ask students, "How do you think those questions relate to understanding the experiences of a child soldier?" Have students individually brainstorm reasons why they think children become child soldiers and explain what situations lead them to become soldiers. List reasons on a chartpak or blackboard, then compare some of the following reasons with those of your students.

REASONS CHILDREN BECOME SOLDIERS

- forced to join armed groups
- abducted by armed groups
- for protection in war
- threatened with destruction of families and communities if they refuse
- cultural and social pressures forcing them to fight
- economic or political pressures forcing them to fight.

(The above reasons provided by ePals.com Classroom Exchange 2004)

Understanding What Life Is Like as a Child Soldier (Lesson)

(The first part of this lesson is taken from the Extension Activity I in the Child at War lesson by Doug DuBrin.)

In addressing the following questions, students should envision themselves (*at their current age*) as participants in combat situations; responses may be given in small groups, as a class, or in essay format. Urge your class to respond to the hypothetical situation as truthfully as possible:

- How would you respond to the lack of sleep, unappealing food, and seemingly endless, exhausting labor associated with combat?
- How would you handle having almost none of the amenities you currently possess (television, the Internet, music, junk food, etc.)?
- How would you respond to taking orders constantly and having virtually no say in your own life?
- If you became ill or wounded in combat, how do you see yourself coping without your family nearby?

- Do you see yourself able to kill another person if you are ordered to do so?
- How do you see yourself responding to the death, pain, and destruction that would surround you in battle?
- What causes, if any, would you be willing to fight for?

To further their understanding, have students read and discuss the following personal testimonies. Ask them to keep in mind their own responses to the previous questions as they read the child soldiers' accounts. Keep in mind that the material is often stark and explicit in its descriptions. Prior to the readings, you might share the information from the passage and paragraph that follow.

> The experiences of [child soldier] children vary widely. Clearly, armed forces and groups have very different practices when it comes to recruiting children and preparing the children for life in the fighting. Many children say that they had or are having uneventful, almost easygoing service. Some children are sent into combat, but not all child soldiers experience fighting on the frontlines. In some cases boys and girls are assigned tasks in base camp or they act as sentries, porters, or spies. Some children have been severely traumatized and are finding difficulties coping with their experiences. (UNICEF 2003)

As you read their stories, please understand that as recruits, many boys and girls were treated inhumanely to condition them and turn them into soldiers. They suffered physical torture for hours, and endured interrogations (Human Rights Watch 2004), threats, mockery, and continuous insults (Brett & McCallin 1998). They became accustomed to sadism by executing animals and people, as well as taking part in acts of cannibalism (Brett & McCallin 1998). New recruits were stripped naked and kept in stocks or in deplorable detention cells with little food and water, to prevent escape. Many of the following narratives contain graphic violence; use your best judgment in deciding which testimonies to share with students.

Your students could discuss the testimonies in small groups or as a class. Written responses could take the form of reflective writing, journal writing, freewriting, or essays.

Child Soldier Testimonies

Than Aung remembers his time there [in Myanmar] in 1997 clearly:

> In the room we were all naked. There were about sixty of us in a room the same size as this one [four to five metres square]. There were two rooms like ours. We couldn't sleep. There were also rats and ants in the

room. The floor was wood. For a toilet they'd dug a hole in the ground and it had a wooden cover over it. The hole was about ten feet deep. There was a terrible smell. Some people smoked in the room, and if they were seen they were beaten. Also if people spoke too loudly, the guards came in and asked, "Who was talking?" then beat them. The food was terrible; there was very little rice, and yellow beans with stones; it was very hard to eat. (© Human Rights Watch 2006)

Emilio, recruited by the Guatemalan army at age fourteen:

The army was a nightmare. We suffered greatly from the cruel treatment we received. We were constantly beaten, mostly for no reason at all, just to keep us in a state of terror. I still have a scar on my lip and sharp pains in my stomach from being brutally kicked by the older soldiers. The food was scarce, and they made us walk with heavy loads, much too heavy for our small and malnourished bodies. They forced me to learn how to fight the enemy, in a war that I didn't understand why was being fought. (© Human Rights Watch 2006)

Tom, a former child soldier in Liberia:

I joined when I was 13 years old. I was just forced to fight because I was separated from my parents and the rest of my family. I had to fight for my own survival. I was given six months of training and became a special forces member. I fought on the front lines, but I wasn't afraid the first time because I had been given drugs. I fired mortar. I experienced some terrible things during the war. I saw some terrible things and did some terrible things. I saw people being killed; I saw fighters eat people's hearts. They burned people and killed young babies. I did these things, too, because we had to obey orders. After the war, I tried to find my family, but they have disappeared. So now I live near a roadside store. That's where I live and sleep. I am haunted by what we did during the war: my heart is constantly joshing me. I have lost my ability to feel. You can cut me with a knife and I won't even feel it. I cry but only when I'm happy. I think about the war from time to time. I talk about it with friends from time to time, but I don't really feel comfortable. Everyone fears me. Yes, up to now, they all [were] afraid of me. I guess it's because my heart is not really clear with people. I don't really like to go around people. I'm sure that one day God will make way for me to sit down to a better place. (Radio Nederland Wereldomroep 1998)

Myo Win's story, as a child soldier from Myanmar:

We were drugged and ordered to move forward on the battlefield. We did not know what sort of drug or alcohol we were given but we drank it because we were very tired, very thirsty, and hungry. We had walked for two whole days under very hot burning sun. The hill (battlefield) had no shade, trees were burnt; and artillery shells were exploding everywhere. We were so scared, very thirsty, and some of us collapsed due to over-tiredness. But we were beaten from behind (by the officers) and had to move forward. One got killed. (BBC World Service 2004)

Girl, Honduras:

At the age of 13, I joined the student movement. I had a dream to contribute to make things change, so that children would not be hungry . . . later I joined the armed struggle. I had all the inexperience and fears of a little girl. I found out that girls were obliged to have sexual relations to alleviate the sadness of the combatants. And who alleviated our sadness after going with someone we hardly knew? At my young age I experienced abortion. . . . In spite of my commitment, they abused me, they trampled my human dignity. And above all, they did not understand that I was a child and that I had rights. (UNICEF 1996)

Boy, Papua New Guinea—joined when he was about fifteen, now twenty-three (at the time of the interview):

We worked together; we would get food and cook together. We slept in huts. There was never a doctor. We patrolled every day, usually five-hour walks. Even in the rainy time we had to patrol. But it wasn't difficult. I had no shoes, wore shorts and t-shirts. I had few clothes. We washed with coconut milk. I couldn't brush my teeth. The other soldiers, all of them, were very nice. Another boy told me when on patrol that my eyes must be in front always and to listen carefully to every sound. If someone gets hit, we have to help them. Afterward, we would talk about the attacks. We attacked in the daytime. I hope I've killed some. I never saw [if I did]. (UNICEF 2003)

Boy child soldier, Philippines—joined when he was fourteen, now sixteen (at the time of the interview):

My comrades went down the mountains to get our food supplies. If we ran out of supplies, we ate sweet potatoes and bananas. Sometimes we had meat. But not the meat sold in the markets. We got to eat meat when we were able to kill a wild boar or snakes. We saw to it that we ate three times a day. Even if we spent days walking, we stopped to have our meal. But we never had a proper meal. It was more for our sustenance, enough for us to live. (UNICEF 2003)

Boy child soldier—joined when he was eleven, now twenty-three (at the time of the interview):

> I realized that traveling around in the nights I spoiled my growth. I didn't rest my body. I had malaria three times. For treatment, I drank bush medicine. When we were sick, they let us rest. During times of being sick it was very hard. I was shot in the right knee in mid-96. It hurt a lot. That time I was thinking of giving up. It was a small injury but I was in a lot of pain. I thought of what the other soldiers would say about me, put me down—I had to go on. (UNICEF 2003)

Other Related Activities and Resources Suggested by Chris Weber

Child Soldier Lessons Available Online

Lesson Plan on Child Soldiers

This comprehensive lesson presents an overview of where, why, how, and under what conditions children are used as child soldiers. Students will identify the physical and emotional challenges that child soldiers face. Students will study the efforts by the international community to eliminate children from armed conflict and strategies used to integrate them back into their communities.

This lesson revolves around the video *Child Soldiers in Sierra Leone*, part of the What's Going On series. In it, Abu declares, "We didn't play. We just fought." Michael Douglas hosts this sobering look at exploited children in a war-torn country where diamonds are traded for weapons. Ordering information is available at: www.un.org/works/goingon/goinghome.html. Lesson plans available at: www.un.org/works/goingon/soldiers/lessonplan_soldiers.html. These lessons include valuable visual aids so students can create maps showing where child soldiers are being used.

Soldiers for Peace Lesson

Students can learn how youths in Colombia have organized the Children's Movement for Peace to create peace in their homes, communities, and country in the "Soldiers for Peace" chapter in *Child Soldiers* by Helen A. Finken, which can be downloaded at www.hrea.org/erc/Library/display.php?doc_id=2248.

- Child Soldiers, www.itvs.org/beyondthefire/Lesson_plan2.html, is a webpage loaded with links to recommended resources, with downloadable lesson plans.

- War Child Canada Student Centre's lesson plans available at www.warchild.ca/studentcentrelessonplans.asp.
- Myanmar's Child Soldier lesson plans available at http: //cnnstudentnews.cnn.com/2001/fyi/lesson.plans/06/13/child.soldiers/.
- Battle to Ban Child Soldiers lesson plans available at http: //cnnstudentnews.cnn.com/2001/fyi/lesson.plans/04/09/ child.soldiers.da/.

Films on Child Soldiers

- *Innocent Voices* (2004). Oscar Torres has cowritten a film, based on his experience, that spotlights the plight of child soldiers. The film was Mexico's entry for the 2004 Academy Award in the Best Foreign Language Film category.
- *Soldier Boy* (1997). Length: 26 minutes. In Liberia, thousands of children are forced to fight in a civil war that has been raging since 1989. This docudrama profiles thirteen-year-old Mike, who, when driven by the militia to join the army, tries to slip away after one bloody assault. Available at www.unicef.org/broadcast/vidcat.htm.

The Voices of Children at War (Dramatic Presentation)

Have your class perform a dramatic presentation titled "The Voices of Children at War" in which they read aloud the words of child soldiers, their parents, and rehabilitation workers. Lesson plans for this activity can be found at: www.cyberschoolbus.un.org/childsoldiers/webquest/voices1.asp.

Research Activities

- Students can create and share PowerPoint presentations about child soldiers, or they can write more traditional research papers. They might research the issue of child soldiers in contemporary conflicts—Afghanistan, Iraq, Nepal, Colombia, Myanmar, Indonesia, the Democratic Republic of Congo, and Sri Lanka. Google a specific topic or create Google alerts at www.google.com/alerts?hl=en, which allow you to receive email updates of the latest relevant Google results (web, news, etc.) based on your choice of query or topic.
- Create a world map of child soldiers using www.un.org/works /goingon/soldiers/childsoldiersmap.html and display it throughout the school.

- Create educational posters that contain information about child soldiers within a specific country and that country's use of them. Students could show their posters to classmates, and give oral presentations. Showcase them at school to educate others about this issue.
- Create a short computer documentary on DVD using editing software and combined with narrated photos and artwork of child soldiers.

Internet Resources

- Recent Human Rights Watch Reports on the Use of Child Soldiers, at http://hrw.org/campaigns/crp/hrw-reports.htm, lists reports on child soldiers in various countries—excellent starting points for research.
- War Child Canada Student Centre webpage, at www.warchild.ca /studentscentregetinformed.asp, has many child soldier links.
- A Research Guide for the Child Soldiers Global Report (2004) can be downloaded at www.child-soldiers.org/resources/global-reports.html.
- Child Soldiers: Issue and Themes webpage contains articles on this topic, at www.essex.ac.uk/armedcon/themes/child_soldiers /default.htm.
- The Coalition to Stop the Use of Child Soldiers, at www.child-soldiers.org/resources/for-schools.html, is another valuable site.
- The Child Soldier Project, sponsored by iEARN at www.childsoldiers.org, lets youth bear witness to the experience of child soldiers and how it affects their lives, their families, their communities, and their countries.

How to Make a Difference

- Outside the Dream, http://www.outsidethedream.org/, is helping to educate former child soldiers. Your students can raise funds to help pay for former child soldiers' education.
- "Make a Difference" One-Minute UNICEF video contest! Get information at http://www.unicef.org/voy/takeactiontakeaction_ 1690.html.
- Write letters to leaders of countries, get involved in a national campaign to end the use of child soldiers, help raise awareness in the media, and join the Human Rights Watch Children's Rights Action Network, at http://hrw.org/campaigns/crp/whatdo.htm.

- Raise funds to support organizations like The Coalition to Stop the
  Use of Child Soldiers, at www.child-soldiers.org, or Save the Children,
  at www.savethechildren.org.

None of Us

No child should go through war, let alone fight in one. Yet too many children
nowadays bear arms around the world. If we do nothing, then governments,
terrorist organizations, and rebel armies will continue this immoral practice.
If students and teachers help nongovernmental organizations on this issue,
they can move mountains. Then fewer children will fight and more will play.
Soldiers or children? That is the question. The answer is in our hands.

8

Understanding Young Refugees

Imagine you've been forced to leave your home because of war or violence. You are desperate to survive. You may have walked for days or weeks holding your children or siblings and the few possessions you could salvage. Family members or friends may have been killed or abducted. Having fled for your life, you need shelter, water, and food and you may need medical care.

You are not alone. An estimated 33 million people around the world have been forced to flee their homes and to seek refuge. (U.S. Committee for Refugees and Immigrants 2005)

Journeys: Lives of Children Refugees

The purpose of this chapter is to provide information to help you understand the plight of refugees. Obviously I cannot cover this issue in the depth that it deserves. Certain aspects, such as refugee camps, grief and mourning, and the demonization and idealization of refugees by asylum country citizens, are not discussed. However, this chapter will serve as a starting point for teachers who want to introduce their nonrefugee students to the plight of young refugees. I purposely included my own insights and experiences of teaching refugee students so you might make your own connections based on prior knowledge and experiences. The chapter also contains lessons, activities, and resources for teachers to use with their students to help aid them in their understanding.

Waves of Memories

Waves of memories of my refugee students pulsed through me as I wrote this section. Young Laotian men in their shades and jeans sat in two rows singing a haunting, traditional farewell song on their last day in newcomer class. I pushed back tears listening to their gift, the first of many given by refugee students. Elementary Vietnamese students taught me both traditional and refugee songs. "Good-bye, my friend, good-bye, my friend, good-byyye, my friend . . ." still haunts me. One Christmas day, Ellen, a former girlfriend, and I invited my middle school Vietnamese boat refugees to our home. Despite the meal and presents we gave them, they gave us more. The same held true when I made home visits. As one colleague said, "Whenever you want to feel welcome, pay a home visit to a refugee student." After each visit, I left their homes lighthearted and feeling treated like a king. Despite their misfortunes and hardships, they showed me compassion and generosity.

Your Richest Resources

You might have or know refugee students or those whose parents were refugees. Consider asking some of them to share their experiences. They will serve as your richest resource for better understanding and empathizing with the refugee experience. At my school, Vietnamese refugee students have given dramatizations of their escapes while others read narratives about their lives. There is so much that refugee students have to offer our students, and in turn, our students can appreciate more of their culture and way of life.

Before I tell you about the power of refugee students sharing their stories, I want to discuss some broader refugee issues. It might answer some questions you have, inspire further investigating on your part, and/or provide information that might be beneficial as you lead the activities and lessons in the next chapter.

Fleeing Throughout History

"One of the UNICEF's young staff members in Herat [Afghanistan] witnessed a family of three children and their parents locked in an embrace and frozen to death" (Steele 2001).

War creates most refugees. Refugees are those who flee their homes and countries because of wars, fear of persecution, famines, or natural disasters (Burger & Rahm 1996; Cutts, et al. 2000). For as long as there have been conflicts, people have fled war and persecution (Wilkinson 2003). One in every 150 people is a refugee. They live in every country in the world (British Refugee Council 1998), and most live in poorer countries of Asia or Africa (UNHCR 2003). There are approximately twenty million uprooted people around the world, and roughly half of these are children (UNHCR 2003).

Who Is a Refugee?

> I will never walk down this street again. Never again will I open this gate, I thought walking up the front steps of our house. That evening we ate the last dinner in our old family house. I walked into my room which had been a messy place of happiness for me. Now it looked lifeless. My dolls and toys, dear childhood friends, were sadly peering at me. They looked abandoned and forgotten. The living room was empty. Suitcases were piled up in one corner. Every object in the house seemed to be saying good-bye, and the house seemed to whisper, "Farewell."
>
> That night I couldn't fall asleep. Thoughts about the upcoming trip to foreign countries upset me. I thought of my beloved hometown, school, and teachers. The uncertainty of the future excited me. I wondered what life would be like in the West. I wondered whether I would have loving, caring friends there. The intensity of my thoughts overwhelmed me. . . . (Excerpt from "Farewell Beloved Russia" by Alla Osenniy, which first appeared in *Treasures 3: Stories & Art by Students in Japan & Oregon*, 1994)

Leaving one's home, possibly for good, is a desperate act driven by threats to life, safety, or freedom. Whether fleeing alone or with others, most refugees are afraid of what lies ahead and sad for what they are leaving behind. Think of what it would be like fleeing your home and country. Making it out alive might be your biggest concern, not only for you, but for your loved ones. What about friends and family you leave behind? Where will you get shelter and food and medicine? How will this affect your children? These questions, worries, anxieties, and more accompany refugees in their flight.

What about children? They may not understand why they are leaving. But they share their parents' fear. During the chaos of escape, they may be separated from their family. They may suffer from hunger, sickness, and nightmares.

> . . . they may have been tortured, physically abused or imprisoned. They have been through terrible experiences, which nobody, least of all children, should ever have to endure. (UNHCR 2000)

Gone is playing with their friends and the safety and comfort of home. Refugee children lose their childhood in a world where hope takes a backseat to the struggle to survive; but given the chance, they can rebuild their lives and become outstanding citizens of their asylum countries.

Yet, wherever they journey, their homeland is always with them, and as Angelina Jolie, Goodwill Ambassador (as of 2006) for the UN High Commission for Refugees, said, "In my experience, going home is the deepest wish of most refugees."

Desperate Acts

> That night, when the sun went down, the wind blew very hard. I was trying to sleep in the tiny boat with thirty people, but I could feel our boat going up and down on the water, and the waves crashing against our boat. I was cold and worried about death. Mom held me in her arms to protect me from falling into the ocean.
>
> In the middle of the night, the captain said the engine was broken. We thought it was hopeless. We thought we were going to die. Death was in front of me. Some people cried while others were silent. When some thought they were going to die, they cried and prayed to God. They talked about tying each other together in a blanket. Then they planned on jumping into the ocean so they would die together. (Excerpt from "Dangerous Journey" by Diem Le, an eleven-year-old girl, which first appeared in *Treasures 3: Stories & Art by Students in Japan & Oregon*, 1994)

Fleeing their homes, refugees run for their lives taking whatever they can carry. They run from bullets, bombs, and missiles. During the 1970s, thousands fled Vietnam in small, crowded, leaky boats. After the downfall of the Pol Pot government in Cambodia, refugees braved landmine-laden jungles to reach Thailand. In the late 1980s, civil war forced thousands of Sudanese boys and girls to leave their villages and trek hundreds of miles through wild African lands. Fighting in Central Africa has forced more than four million people out of their homes, and more than one million people fled the 1999 war in Kosovo (Porter 2003). U.S. air strikes caused hundreds of thousands of Afghans to flee to Iran and Pakistan in 2001. Recent wars have created countless refugees from regions including Afghanistan, Iraq, Darfur, Sierra Leone, and Palestine (UNHCR 2004).

Living in Refugee Camps

> Imagine living with your family, brothers, sister, children, their wives and husbands, and children, in a tent the size of a car trunk. Imagine that tent is waist-high made from sticks and scraps, sacks, blankets, has no floor and no sides so that the freezing wind and dust storms find it no opposition at all.... (Perry 2001)

As refugees seek safety, they find or make crude shelter wherever possible. For Bibi Gul and her family, home was a dirty gray blanket on the hard desert floor in Afghanistan (Lamb 2001). Grass, wood, metal sheets, branches, and plastic shelters serve as makeshift houses. Their own homes must seem like an agonizing, distant dream.

After fleeing, most refugees live in refugee camps until a country can provide asylum for them. For many, these camps become almost permanent homes (Burger & Rahm 1996). Refugee camps, often tent cities, range from 200 to as many as 800,000 people (Mayell 2004). Providing clean water, substantial food, and medical treatment are priorities but not guarantees. Living in cramped quarters challenges the inhabitants and the local environment. Because displacement can be very traumatic for children, refugee camps' staff try to involve them in educational activities (Mayell 2004).

Vast Differences

Those few refugees that are granted asylum come with different experiences, outlooks, cultural values, and backgrounds. It's important to see each student refugee, even those from the same country or ethnic group, as very different. Some were in refugee camps for years, others only months. Many are scarred from the impact of war while others remember being persecuted in their native lands. Some arrive in the United States as unaccompanied minors, some with their families (sibling[s], parent, or intact family), while others come in groups. The educational background of parents and children, even from the same country, varies.

For example, the first wave of Vietnamese refugees originated from South Vietnam. The parents were highly educated and older children had attended school in Vietnam. Later waves of Vietnamese refugees came from middle and northern Vietnam. Most children arrived in the States with little or no education. In their home countries the parents may have been farmers, mechanics, or doctors. Their socioeconomic backgrounds, English, and professional skill levels varied. Coping mechanisms vary as will their stage of acculturation. When you work with student refugees, drop all assumptions you have because each one is very different.

From a Fire into a Fire

I didn't have any shoes on when I stepped out of the airplane. I had shorts on and it was snowing in Washington State. It was snowing and freezing. (Excerpt from "My New Life in America," by Huong Nguyen, which first appeared in *Treasures 2: Stories & Art by Students in Oregon*, 1988)

On their never-ending journeys, refugees carry their sadness, losses, anxiety, and hopes. Those fleeing war-torn lands might still be suffering from war-related trauma. A Liberian refugee student first gazed at me with a haunting look of sorrow, his face like that of an old man aged with sadness beyond description. I wondered what terrible things he had seen. Later, I learned his father was killed during the civil war, and he had witnessed countless acts of violence.

Refugees who find asylum in America, as Piper (2002) wrote, "come from a fire into a fire." Every day they encounter new challenges. Learning English, adjusting to rules, and making friends are just a few of the many hurdles they endure daily. Additionally, there are many shocks in store. While many imagine their parents will get rich in a short time, refugees find it hard to obtain work, and even well-educated professionals cannot work in the same profession. Although they were doctors and lawyers, many must work in restaurants or factories.

As students learn more English than their parents, there can be power struggles between parents and children. Even shopping poses problems. Meat wrapped in plastic isn't recognizable to refugees used to purchasing live or freshly killed animals. Check-out stands, especially the self check-outs with scanners, can be confusing. Everything about our way of life is new and different to refugees from third-world countries.

It's difficult to understand how hard it is for refugees. Imagine being transported to a mountain village in Nepal. You know nothing about the culture nor do you speak Nepalese. You have little or no money. Where do you get clothes; what should you wear? How would you obtain food? If you get altitude sickness, how would you treat it? How would you secure shelter? How would you survive, even prosper, in this land where customs, everyday tasks, relationships between people, and laws are very different? If you can imagine yourself in that situation, you know what it must be like for refugees in America.

Despite All of Their Misfortunes and Tragedies

Despite all of their scars and sorrows, many refugee students triumph and contribute to our society. These students are survivors and have important stories to tell. We can learn much from them. Their stories tell much about them, and their way of life, values, and perspectives. They are windows into their cultures. I have been fortunate to have read, heard, and published refugee students' stories. Vietnamese boat children retold their perilous journeys. Cambodian students recalled the horror of living under the Khmer Rouge regime. Russian students described leaving their homes and Mother Russia for the last time. A Bosnian boy described his father's scars from battle. Many recounted stories about their new lives in the United States. Listen to your refugee students' stories and share them.

Treasure Boxes Opened and Their Wealth Shared

William Rubel and Gerry Mandel, editors of *Stone Soup: Magazine for Children,* told me of a letter they received from a teacher in Wyoming. After she read aloud a story in *Stone Soup* by a Vietnamese girl living in Oregon (a former student of mine), the teacher's own Vietnamese student wrote page after page. It was like a floodgate had opened up inside this quiet girl.

I have witnessed students and adults of all races and genders being moved and inspired by young refugee authors. As you read their stories and listen to what they have gone through, you walk in their shoes. You cannot help but better understand and appreciate them and their cultures. For example, on a visit to Vestal School in Portland, Oregon, I spoke at a school-wide assembly about the *Treasures* books, a series I had edited. I noticed most of the students were polite, some intently listened, a few talked. Near the end, I introduced one of their fellow students who had been published in *Treasures: Stories & Art by Students in Oregon.* As this refugee student walked up to the podium and began reading her story, there wasn't a breath to be heard. No one moved or said a word; all eyes were on her. The auditorium had come to a complete halt, as if it were frozen in time, except for her. The student's soft voice and strong story filled the auditorium; it belonged to her. As she read her last word, closed the book, and bowed her head, the auditorium came to life. I have seen such applause and admiration many times since and have heard many teachers tell similar stories.

I will always remember and admire the courage of Thu Thuy Nguyen, a Vietnamese high school student who read her heart-wrenching poem, "When Time Is Gone," at Powell's Bookstore in Portland, Oregon. Thu Thuy relived her experience as tears fell down her cheeks. She struggled to speak through her sorrow. When she read of her final farewell, we were moved, for her and our own partings in life. Her voice trembled as she wiped away her tears, and we wiped away ours.

WHEN TIME IS GONE

How I felt the day before I escaped on the boat from my country.
The evening ended the day,
That evening I can never forget.
All my family were sitting together.
We just looked at each other.

No one talked and laughed,
Just sad and quiet,
I could hear their breath
and their hearts beating.

That was the last day,
hour, minute, I had together
with my family.
They all gave advice to me.
I was ready to go in a few minutes.
They knew when I left
There would never be a day to be back.
But they had a plan for my future.

I didn't know what it would be like going away
from my country, my family.
I thought when I left my country
it would be like I went to visit friends
and came back in a few days.
But I was wrong.
When time is gone
It can never come back.

(Thu Thuy Nguyen, seventeen, *Treasures 3: Stories & Art by Students in Japan & Oregon*, 1994)

Lessons and Activities to Help Increase Students' Understanding of the Refugee Experience

Refugees' Wide Range of Experiences (Activity)

Refugees have a wide range of experiences, each one different from another. Ask students to write down what they think refugees experience and discuss this topic as a class. Afterwards, share the following handout and compare their ideas with the list below, based on "Helping Adults Help Children: Refugees and Immigrants Have Different Experiences" by Beryl Cheal.

Refugees:

- flee their home communities because they fear for their safety
- take only what belongings they can carry, sometimes only the clothes they are wearing
- don't have time for farewells with friends or relatives
- usually want to stay in their home country

- often are hurt during flight and sometimes they take part in violence
- may lose family members during flight by getting lost, dying, or straggling too far behind
- may leave family members behind
- may not have enough food while they are fleeing
- arrive in a place where they may or may not be wanted
- often experience malnutrition, disease, and other hardships in over-crowded refugee camps
- usually do not know what their future will be
- have health problems with little, if any, medical facilities
- find it difficult to maintain ties with the home country
- frequently come to their sanctuary country with skills they can use in gaining employment.

Teaching Empathy for Refugees Through Ecphrastic Poetry

Before students can understand and later help refugees, they need to empa-thize with them. One of the best ways is through ecphrastic poetry lessons. For a more comprehensive description, please read Nancy Gorrell's article in Chapter Four. Here are guidelines for this activity, which I took from Gorrell's piece.

- Display a photo of a refugee (especially a child or teen).
- Ask the class, "How do you think that refugee might feel?"
- Once they have discussed the photo, you may take a photo for which you have written an ecphrastic poem and share both photo and poem with students. The power of such modeling for the class cannot be underestimated.
- Display copies of refugee photos and let students choose which photo to use.
- Have them study the photo for a few quiet minutes. Then have students write questions or reactions they have to their photo.
- Keeping instructions open and simple, pose the following questions:
    1. If you could speak to the refugee, what would you say?
    2. If you could speak to anyone in the photograph, what would you say?
    3. If you could imagine any of the subjects speaking, what do you think they would say?

4. In your journals, write any poem reflecting your viewing of this photograph. You may reread your wonder questions and reflections to help you get started.

- Sitting in a circle, have students share and discuss each other's poems.
- Encourage them to continue revising their poems.
- Ask students to make an artistic display with photos and poems.

Examples of Ecphrastic Poetry

Nancy Gorrell's (see Chapter Four for more information about her) students at Morristown High School, Morristown, New Jersey, wrote poems in response to viewing photos of young refugees. Jaclyn Lawlor and Sarah Knapp wrote the following poems and prose to the Ugandan refugee boy who appears on the front cover photo.

HEAVY EYES

Jaclyn Lawlor, seventeen, Morristown High School, Morristown, New Jersey

A baggy shirt clings to your frail body
You are a night commuter
Camouflaged into the sunset, hiding from the unknown
Heavy eyes tell stories of fear
Fear of unknown, fear for their families
Knapsack on your lap, you carry a load
A load heavier than most can imagine
Your eyes tell everything
Trudging through dusty roads to find shelter
You are on your own in a large world
Everyday clinging on with hope
In the war of children
A life of fleeing and hiding
Is not one of a young boy
You stare straight into my heart
And I'd like to ask you
"Is this all that you know?"
But I don't have to
Because
Your eyes
Say
Everything

THE NIGHT MARCHED IN CARRYING THE UNKNOWN CHILD

Sarah Knapp, seventeen, Morristown High School, Morristown, New Jersey

He was young. His life began in the morning when he went to school. He followed his daily routine just like any other child in any other place. He learned many things. After school he would return home and the anxiety would begin to build. When death looms in front of an old man, he feels this same fear.

Yet this was only a child, fearing the night and the darkness.

Like any other child fearing the hidden monsters, craving a nightlight or a mother when the darkness is fiercest. The day protected him with its daily routine and then as the night marched in, he could hear it carrying the unknown. He rolled up his woven rug and pulled on his patterned jacket. He tried to look tough, prepared for any challenge that the darkness might bring. He knew he had no choice that some things were inevitable, that light would fall to dusk and that dusk would give in to night.

He was a boy who knew all this.

He threw his rug over his shoulder like a true adventurer would and he walked out to the road. The hard packed yellow road was depleted of any true color, rotting in that country. The road that could lead him to any great city was instead his path into the darkness. He stood there letting his heart beat quickly but trying to control the rest of his body. He was ready for any challenge.

A boy made to be a man.

Yet his heart raced every time because the walk never became routine. Every night it was daunting and every night remained dark. Yet he was hardened because he knew every step to take and every feeling to try to suppress. Though his heart confirmed his fear he now could control his hands. He had learned to control his eyes and his frown. His fingers held onto the woven strap of his rug and he looked out upon the road. He stared at the world and even though they would not look back he still shouted at them that he was courageous. His eyes told all—he could still be strong.

He whispered that although he might look like a boy, in the darkness no one could tell that he wasn't a man.

HIS EYES

Sarah Knapp, seventeen, Morristown High School, Morristown, New Jersey

His eyes see
They see his home and his family
his friends and his life
his age
his vulnerability
So they harden to deny this weakness
They harden to show his determination
 to prove that he will survive
That he can survive
That he is not afraid
And they watch the night
They watch the others
They witness their country
Taken over by cruelty and destruction
They know his age
his innocence
They know that although he leaves home at night,
He returns there in the morning
That his innocence remains
Because he has never held a gun
That here in this place
Innocence is measured in such terms
And that sleeping in fear and anxiety
That knowing what those soldiers do
That seeing friends be taken
Is still steeped in naivety
Because they have never seen a gun in his hands
Because they see his home every morning
Because they survive and he survives
They remain pure
Because they have not witnessed the ultimate brutality
And that devastation is nothing in comparison
They look out in hardened determination
To walk
To sleep
To survive
To see the world without its bullets.

Internet Sources of Photos

Great Internet sources of refugee photos are: UNHCR website and UNCHR's *Refugee* magazine, available for free; Doctors Without Borders website; Google images, and so on.

Invisible Children *DVD (Activity)*

Watching *Invisible Children* is an incredible, heartfelt experience, which speaks for all refugee children around the world. Your students will feel the sorrow, fear, and joy on the faces of northern Ugandan children refugees. You will also learn how you can help, and after seeing *Invisible Children*, your students will want to help. You can order a copy at www.invisiblechildren.com/.

Who Is a Refugee? (Activity)

(Reprinted with permission from the "Refugee Activity Pack," Save the Children UK, 2002)

Purpose: To enable young people to think about what causes a person to become a refugee, propose a definition, and discuss this with other participants.

Time scale: 10–12 minutes for the activity and 10–20 minutes for feedback and discussion.

Materials: Chartpak paper, thick color marker pens.

Activity: Ask the class to work in small groups. Each group should brainstorm what they understand by the word "refugee." When the groups have finished, the flipchart paper should be pinned up around the room so all students can see ideas from other groups.

Advice to the teacher: Ask for feedback from each group as you go through the chartpak papers. Draw out any common themes—fear or persecution, imprisonment, dangerous escapes, or being outside country of origin or needing protecting from another country—similar definitions, or any differences between the groups. These can then be used to create a definition, which might contain some of the elements of the United Nations' definition of "refugee."

The United Nations defines a refugee as a person who is outside his or her country and cannot return because of a "well-founded fear of persecution for reasons of race, religion, nationality, membership of a particular social group or political opinion." A refugee either cannot return home, or is afraid to do so.

What Makes a Home? (Activity)

(Reprinted with permission from the "Refugee Activity Pack," Save the Children UK, 2002)

> We left our village when the bombs began falling. Some people stayed, but we were afraid of being killed. The bombs were like earthquakes that didn't stop. You spend many years building up a home, and then, in one moment, it is destroyed.

seventeen-year-old Aygun, Azerbaijan (Machel 1996)

Purpose: For students to understand what makes a home for them and for other group members. To consider the feelings they would have about their home if they had to move to another country.

Time scale: 45–60 minutes.

Materials: Chartpak paper, marker pens, post-it notes, sticky dots.

Activity: Have students get into groups of four. Each group should have chartpak paper, marker pens, and post-it notes. One member of each group should draw a large house on the paper. First, members of each group think about what makes a home for them (e.g., relatives, friends, places, objects, emotions, and memories). They should jot down these ideas on individual post-its and stick them on the house. Once the group is done, ask students to group similar post-its and encourage them to discuss different things that mean "home" to them. Ask students to stick three colored dots by the three post-its mentioning those things they would miss most about their home if they had to leave. After this "voting" is complete, ask the groups what seemed most important to their group and what seemed least important.

Advice to the teacher: Be sensitive to the fact that some students might have difficulties at home and may not want to participate in this activity. Nobody should be forced to take part.

Encourage each group to give feedback to the whole class. Use the following prompts:

- What would your group miss most about home if they had to leave today?
- How would you feel if you had to go to a new country?

Why Do People Leave Their Homes? (Activity)

(Reprinted with permission from the "Refugee Activity Pack," Save the Children UK, 2002)

Purpose of this activity: To examine different factors that influence people's decisions to leave their country and seek a place of safety as refugees.

Materials: Chartpak, marker pens.

Activity: Prior to this activity, have students research the question, "Why do refugees leave their homes?" on the Internet. Divide the class into pairs and ask them to think of three to five reasons why people have to flee their country and seek a place of safety as a refugee, and to write answers on index cards. Ask each pair to tell the class the situation they imagined which forced them to become refugees.

Advice to the teacher: If students need assistance, prompt them to think about events in the past that may have caused people to leave their countries in fear of their lives, e.g., wars in Afghanistan, Kosovo, and Iraq and genocide in Rwanda and Sudan.

Draw attention to common themes such as war, membership in a political group, torture, and fear of being hurt. Some students may give economic reasons (e.g., to get a better job or raise their standard of living). However, it should be explained that people who leave for financial reasons are "economic migrants" and not refugees.

Discussion Points:

- Refugees are not all the same. They vary in social background, educational experience, and ways of coping. Even refugees from the same country will have different experiences and may be from opposing factions.
- Families may make enormous sacrifices to protect their children.
- Refugees may have experienced extreme situations and witnessed acts of violence in their home country or on their journey to safety.

What to Take? What to Leave Behind? (Activity)

(Reprinted with permission from the "Refugee Activity Pack," Save the Children UK, 2002)

Purpose: To raise students' awareness of what they value and what it might be like for a refugee having to make decisions about what to take and what to leave behind when leaving their home.

Time scale: 1 hour.

Materials: Pieces of paper for each group large enough so the group can draw around one person (wallpaper or flipchart paper taped together will work), different color marker pens, post-it notes.

Activity: Divide students into groups of five. Ask one member of each group to lie on the paper and have others draw around his/her body. Ask the group to draw a suitcase and waste bin beside the outline of the body, a heart on the body, and a question mark by the head. Now have each member of the group individually write or draw ten items on their post-it notes they would want to take with them if they had to leave their home in a hurry. They have one hour to leave and can only take one small suitcase or backpack with them. They cannot take any item(s) that have to be carried separately. Members of their family may not carry anything for them.

Ask each group to put the post-it notes into the suitcase. Encourage the groups to discuss similarities and differences in their choices.

Tell the groups their bags are too heavy and they need to leave behind some items. The whole group must discuss and agree on what they should take and what to leave behind. The group is allowed a total of ten items in their suitcase. Remaining items should be put in the waste bin on their sheets.

Once groups have made their decisions, ask them to report to the wider group, telling why they selected certain items to take and why they decided to leave others behind.

For the next part of the activity, ask participants to change groups to work with different people.

Ask participants to write on post-it notes how it would feel to make a decision about what to take and what to leave behind. Did they have to leave something important behind because the rest of the group did not feel it was important? Stick these post-its by the heart on their body. Finally, ask participants to think about what it might be like for a refugee having to leave important, valuable, and personal possessions behind. Ask what the activity has made them think about; for instance, what things are important to have with you and how long would you survive with just your suitcase and the items in it? The group should put any thoughts about this activity on post-it notes and stick them next to the head. Groups should take the opportunity to look at other groups' work.

Compile a class list of reasons and items categorized by theme (e.g., food, memorabilia, and so on). Compare students' items with those taken by actual refugees (Global Express 2004):

- clothes to help with disguise or concealment
- travel documents (passport, identity cards)
- photographs
- presents given to them or other items of personal significance
- food and clothing.

Advice to the teacher: This activity relies on groups working together, discussing, and negotiating to make decisions. It is important that you emphasize that everybody should have a say within the group. You may need to prompt groups at different stages of the activity. Ask the group why they think refugees have to leave their homes and countries in a hurry—for example, because of war, conflict, persecution, and genocide.

Backpack Project that Lends a Hand

Jean Daigneau, a staff member at St. Patrick School (Kent, Ohio), described a related backpack project her school's students participated in, based on an idea from the United States Conference of Catholic Bishops. Daigneau wrote, "Students envisioned themselves having to leave their countries on short notice because of political turmoil and having one hour to pack a backpack to take whatever they could carry. Students then actually packed backpacks and donated them to a migrant center in our area." Your students could take part in a similar activity and then donate their stuffed backpacks to a local refugee organization. What a great way to help refugees!

Passages

USA for UNHCR (The UN Refugee Agency), www.unrefugees.org/usa forunhcr/dynamic.cfm?ID=347, has developed an excellent set of comprehensive, across-the-curriculum lesson plans for middle and high school students. You can download *Passages Game*, an excellent simulation game designed to create better understanding of the problems facing refugees. Participants simulate the refugee experience, from flight to arrival in the refugee camp, along with the difficulties of integration and repatriation of refugees.

Read Refugee Narrative, Discuss, and Write About It (Activity)

It is one thing to role-play being refugees and quite another to listen to their experiences. Refugees have suffered and triumphed over unimaginable experiences. In finding sanctuary in a foreign country, they left behind their culture, relatives and friends, and home. The primary purpose of this activity is for students to empathize with the refugee authors and their experiences.

- Have students write a reflective piece about a refugee story. Refugee stories can be read at www.usaforunhcr.org/usaforunhcr /dynamic.cfm?ID=95.

Guiding Questions for Reflective Writing

- What did you previously know about refugees?
- What have you recently learned about refugees, including those whose writings you read?
- How have your perceptions about refugees changed and why?
- What were the reasons for the way you responded to the refugee author?
- What feelings and thoughts do you have about the author and why?
- Since learning about refugees and reading their stories, how have you changed?
- Why is it important to learn about them?
- What "good" has come from studying refugees?
- What would you like to do to help refugees? What needs to be done by you to succeed? What do you hope to achieve?
- Describe a powerful moment for you as you read their pieces.

Go public with your students' pieces, share them with the class, and post them on your school and global websites.

In the Heart of the City (Curriculum)

Doctors Without Borders/Médecins Sans Frontiéres (MSF) provides an outstanding refugee camp curriculum packet, which can be downloaded at www.refugeecamp.org/curriculum/. The curriculum is divided into eight units that encourage students to think about a variety of issues that affect the lives of refugees: how refugee camps are set up; how food, water, and sanitation are handled in the camps; how disease is prevented in such crowded, unsanitary settings; the tensions that can arise between refugees and local populations; and finally, how it feels to be a refugee. An accompanying virtual visit at www.refugeecamp.org is designed to supplement the activities presented in the curriculum.

Debunking Misperceptions and Myths About Refugees (Activity)

There are almost half a million refugees from various countries in the United States today (USA for UNHCR 2004). Myths and misperceptions about them abound, but we need to drop any assumptions we have in order to live with our guests who contribute much. Below are common myths you might explore with your students. Discuss their views on the assumptions below and have them explain why they think some are accurate and others inaccurate. Have students research these assumptions to provide information that supports or refutes them.

REFUGEE MYTHS

BARBARA B. BIEBEL (DIRECTOR, CATHOLIC CHARITIES OF GREEN BAY)

Myth: Refugees come here for economic reasons.

Fact: Refugees are individuals or families who come here because they had to flee their homeland and are unable to return because of persecution or fear of persecution. Most refugees would rather live and work in their native countries.

Myth: The United States is the only country that accepts refugees.

Fact: Twenty countries resettle refugees including Australia, Canada, China, France, Germany, Japan, New Zealand, Switzerland, and the United Kingdom. The United States takes fewer than 1 percent of the world's refugees each year.

Myth: Refugees automatically receive special money from the U.S. government.

Fact: The U.S. government does not automatically provide refugees with money when they arrive. However, benefits are available for needy refugees including food stamps and job training. Refugees must apply for these benefits and meet income and resource requirements to qualify just as American citizens do.

Myth: Refugees do not pay taxes.

Fact: Refugees pay taxes—federal, state, and local—like any citizen in the United States. There are no special rules that give refugees tax breaks.

Myth: Refugees take jobs away from Americans.

Fact: Refugees must apply and compete for jobs the same as anyone else. Refugees also create jobs by opening new businesses that employ other refugees and residents in their community.

Myth: Refugees do not want to learn English.

Fact: Most refugees want to learn English, and many enroll in English as a Second Language classes.

Exploring the Refugee Experience Through DVDs/Videos

There are several worthwhile, powerful movies that capture the plight of refugees, which your students might experience, discuss, reflect, and respond to.

- *What's Going On? Refugees in Tanzania* takes place in the heart of Africa, where Angelina Jolie works with children victimized by long years of civil strife. She introduces the Fataki children—Tutsis who live in a sprawling refugee camp in Tanzania. Ordering information and other materials available at: www.un.org/works/goingon /goinghome.html.

- *Into this World* follows the hazardous journey of two Afghan boys from Pakistan through Iran, Turkey, Italy, France, and the United Kingdom in search of refuge in London. Video available at amazon.com.

- *Lost Boys of Sudan*, which premiered on PBS' P.O.V. series in 2003, is a gripping documentary about young refugees from the Sudanese conflict and a moving story of survival and acclimation in a strange and daunting land. Video available at amazon.com.

- *I Am David* is adapted from Anne Holm's internationally acclaimed novel *North to Freedom*. Available at amazon.com.

- *Terror's Children*, a documentary portrait of young refugee children who are often the overlooked victims in the war on terrorism, is the work of Sharmeen Obaid, a twenty four-year-old Pakistani woman.

What You Can Do to Help (Activities)

The UNHCR suggests you can do the following to help refugees:

- Write to local and national elected officials, urging them to support solutions for refugee crises. You can find their contact information at http://capwiz.com/savethechildren/home/.

- Prepare a school display. Pinpoint refugee locations on wall maps or create a large mural showing some of the problems faced by refugees.

- Organize a fundraising activity such as a car wash or bake sale. Buy books for local refugees (or abroad) or donate the money to UNHCR or another organization (listed in the next section) that helps refugees.

- Collect donations of clothing and toys for refugee children in your community or state.

- Be a friend to a refugee family in your community. Your friendship can help family members adjust to their new life. To find refugee families, contact a refugee organization in your community.

- Invite refugees to your class to talk about their experiences. Find out what they went through to reach your community. Ask them to describe their lives before they became refugees. Hearing stories from refugees can give you a new outlook on your own life.
- Write a letter introducing yourself to a refugee child and send it to:

  United Nations High Commissioner for Refugees
  Children's Letterbox
  Case Postale 2500
  CH-1211 Geneva, Switzerland

- Most importantly, make yourself aware of refugee situations and special problems that refugees face. Read newspapers, news magazines, and websites, such as www.unhcr.ch/cgi-bin/texis/vtx/home. Try to include discussions of refugees in your classes. If possible, volunteer with a refugee organization. (See the following list of organizations and check your local phone book to see if local refugee organizations exist.)
- World Refugee Day Poster Contest: www.unrefugees.org/usaforunhcr /dynamic.cfm?ID=351.
- If your class joins iEARN, www.iEARN.org, it will be able to participate in ongoing projects to assist refugees.
- "Make a Difference" one-minute video contest! Looking for a way to make a difference? Create a one-minute video telling the world how young people are speaking out, taking action, and making a difference. The winning video will be the official Voices of Youth public service announcement, receive prizes, and will be made available for broadcast around the world on The International Children's Day of Broadcasting. Get additional information at www.unicef.org/voy/takeaction /takeaction_1690.html.

Your Students Can Help These Organizations

- The Memory Project, www.thememoryproject.org/. Your students work together to create books with uplifting stories and beautiful artwork for children in orphanages, refugee camps, and areas of war. My students enjoyed this wonderful project.
- Save the Children: Save the Children © Legislative Action Center, www.savethechildren.org/action/, or Make a Difference donation, https://secure.ga3.org/01/support_now?stationpub=hp_owow.
- CARE, www.care.org.
- Doctors Without Borders, www.doctorswithoutborders.org /index.shtml, for donations or volunteer work.

- Catholic Relief Services: Ways to Get Your High School Involved, www.catholicrelief.org/get_involved/high_school/index.cfm.
- Refugees International, www.refugeesinternational.org.
- Amnesty International: Act now for human rights, www.amnesty.org /actnow/.
- The World Food Programme, www.wfp.org.
- USA for UNHCR: the UN Refugee Agency, www.usaforunhcr.org. Its Teachers Corner offers a wealth of educational resources and materials to help teachers, parents, and students learn more about refugees.

9

Nuclear Weapons:
The Greatest Level of Savagery

I do not know with what weapons World War III will be fought, but World War IV will be fought with sticks and stones.

—Albert Einstein

This chapter provides you with background information on nuclear weapons and related lessons and activities.

Haunting Silence

Garlands of paper cranes made by Japanese school children swayed in the gentle breeze. The wire framework of the A-Bomb Dome hurtled me to the past and helped me understand why I had come to the Hiroshima Peace Memorial Park and Museum. As I walked through the park, parades of school children quietly followed teachers while couples talked in whispers. In the West Building of the museum, I cringed in horror at the drawings by survivors. Moving from one exhibit to the next, I was overcome with the horror and utter devastation that we wrought. All throughout this afternoon, one sound echoed—the sound of haunting silence, which Ako, a student, describes in her story about her visit to Nagasaki's Peace Museum.

> I moved into the hushed building. The exhibits went from the second to fifth floors: glass with a melted surface, clothing torn into tatters. Horrifying photographs like those we saw in the video at school: pictures of the pattern from people's clothes burned into their skin, pictures of grief-stricken mothers holding their dead children, pictures that made me wonder how anything like this could have happened. A strange chill began to creep over me as I moved slowly from one picture to the next. All the things I was seeing gradually became more

and more real in my mind. The hush inside the building began to seem kind of scary.

One particular picture caught my eye. It was labeled "Child's Burn Treatment," and showed a badly hurt child being treated. The pain must have been too much for the child, and, like little children often do, she was trying to pull away, screaming. It was a painful sight to see. Looking at that child's face, I felt so sorry for her that tears came to my eyes. I started to get really mad at the atomic bomb that took away the life of even such an innocent child. I was seeing the terrible power of the atomic bomb, which sent a chill up and down my spine. (Ako Kobayashi, ninth-grade girl, Shuzan Junior High School, Kita, Kyoto Prefecture. Keiko Nakamura, teacher. Excerpt from "School Trip to Nagasaki," which first appeared in *Treasures 3: Stories & Art by Students in Japan & Oregon,* 1994.)

Nuclear Winter

Do more Hiroshimas loom in the future? Reading plausible nuclear war scenarios conjures up horrifying, unimaginable nightmares. Dr. Martin Luther King said that we can choose between a future of diplomacy and cooperation, or "spiral down a militaristic stairway into a hell of nuclear annihilation" (King 1964). While the Cold War is over, the nuclear threat is not. A majority of Americans believe that by 2010 one country will use nuclear weapons against another, and most Americans do not want any country, including the United States, to possess nuclear weapons (Associated Press 2005). On the other hand, the U.S. government is moving toward a policy where nuclear weapons could be used in preemptive strikes.

> The Pentagon has drafted a revised doctrine for the use of nuclear weapons that envisions commanders requesting presidential approval to use them to preempt an attack by a nation or a terrorist group using weapons of mass destruction. The draft also includes the option of using nuclear arms to destroy known enemy stockpiles of nuclear, biological or chemical weapons. (Pincus 2005)

Barbara Smith stated, "It's [the spread of nuclear weapons] too dangerous, too many things can go wrong" (Associated Press 2005). What are the dangers that threaten us with nuclear devastation?

- Experts think terrorists pose the greatest threat because they would not hesitate to use them or care about the consequences (Lester 2005).
- In a report, the RAND Corporation stated that the 4,000 Russian and U.S. strategic missiles on hair-trigger alert could be launched in a few

minutes and would destroy both countries within an hour (Joint Project of Association of World Citizens and Friends of the Earth Anti-Nuclear Weapons Campaign 2005). "Hair-trigger" or "launch on warning" alert status means that in less than fifteen minutes following the detection (real or false) of a missile attack, leaders of the United States or Russia must decide to launch missiles in a counterattack or lose them.

- In the past, there have been many close calls (e.g., false alarms, nuclear accidents and misfirings, warning system errors, human error, and so on) that might have started nuclear war (Phillips 1998; Moore 2004).

- The megatonnage of the U.S. and Russian nuclear arsenals alone "is more than enough to destroy civilization and perhaps the human race" (Joint Project of Association of World Citizens and Friends of the Earth Anti-Nuclear Weapons Campaign, 2005). ". . . fewer than 200 of these weapons [United States and Russian nuclear weapons] could devastate either country" (Union of Concerned Scientists 2005).

- The U.S. government has failed to retrieve uranium that it sent abroad (Rachel's Environment & Health News 2004).

> As the United States presses Iran and other countries to shut down their nuclear weapons development programs, government auditors have disclosed that the United States is making little effort to recover large quantities of weapons-grade uranium—enough to make roughly 1,000 nuclear bombs—that the government dispersed to 43 countries over the last several decades [including Iran and Pakistan]. (Brinkley & Broad 2004)

- Tens of thousands of nuclear weapons and material for thousands more are kept in poorly guarded facilities in Russia (Friends Committee on National Legislation 2003).

- Bunn, Wier, and Holdren (2003) state that a quarter of a million nuclear weapons can be produced out of the separated plutonium and highly enriched uranium held in the world's arsenals.

- U.S. nuclear weapons are no longer seen as deterrents—weapons of last resort—but could be used in preemptive strikes, thus reversing a decades-old trend (Steinberg 2003; Arkin 2002). The Nuclear Posture Review of the U.S. government describes possible plans for nuclear strikes against China, Russia, Syria, Iran, Iraq, North Korea, and Libya. This might encourage other states to adopt similar policies, which might destabilize and increase the chance for one country to use nuclear weapons. Once a country uses nuclear weapons, others might feel the need to use theirs. There's no telling how widespread a nuclear war would be, but the devastation would be horrific.

Questions and Concerns

The U.S. nuclear weapons policy and program raises questions and concerns, sends the message of proliferation around the world, and undermines our goal of stopping the spread of nuclear weapons. The Reliable Replacement Warhead program outlines plans for design, production, and deployment of a new generation of warheads (Borger 2005). While the Bush administration is pushing for research on mini-nuclear weapons, legislation has kept alive the feasibility of conducting research on a bunker-busting nuclear weapon (Taylor 2005). If the U.S. government were to begin research, which almost always leads to testing, "this would be a signal to other nuclear weapon states to do the same. China is almost certain to resume testing. After the U.S. decision to develop ballistic missile defenses, China feels vulnerable, and is likely to attempt to reduce its vulnerability by a modernization and build-up of its nuclear arsenal. Other states with nuclear weapons, such as India or Pakistan, may use the window of opportunity opened by the U.S.A. to update their arsenals. The danger of a new nuclear arms race is real" (Rotblat 2004).

Considering how powerful our military arsenal is, why do we need to even think about conducting nuclear weapon research?

> No other military is even close to the United States. The American military is now the strongest the world has ever known, both in absolute terms and relative to other nations; stronger than the Wehrmacht in 1940, stronger than the legions at the height of Roman power. For years to come, no other nation is likely even to try to rival American might. (Easterbrook 2003)

Along with the conventional arsenal, the U.S. government has at its disposal approximately 10,300 nuclear weapons (Arkin and Norris 2005), and a limited strike alone could kill tens of millions of Russians or Chinese.

Just How Horrible Would Nuclear War Be?

Alan F. Phillips, M.D. (2001) answers that question in his article, "The Immediate Effect: Medical Problems After Nuclear War," displayed at www.3ammagazine.com. After reading his article you might come to the same conclusion: There would be no solutions to the sustained medical injuries and illnesses of the survivors of a nuclear holocaust. The following excerpts are reprinted with permission from *3:AM Magazine*. They are a sobering wake-up call.

> A nuclear war between U.S.A. and Russia—or, say, one or more of the new nuclear powers to have emerged in recent years—would cause

more human deaths and injuries in a few hours or days than have occurred in all the wars in the history of the world.

. . . The conclusion reached by medical societies, health services,
and universities, which is also my own conclusion, is that there would
be essentially NO medical response.

. . . Calculations for a Nuclear War appear unbelievably callous. The
U.S. "Federal Emergency Management Agency" has described various
scenarios, and a typical one might result in 86,000,000 people dead and
34,000,000 severely injured in the United States (CRPB-2 Model,
quoted by Abrams & Von Kaenel, 16). "Acceptable" or not to the military minds, there is no way that this number of injured could be ac-
commodated or treated in all the hospitals of the world. There are
about 2,000,000 hospital beds in Canada and the U.S.A. combined.

Obviously no existing or conceivable medical service could handle
a disaster even one-tenth of this size.

What would happen to individuals in an attacked city?

The lucky ones would be those killed outright; they might be vapor-
ized, or be left represented by a shadow burned onto a wall like the
well-known picture from Nagasaki. The slightly less fortunate would
be severely injured and regain consciousness in great pain and terror, in
time to see and feel fire bearing down on them, and they would die
without hope, but quickly. Some would be injured in the streets, and
unable to walk. No help would come to them. Others might be trapped
by fallen masonry, caught by the legs, pinned down by a fallen utility
pole, or enclosed in a collapsed basement, perhaps not mortally
wounded but with no hope of moving the obstructions until they died
from fire, radiation sickness, or thirst. The terror and desolation of
hundreds of people in such a situation, in the dark, some of them in
hearing of others, some alone, is difficult to conceive.

. . . There is no end to the scenes of pain and horror that one can see
in imagination. The Canadian picture of a serious injury, in an auto accident, an industrial accident, or a severe burn at home, is of pain,
fright, and chaos lasting for many minutes or at most an hour or two
until the ambulance arrives, skilled help is at the scene, and the problems begin to be controlled. After the destruction of a country by
nuclear bombs, only a small proportion of people would ever get help.
The great majority of injured would die where they lay, slowly, without
any comfort or pain relief whatever; others would struggle for miles
through fire and rubble, and find no help, whether they reached their
home or a suburban hospital surrounded by uncountable crowds of injured and hopeless people. No-one, not even the doctors, would know
who had received a serious or a fatal dose of radiation; so patients who

received first aid to the extent of arresting haemorrhage and rough splinting of broken bones, would not know if slow inevitable death awaited them in a few days or weeks. They could assume that any rain that fell would be lethally full of radioactivity (even to causing beta-ray burns on the skin) but would have no way of knowing whether food, or water from other sources, was radioactive.

Phillips cites the Health Policy of the American College of Physicians, which states "that education is a key to prevention of nuclear war, and endorses increased professional and public education on the medical consequences of nuclear war" (American College of Physicians 1982). Armed with such knowledge, perhaps students and educators will effectively urge our government to reduce the risks of nuclear war. At the very least, students need to know the consequences and tolls that nuclear weapons wreak.

Lessons and Activities on the Dangers that Nuclear Weapons Pose

Discuss the Danger

Since the very first atomic bomb test, people have described the destructive powers and effects of nuclear weapons. As Einstein said, once we unleash them in a nuclear war, what will be left? William Burchett, an independent Australian reporter, told the world what was left of Hiroshima as he typed out his story amongst the rubble (Goodman & Goodman 2004).

> Hiroshima does not look like a bombed city. It looks as if a monster steamroller has passed over it and squashed it out of existence. I write these facts as dispassionately as I can in the hope that they will act as a warning to the world.

Have your class discuss any or all of the following quotes and how they apply to their lives. This activity can serve as a warm-up to the lessons that follow and will tell you what your students know and don't know about nuclear weapons.

- "Nuclear war cannot be won and must never be fought." —President Reagan
- "We can sum it up in one sentence: Our technical civilization has just reached its greatest level of savagery. We will have to choose, in the more or less near future, between collective suicide and the intelligent use of our scientific conquests. . . . Before the terrifying prospects now

available to humanity, we see even more clearly that peace is the only goal worth struggling for. This is no longer a prayer but a demand to be made by all peoples to their governments—a demand to choose definitively between hell and reason." —Albert Camus, *Combat*, 8 August 1945.

• "The survivors [of a nuclear war] would envy the dead." —Nikita Khrushchev, Pravda, 20 July 1963.

• "In an all-out nuclear war, more destructive power than in all of World War II would be unleashed every second during the long afternoon it would take for all the missiles and bombs to fall. A World War II every second—more people killed in the first few hours than all the wars of history put together. The survivors, if any, would live in despair amid the poisoned ruins of a civilization that had committed suicide." — President Jimmy Carter, Farewell Address to the American People, 14 January 1981.

• "If men can develop weapons that are so terrifying as to make the thought of global war include almost a sentence for suicide, you would think that man's intelligence and his comprehension . . . would include also his ability to find a peaceful solution." —President Dwight D. Eisenhower, Press Conference, Washington, DC, 14 November 1956.

• "I want to go to zero, and I'll tell you why: If we and the Russians can go to zero nuclear weapons, then think what that does for us in our efforts to counter the new war. . . . Think how intolerant we will be of nations that are developing nuclear weapons if we have none. Think of the high moral ground we secure by having none. . . . It's kind of hard for us to say to North Korea, 'You are terrible people, you're developing a nuclear weapon,' when we have, oh, 8,000." —General Charles Horner, U.S. Army (Ret.) Former Commander, U.S. Space Command, 15 July 1994.

Valuable Lessons

The lessons that follow were designed by Alan Shapiro to introduce your students to current U.S. nuclear policy and its pros and cons. They are especially valuable because they allow students to decide for themselves and discuss with each other their opinions of the information contained within the readings. His questions stimulate student research. Lastly, he suggests ways in which they can respond publicly.

NUCLEAR WEAPONS CONTROVERSY: THREE LESSONS ON NEW U.S. POLICY

ALAN SHAPIRO, EDUCATORS FOR SOCIAL RESPONSIBILITY, METROPOLITAN AREA

(These lessons were written for Educators for Social Responsibility, Metropolitan Area, which works to make social responsibility an integral part of education through programs in conflict resolution, diversity, and social awareness. Visit their website of free teacher resources at www.teachablemoment.org. For more information, contact ESR Metro (475 Riverside Drive, Room 550, New York, NY 10115; phone: 212-870-3318) or visit at www.esrmetro.org. © Educators for Social Responsibility. Reprinted with permission.)

To the Teacher

Students probably know that nuclear weapons have great destructive power, and may know that they produce radioactivity, but may not be aware of how lethal and long-lasting it is or of other significant effects. And while students may have some information about what U.S. nuclear weapons policy has been, they probably know little about controversial changes in that policy under the administration of President George W. Bush. Perhaps the most notable of them became public on March 10, 2002, when an unclassified section of the Pentagon's Nuclear Posture Review was published (key portions remain secret).

Earlier changes in nuclear weapons policy and those announced on NPR in 2002 are clearly momentous and warrant examination, discussion, and the judgment and response of citizens. The lessons here are intended to provide students with some specifics on the effects of nuclear weapons explosions and background on U.S. nuclear weapons policy in the past; information about changes in that policy and pros and cons about them; and opportunities for student discussion, coming to judgment, and response to an issue of paramount importance to Americans and the world.

Lesson One

1. Distribute Student Reading 1 for students' responses.

Student Reading 1: A Questionnaire

Directions: Mark each of the following statements T (true), F (false), or ? (don't know).

1. The only difference between nuclear bombs and other bombs is that nuclear bombs are far more powerful.

2. The U.S. has signed a treaty that commits it to work for nuclear disarmament.

3. The U.S. has pledged never to use nuclear weapons against a country that does not have them.

4. The U.S. has voluntarily suspended nuclear weapons testing.

5. Most nations in the world now have nuclear weapons.

6. The U.S. is the only nation ever to have used nuclear weapons against another nation.

7. The U.S. has signed a treaty that bans building a missile defense system.

After they have completed the questionnaire, discuss students' responses without indicating their correctness or incorrectness.

- Which answers are they sure of? How do they know?
- What misinformation do students have? Why?
- What do they not know or understand?

On each item, but perhaps especially the first, it will probably be useful to ask for details. For example, ask students who think #1 is false what the differences are. Ask students who think #2 is true what the name of the treaty is and what they know about it; or ask students who think #2 is false for the basis of their response. This process will clarify what students know, what they don't, and where they are misinformed.

2. Distribute Student Reading 2 for reading and study.

When students have finished, ask them to mark their responses for Student Reading 1 a second time. Are there questions or problems with any answers? Clarify.

Student Reading 2: Information About the Questionnaire

1. Differences between nuclear bombs and other bombs. The effects of an ordinary or conventional bomb, whatever its size, are to produce a blast after it explodes and, in the immediate vicinity, to wound and kill people and to damage and destroy property.

   The effects of nuclear bombs are far more extensive. On August 6, 1945, at 8:16 A.M., an atomic bomb was detonated about 1,900 feet above the central section of Hiroshima, Japan. In that instant, tens of thousands of people were burned, blasted, and crushed to death. Tens of thousands more suffered injuries of every description or were doomed to die of radiation sickness. The center of the city was flattened, and every part of the city was damaged. Half an hour after the blast, fires set by the thermal pulse and the collapse of buildings began to coalesce into a firestorm that lasted six hours. Starting about 9 A.M. and lasting until late in the afternoon a "black rain" fell on the western portions of the city, carrying radioactive fallout from the blast to the ground. For four hours at midday, a violent whirlwind, born of the strange meteorological conditions produced by the explosion, further devastated the city.

The number of people who were killed outright or who died of their injuries over the next three months is estimated to be 130,000. Over the next five years it is estimated that another 140,000 who had suffered burns, nausea, vomiting, bloody discharges, overall weakness, hair loss, and disfiguring scar tissue died. Decades after the attack, survivors suffer higher rates of cancer than those not exposed to the bombing, and many of the approximately 4,000 who were fetuses and are still alive were born mentally retarded and with smaller heads.

A medium-sized nuclear bomb today has an explosive yield of one megaton (a million tons of TNT), or 80 times that of the bomb that destroyed Hiroshima. A one megaton bomb would, like a conventional bomb, wound and kill people and destroy property, though much more extensively. In addition to those effects, it would:

- produce a fireball with temperatures exceeding 27 million degrees Fahrenheit, vaporizing everything within 1.5 miles of ground zero
- kill unprotected human beings in an area some six square miles with "initial nuclear radiation"
- produce radioactive fallout—dust and debris created by the blast and thrown up into the atmosphere—which exposes people to various fatal radiation illnesses
- release radioactive elements that remain for thousands of years; produce cancers, leukemia, and mutagenic effects; and make a city and the area around it uninhabitable
- create a thermal pulse—a wave of blinding light and intense heat—that causes second-degree burns in exposed human beings nine and one-half miles from the center of the explosion
- produce such strange meteorological conditions as those experienced at Hiroshima—radioactive black rain and violent winds that hurl debris at 600 m.p.h.

- generate an electromagnetic pulse that knocks out electrical equipment over a wide area.

If many nuclear bombs were exploded around the world in a full-scale nuclear war, scientists predict that at least three additional global effects would occur:

- worldwide fallout contaminating the whole surface of the earth
- general cooling of the earth's surface resulting from millions of tons of dust blocking the sun's rays (referred to as "nuclear winter")
- partial destruction of the ozone layer that protects living beings from radiation.

2. U.S. commitment to nuclear weapons disarmament. In 1945, only the U.S. possessed nuclear weapons. This monopoly lasted until the Soviet Union became a nuclear power in 1949. Great Britain, France, and China soon followed. The growing number of nuclear nations and the dangers associated with nuclear weapons led to the Non-Proliferation Treaty, or NPT, in which non-nuclear nations agreed not to receive nuclear weapons or manufacture their own, and nations with nuclear weapons agreed to make serious efforts at nuclear disarmament. This agreement went into effect in 1970 and has now been signed by 187 nations, including the U.S.

In May 2000, after a month-long conference, the five original nuclear weapons powers—the U.S., Russia, Great Britain, France, and China—strengthened their pledge of 30 years ago by committing to "an unequivocal undertaking to accomplish the total elimination of their nuclear arsenals."

3. A U.S. pledge. Since 1978, the U.S. has pledged not to use nuclear weapons against any non–nuclear-weapons state that signed the NPT. Among those states are Iraq, Iran, Libya, and North Korea. The most recent pledge was in 1995 during the Clinton administration by Secretary of State Warren Christopher.

4. U.S. policy on nuclear weapons testing. From 1951 to 1963, the U.S. conducted more than 200 above-ground tests of nuclear weapons, as did the Soviet Union. Although the two nations agreed in 1963 to stop such testing, underground tests continued. Since 1992, the U.S. has voluntarily refrained from further nuclear weapons tests. But it has not agreed to the Comprehensive Test Ban Treaty (CTBT) banning "all nuclear weapon test explosions," signed by 164 nations and all major nations except the U.S. and China. The main reasons for a test ban are: 1) to prevent nuclear weapon development, which requires a test

program, and 2) environmental and health concerns. For example, the Center for Disease Control and Prevention has found that virtually every person who has lived in the U.S. since 1951 has been exposed to radioactive fallout from global nuclear weapons tests. This fallout, the Center's study says, could eventually be responsible for 11,000 cancer deaths in the U.S. Though President Clinton urged approval of the CTBT, a majority of the Senate rejected it in 1999 on the grounds that the U.S. might need to test nuclear weapons in the future, a decision President Bush agrees with.

5. Nations with nuclear weapons. In addition to the five original nuclear weapons states, three others now have nuclear weapons—Israel, India, and Pakistan.

6. Use of nuclear weapons against another nation. Near the end of World War II, the U.S. dropped atomic bombs on the cities of Hiroshima and Nagasaki, Japan.

7. U.S. position on missile defense. For a quarter century and until recently the Anti-Ballistic Missile Treaty (ABM), agreed to by the U.S. and the Soviet Union, prohibited each country from developing a missile defense system to defend its national territory against nuclear attack. The idea was that stability depended on each country's being equally vulnerable to attack.

But on December 12, 2001, President Bush declared:

> Today I have given formal notice to Russia, in accordance with the [ABM] treaty, that the United States of America is withdrawing from this almost 30-year-old treaty. I have concluded that the ABM treaty hinders our government's ability to develop ways to protect our people from future terrorist or rogue-state missile attacks. The 1972 ABM treaty was signed by the United States and the Soviet Union at a much different time, in a vastly different world. One of the signatories, the Soviet Union, no longer exists. And neither does the hostility that once led both our countries to keep thousands of nuclear weapons on hair-trigger alert, pointed at each other. . . . We know that the terrorists, and some of those who support them, seek the ability to deliver death and destruction to our doorstep via missiles. And we must have the freedom and flexibility to develop effective defenses against those attacks.

New York Times columnist Bill Keller presented another view of the reasoning behind the missile defense decision (12/29/01):

The real logic of missile defense . . . is not to defend but to protect our freedom to attack. For example: Taiwan decides to risk a climactic break with mainland China. The mainland responds with a military tantrum. America would like to defend the island democracy against the Communist giant—but we are backed down by hints that Beijing cares enough about this issue to launch nuclear missiles. American voters may or may not support a conventional war for Taiwanese independence; they're much less likely to support one that risks the obliteration of our cities. Ah, but if we have an insurance policy, a battery of anti-missile weapons sufficient (in theory) to neutralize China's two dozen nuclear missiles, we would feel freer to go to war over Taiwan.

Or would the U.S. have gone into Afghanistan so quickly if it knew the Taliban had a single missile capable of pulverizing Washington? But if the U.S. had a missile defense system able to protect against a limited attack, the theory goes, the Taliban's single missile would not be a deterrent to a U.S. attack. Missile defense, in other words, is not about defense. It's about offense.

3. Distribute Student Reading 3.

Student Reading 3: Support and Opposition

Directions: Read and study the following pros and cons on U.S. nuclear policy and review the earlier student readings. Then consider the following questions, decide on and make note of your answers, and come to class prepared to support your points of view. Be ready to explain why or why not regarding your answers.

1. Should the U.S. develop new nuclear bombs?
2. Should the U.S. cut its nuclear stockpile to a minimum?
3. Should the U.S., if necessary, resume testing of nuclear bombs?
4. Should the U.S. continue its efforts to build a missile defense system?
5. Should the U.S. ever use nuclear bombs again?
6. Should the U.S. take serious steps to lead other nuclear powers in fulfilling their pledge in 2000 of an unequivocal undertaking to accomplish the total elimination of their nuclear arsenals?

Support for New Nuclear Policy

- "We've got all options on the table because we want to make it very clear to nations that you will not threaten the United States or use weapons of mass destruction against us or our allies." —President Bush, *The New York Times*, 18 March 2002

- "This administration is fashioning a more diverse set of options for deterring the threat of weapons of mass destruction. That is why the administration is pursuing advanced conventional forces and improved intelligence capabilities. A combination of offensive and defensive and nuclear and non-nuclear capabilities is essential to meet the deterrence requirements of the 21st century." [These requirements include the creation of a missile defense system.]—*The Nuclear Posture Review*, 2002

- "We should not get all carried away with some sense that the United States is planning to use nuclear weapons in some contingency that is coming up in the near future. It is not the case. What the Pentagon has done with this study is sound, military, conceptual planning and the president will take that planning and he will give his directions on how to proceed." —Secretary of State Colin L. Powell, *Face the Nation*, CBS, 10 March 2002

- "This is . . . not a plan. This preserves for the President all the options that a President would want to have in case this country or our friends and allies were attacked with weapons of mass destruction."—General Richard B. Myers, Chairman of the Joint Chiefs of Staff, CNN, 10 March 2002

Opposition to New Nuclear Policy

- "Did the decision-makers in Washington reflect, when they gave themselves the right to launch nuclear attacks on the Middle East and elsewhere, that they might inspire those targeted to do likewise to us? Did they forget that there is no defense against nuclear arms and no rescue for those attacked by them? . . . No country is omnipotent. None are invulnerable. What the United States has done to others at Hiroshima and Nagasaki—and what we may yet do to others at Teheran and Tripoli—others can do to us."—Jonathan Schell, *The Nation*, 1 April 2002

- "If the *Nuclear Posture Review* is the best that we can do, it is a political roadmap to ultimate catastrophe. . . . In the wake of announcing a withdrawal from the Anti-Ballistic Missile Treaty (ABM), Bush administration policies such as refusing to ratify the CTBT, developing new nuclear arms, and implicitly threatening nuclear use against non-nuclear states, threaten to undermine the credibility of the United States. . . . Nothing could be more dangerous than a world without legal constraints on developing nuclear arsenals." —Jonathan Granoff, President, Global Security Institute, March 12, 2002

- "If another country were planning to develop a new nuclear weapon and contemplating pre-emptive strikes against a list of non-nuclear powers, Washington would rightly label that nation a dangerous rogue state. Yet such is the course recommended to President Bush by a new Pentagon planning paper. . . . Nuclear weapons are not just another part of the military arsenal. They are different, and lowering the threshold for their use is reckless folly." —*The New York Times* editorial, 12 March 2002

- A response from China: "China wants to make it very clear that China will never yield to foreign threats, including nuclear blackmail. The days when China could be bullied are gone." Chinese Vice Foreign Minister Li Zhaoxing, *The New York Times*, 17 March 2002

- A response from Russia: "A spokesman for the Russian foreign minister . . . called on the Bush administration to explain the report and that it remained to be seen to what point this information corresponds to reality. If it does, how can you reconcile it with declarations of the United States that it no longer considers Russia as an enemy?"—*The New York Times*, 12 March 2002

Lesson Two

1. Conduct a moving opinion poll with students.

It is a way to get students up and moving as they place themselves along a STRONGLY AGREE–STRONGLY DISAGREE continuum according to their opinions about specific statements. Create a corridor of space in your room from one end to the other, long enough and wide enough to accommodate the whole class. Make two large signs—STRONGLY AGREE and STRONGLY DISAGREE—and post them on opposite sides of the room.

Explain to students: "You will be participating in a moving opinion poll. Each time you hear a statement you are to move to the place along the imaginary line that most closely reflects your opinion. If you strongly agree you will move to that side of the room; if you strongly disagree you will move to that side of the room. You can also place yourself anywhere in the middle, especially if you have mixed feelings about the statement. After you are all placed, people will share why they are standing where they are. This is not a time to debate. Rather, this is a way to check out what people are thinking and get a sense of the different ways people view the issue."

You may want to use all or some of the following statements. The object of changing statements is to introduce qualifying conditions and contexts and see if students' opinions shift. You may want to begin with statements that indicate personal preferences on matters of less importance than nuclear weapons policies and give students an opportunity to familiarize themselves with a moving opinion poll, especially if they haven't participated in one before.

Sample statements:

- The best TV program is "The Simpsons."
- Getting music for free by downloading it from a computer is unfair to musicians and record companies.
- Basketball is America's most exciting sport.

Nuclear weapons policy issues:

- The U.S. should rely on its current stock of nuclear bombs and not build.
- The U.S. should develop new nuclear bombs as its leaders see a need.
- The U.S. should eliminate nuclear bombs and use only conventional weapons for defense.
- The U.S. should cut its nuclear weapons stockpile to a minimum if other countries are willing to do the same.
- The U.S. should cut its nuclear weapons stockpile to a minimum no matter what other countries do.
- The U.S. should maintain its current nuclear weapons stockpile and add to it as necessary.
- The U.S. should voluntarily refrain from nuclear weapons testing.
- The U.S. should sign the CTBT.
- The U.S. should test nuclear weapons whenever it needs to.
- The U.S. should resume its ABM agreement with Russia.
- The U.S. should use nuclear weapons only against an enemy who also has them.
- The U.S. should never again use a nuclear bomb.
- The U.S. should use nuclear weapons only in a desperate situation.
- The U.S. should gradually eliminate its nuclear weapons if other countries are willing to do the same.

- The U.S. should immediately eliminate all of its nuclear weapons.
- The U.S. should take the lead in a global effort to eliminate nuclear weapons.

2. *Assignment*

Write an essay of 300–500 words addressing the following: Should the U.S. take active and serious steps to lead other nuclear powers in fulfilling their pledge in May 2000 of "an unequivocal undertaking to accomplish the total elimination of their nuclear arsenals"? If your answer is "yes," explain why. If your answer is "no," explain why not. If you have mixed feelings and thoughts, explain them.

Suggestions for further student investigation:

- What was the Manhattan Project and why was it launched?
- Describe the atomic bombing of Nagasaki, Japan.
- What do nuclear weapons cost the U.S. each year?
- What has been their cost since World War II?
- What environmental and health problems are associated with nuclear weapons production?
- Why do U.S. leaders generally regard the nuclear weapons policy of deterrence to have been successful?
- What is the status of nuclear weapons programs in North Korea? Iraq? Iran? Syria? Libya? China? Russia?
- What efforts are being made by private organizations to abolish nuclear weapons?

Some suggestions for student responses to what they have learned:

- Write letters to representatives, senators, the president.
- Organize a program for a club, school assembly, or the PTA.
- Create a hall or library display.
- Dedicate/publish a special issue or section of the school newspaper.
- Organize programs in any groups to which students belong (or groups parents or friends belong to).
- Get in touch with ESR Metro (212-870-3318 ext. 14335) for news of student activities and possible participation.

Resources for Teachers

The following websites will offer information about nuclear issues, both past and current; sample lessons; study guides; PowerPoint presentations; films; course syllabi; and more. Most importantly, they will provide ways for students to get involved and speak directly to leaders about this paramount issue.

- The Nuclear Age Peace Foundation at www.wagingpeace.org/. Check out its comprehensive web links page at www.wagingpeace.org/menu /resources/web-links/.
- Educators for Social Responsibility (ESR Metropolitan Area), at www.esrmetro.org/resources.html, has teacher sourcebooks and lessons on nuclear issues.
- NuclearFiles.org at nuclearfiles.org/.
- Nuclearpathways.org at nuclearpathways.org/.
- Reaching Critical Will at www.reachingcriticalwill.org/.

Closing Thoughts by Chris Weber

This chapter opened with my describing my visit to the Hiroshima Peace Memorial Park and Museum. In closing, I believe that you, like me, will be moved by the message from a high school student in Hiroshima.

> In my hometown, Hiroshima, we engage in various activities to promote world peace. In school, every student participates in Peace Education programs. We listen, for example, to tragic narratives by survivors of the bomb that fell on Hiroshima. We also visit Hiroshima's Peace Memorial Museum and the A-Bomb Dome Memorial.
>
> Last year was the 60th anniversary of the bombing, which happened on August 6, 1945. The newspapers and TV had almost daily articles and programs about war, peace, and the use of nuclear weapons, and during the summer I had the opportunity to take part in PEACE SITE HIROSHIMA 2005, an art project to commemorate the anniversary. For this international collaboration, six students came from Montreal, Canada, and six came from Hanover, Germany. (They stayed in my fellow students' homes.) Together, we created artwork embodying our fervent wish for world peace which was then publicly displayed for four days near the A-Bomb Dome Memorial.

This experience gave me the precious opportunity to appreciate other people's aspirations for peace and to ponder deeply the problem of nuclear weapons and war. During the project, we listened to the narratives of people who survived that devastation 60 years ago, and one woman spoke of losing her beloved family members and friends. As they described their agony, their sorrow, and their hatred of war, they urged us never, ever to let this tragedy be repeated.

There are those who say that looking back on the past is meaningless for achieving world peace. I don't think so. To promote peace, it is essential to face fully the history of nuclear weapons and war. Learning about the past will never be wasted. However, facing the terrible history of the atomic bombings should never be used to fuel feelings of hatred but rather to obtain precious knowledge that will help keep our future world in peace.

Achieving peace won't be easy. In spite of our wishes and our activities for peace, more nations seek to become nuclear powers and small-sized nuclear bombs are being developed. We must be prepared to stand up and work for world peace whenever it is endangered. To that end, it is essential that we learn about the realities of nuclear devastation, study the world situation today, and make ourselves aware of peace activities everywhere.

I believe that education, not only in schools but also in local communities, plays an enormous part in nurturing people's desire to work for peace by giving them the chance to acquire knowledge and to actually act for peace.

Miki Kohno, eighteen-year-old female student, Hiroshima Municipal Motomachi Senior High School, Hiroshima, Japan. Yoji Matsumoto, principal. I-Kwang Kim provided the superb translation and acted as an invaluable go-between.

10

Developing Media-Literate Students

Our government has declared a military victory in Iraq. As a patriot, I will not celebrate. I will mourn the dead—the American GIs, and also the Iraqi dead, of which there have been many, many more.

I will mourn the Iraqi children, not just those who are dead, but those who have been blinded, crippled, disfigured, or traumatized, like the bombed children of Afghanistan who, as reported by American visitors, lost their power of speech. The American media has not given us a full picture of the human suffering caused by our bombing; for that, we need to read the foreign press.

—Howard Zinn 2003

Empowering Students Through Media Literacy

On the second day of the Iraq War, I walked into a classroom and recalled an astonishing scene. The TV was displaying bomb explosions. A second-grade girl jumped up and down saying, "Oh, a house is on fire," as it exploded under our bombardment. I was shocked because this very caring girl said her words with such glee, having no idea how much suffering the bombardment caused. The chances are that American students continued viewing similar scenes and images of our military might throughout the war. Sanitized media coverage of the Iraq War was similar to that of the Persian Gulf War. One would expect even tighter government control over the media in future conflicts.

For the most part, Americans heard interpretative commentary by ex-generals and military experts. Americans saw, heard, and read very little of the Iraqi victims and American anti-war protestors. Rendall and Broughel (2003) stated, "The anti-war percentages ranged from 4 percent at NBC, 3 percent at CNN, ABC, PBS and FOX, and less than 1 percent—one out of 205 U.S. sources—at CBS." Again, what we heard during the Iraq War mirrored the Gulf War media coverage in many ways. Expect more of the same.

Since the Vietnam War and subsequent conflicts, the media has rarely informed us of how many civilians have been killed. How many soundbites or printed words did the media devote to the more than 100,000 Iraqi men, women, and children killed by the coalition? In his poem "From Iraq," Michael Rosen wrote:

> We are the unfound
> We are uncounted
> You don't see the homes we made
> We're not even the small print or the bit in bracket . . .
> because we lived far from you . . .
> because you have cameras that point the other way. . . .

While Americans were told there was no alternative to attacking Iraq, European youth were told there were numerous options to war (Bowie 2003). They learned about the campaign of disinformation and propaganda coming from the U.S. military. Young people in the rest of the world saw TV reports with more emphasis on civilian casualties and suffering. U.S. and international media tend to cover wars in whatever ways suit their interests, their owners, their sponsors, and their audience. Regardless of the media bias and motives from country to country, let's teach students to be media savvy; otherwise, will there be more of the following?

> A third school of thought was expressed to me rather succinctly the other day by the owner of the music shop where I take my guitar lessons: "I don't believe the polls. I don't think Americans really do support the war, no people can be in favor of war—but they don't really see the war, do they? They just believe what the American media tells them." (Reynolds 2003)

Media plays a huge role in the lives of young children and teens, who spend enormous numbers of hours in front of a screen, either computer or television. At the same time, teens are bombarded daily with carefully constructed advertisements, including military recruitment. In fact, Dr. Whitehurst (2005) writes that ". . . Channel One News, the 'educational' TV show that my daughter Isa and millions of other American kids watch every morning at school, is busy recruiting our teenagers into the military." Media messages are carefully crafted whether to sell a pair of jeans or the government's spin. Moreover, the military constantly run ads trying to lure teens to be "the best you can be."

Rather than letting students soak up news like mindless sponges, engage them in media literacy activities where they will be able to:

- analyze words and images
- question motives, values, sources, and corporations behind the messages
- critically view the media messages—think about them
- detect bias and disinformation in the news media
- use the media wisely and apply its messages to their own lives.

Discussing Quotes About War

The first casualty when war comes is truth.
—Senator Hiram Johnson, 1917

Senator Johnson made that remark during World War I, and his statement applies to any war.

Have your class discuss any or all of the following quotes and how they apply to the current news media and its viewers and readers.

- "If we let people see that kind of thing, there would never again be any war."—Senior Pentagon official explaining why the U.S. military censored footage from the Gulf War showing Iraqi soldiers sliced in two by U.S. helicopter fire
- "If you tell a lie big enough and keep repeating it, people will eventually come to believe it."—Nazi Propaganda Minister Joseph Goebbels, January 12, 1941
- "In a time of war, free speech comes under fire by our government in the forms of censorship, false reporting, and untruths and unbalanced news. The truth needed for a vibrant democracy has dissipated, leaving behind an antiseptic and sanitized version of the war in Iraq, brought to us by media corporations—often referred to as 'mouthpieces for the U.S. government.' " —Mariellen Diemand, 2003
- "Our government is in the business of propaganda, which is not the same thing as lying, but definitely not the same thing as truth." —Former U.S. State Department Spokesman
- "Do not fear the enemy, for your enemy can only take your life. It is far better that you fear the media, for they will steal your Honor. That awful power, the public opinion of a nation, is created in America by a horde of ignorant, self-complacent simpletons who failed at ditching and shoemaking and fetched up in journalism on their way to the poorhouse." —Mark Twain
- "Naturally the common people don't want war. But after all, it is the leaders of a country who determine the policy, and it's always a simple matter to drag people along whether it is a democracy, or a fascist

dictatorship, or a parliament, or a communist dictatorship. Voice or no voice, the people can always be brought to the bidding of the leaders. This is easy. All you have to do is tell them they are being attacked, and denounce the pacifists for lack of patriotism and for exposing the country to danger. It works the same in every country." —Hermann Goering, Hitler's Reichsmarschall, at the Nuremberg Trials after World War II

- "I'm still taken aback at the extent of indoctrination and propaganda in the United States. It is as if people there are being reared in a sort of altered reality, like broiler chickens or pigs in a pen."—Arundhati Roy

- "Next the statesmen will invent cheap lies, putting the blame upon the nation that is attacked, and every man will be glad of those conscience-soothing falsities, and will diligently study them, and refuse to examine any refutations of them; and thus he will by and by convince himself that the war is just, and will thank God for the better sleep he enjoys after this process of grotesque self-deception." —Mark Twain, *The Mysterious Stranger*

- "War, we have come to believe, is a spectator sport. The military and the press—remember in wartime the press is always part of the problem—have turned war into a vast video arcade game. Its very essence—death—is hidden from public view."—Chris Hedges, a Pulitzer Prize–winning reporter for *The New York Times*

Moving Students Toward Media Literacy

Read the following piece by Polly Kellogg to learn ways to help students become more media literate, especially regarding war or conflict coverage. You can utilize her ideas and activities when teaching about not only war coverage but also war-related topics. It's important that we give our students the skills to examine the media and their messages so that they can make more fully informed decisions. Kellogg's ideas and activities are a wonderful start in this direction.

DRAWING ON HISTORY TO CHALLENGE THE WAR

POLLY KELLOGG

As I watched the mainstream media minimize the tremendous opposition to the Bush administration's drive to attack Iraq, I became determined to encourage my students to think critically about the war plans and to seek out alternative media perspectives. I created an effective unit using 1) a video on disinformation about the Gulf War, 2) a media project to explore alternative media perspectives on the Internet, and 3) an action project to educate others about Iraq. Although I teach university students, this unit can be used with high school students.

[Note: In this lesson, the author uses *Hidden Wars*, a film on disinformation regarding the Gulf War. You could show similar videos like *Uncovered* instead. Following this article is a list of films providing alternative viewpoints and centered on media coverage of conflict. Any of these films will raise questions and encourage critical thinking and discussion about the U.S. government's motives for military action.]

Hidden Wars of Desert Storm, a revealing documentary on the history of U.S. maneuvers to control oil in the Middle East and hidden manipulations surrounding the Gulf War, raises questions about the Iraq war rhetoric and possible motives behind the call to war.

To engage students' empathy, I began with the last 17 minutes of the 64-minute video, because this segment on war disabilities is emotionally compelling. It shows both U.S. veterans and Iraqis made ill from depleted uranium, which the U.S. military uses to harden bullets, tanks, and missiles. After seeing video images of Iraqi children dying of leukemia caused by depleted uranium, it was hard for students to see Iraqis as "the enemy." One student said, "I had no idea children were dying." Another asked, "How does the military get away with being so cruel? They didn't even warn people about the radiation."

The second day, I showed the first part of *Hidden Wars*, a crucial history of U.S. activities in the Middle East our mainstream media ignores. To control Mideast oil, from WWII to 1988, the U.S. encouraged war, helped install dictators (Hussein and the Shah), and supplied them with billions of dollars of weaponry. In the 1980s, U.S. corporations supplied Iraq with biological, chemical, and nuclear components.

Twenty-two minutes into the video we watched the first President Bush bullying the United Nations into supporting an invasion. I stopped here to let students discuss obvious parallels to the present tug-of-war between the younger Bush and the United Nations over how much time to allow for inspections. They had many questions about why the United States has so much power over the United Nations. I suggested they think about Bush's struggle with allies in the United Nations in light of the administration's goal of U.S. global dominance. As part of this discussion, I asked them to brainstorm the pros and cons of U.S. global dominance.

The rest of the video carefully documents its thesis that the U.S. government secretly wanted Hussein to invade Kuwait because the U.S. military would have an excuse to get a long-desired base in oil-rich Saudi Arabia. For example, we see an interview with the reporter who discovered that U.S. generals showed the Saudi monarchy falsified satellite photos of Iraqi troops poised to attack the Saudi border in order to get the Saudis to accept a U.S. military base.

Challenging War Rhetoric

I wondered how students would relate to revelations about a war they knew little about. When the video ended, they jumped right into an angry critique of the rhetoric surrounding the present war. One indignant student asked, "If our companies gave Hussein weapons of mass destruction, why are we going to bomb him because he might still have some?" Another said, "Our government is certainly not fighting for democracy in Iraq, because that's never been their goal." A woman said, "If this war turns out to be about oil, I'm going to be really mad."

Alternative Perspectives

I introduced the media project by saying the Internet makes it possible for us to seek out different perspectives from non-corporate, alternative media, and from media of other nations, instead of the "official story."

I asked students to collect examples of how the mainstream media and the alternative press were covering the war buildup. They were to clip articles about Iraq from the local newspaper and alternative media websites whose addresses I supplied. After several weeks of following the news, they would write a paper analyzing contrasts between the two types of media. What differences did they see in what is emphasized? What differences did they see in headlines? Did pictures differ? I encouraged them to highlight and mark articles with their comments. They were to examine such things as loaded language, plays on emotion, historical context (or lack of), and depth of investigative reporting. I included some lively anti-war websites to convey a sense of anti-war activism.

To get students started, I showed examples of alternative press headlines about oil—a topic the mainstream media practically ignores. Anticipating the assignment might seem overwhelming, I asked students to share their findings in small groups for 10 minutes at the start of each class for a couple weeks. In these groups, the web exploration came alive. Students who loved the Internet gave tips to those less experienced. As they shared their "finds," they spurred each other on. Students found pictures of large anti-war protests around the world that the mainstream press all but ignored. One student found a picture of an Iraqi girl that held great meaning for him. At the Fairness and Accuracy in Reporting (FAIR) site they discovered critiques of mainstream coverage. One student proudly announced she read that Bush had used the word "terrorist" 30 times in a 30-minute speech on Iraq, to link people's feelings about bin Laden to Hussein. Several students brought in lists of "talking points" on why we should not attack Iraq. Students noticed the lack of mainstream publicity about polls, now that most Americans oppose a unilateral attack. Colorful anti-war posters and bumper stickers from the activist sites were popular.

When I teach this unit again, I plan to increase the focus on international media. I feel strongly that we need to find ways to bring international news into our schools and make it a part of our lives.

Action Project to Educate

As their awareness grew, many students argued about the war. This inspired an assignment to make these discussions focused and productive. They had to plan an educational session to teach others about Iraq, putting thought into how best to share the information they discovered. They needed to back up their arguments and their educational sessions had to be substantial, not brief. I offered the option of writing to an editor or public official, but they all jumped at the option of talking to friends. Some showed a video on the impact of sanctions. Many used alternative press articles to start discussions.

Their papers radiated enthusiasm: "I was so proud to know how to argue with my dad. I told him 'I'm telling you realities. You think what they want you to think,'" and "My mom actually checked out the Zmag website herself!" Students were also discouraged at how little people knew. "My friend thinks he knows everything and won't listen to reason." As our country moves headlong toward war, we need informed people—both young and old—speaking out against it. I believe many of my students will make their voices heard.

Polly Kellogg teaches in the Department of Human Relations and Multicultural Education at St. Cloud State University and is a member of Women Against Military Madness. "Drawing on History to Challenge the War" first appeared in *Rethinking Schools* magazine, Winter, 2001/2002 and is reprinted here by permission of Rethinking Schools.

Hidden Wars of Desert Storm, 64 minutes, directed by Gerard Ungerman and Audrey Brohy, narrated by John Hurt. $25, www.hiddenwars.org or from www.teachingforchange.org.

Films, Lessons, and Alternative Media Suggested by Chris Weber

Alternative Films Focusing on Recent Wars and Media Coverage

- www.jibjab.com. At this site, you will laugh and cry at the opinions presented through side-splitting parodies in the form of flash movies.
- *Fahrenheit 9/11*. Available at www.amazon.com.
- *Why We Fight*. This award-winning film provides an inside look at the anatomy of the American war machine. Free online viewing at http://informationclearinghouse.info/article8494.htm.
- *When Lies Become Truth*. (Video—Orwell Rolls in His Grave—Part I) A must-watch documentary. Free online viewing at http://information clearinghouse.info/article8560.htm.
- *OUTFOXED —Rupert Murdoch's War on Journalism*. Available at www.amazon.com.
- *Uncovered: The Whole Truth About the Iraq War*. Free online viewing at www.informationclearinghouse.info/article6423.htm.
- *The Fog of War*. Robert Horton, amazon.com reviewer, writes, "*The Fog of War*, the movie that finally won Errol Morris the best documentary Oscar, is a spellbinder." Available at www.amazon.com.
- *Purple Hearts* by Roel van Broekhoven. A photo series that New York–based Nina Berman made of wounded Iraq veterans led to the making of this documentary. View online at www.informationclearinghouse .info/article7799.htm.
- *Iraq: Two Years On: What Have I Become*. A flash presentation viewed online at: http://bushflash.com/y2.html.
- *911 in Plane Site*. What no other video exposé on September 11th has provided to date is exposure to a barrage of news clips from a majority of the mainstream news outlets. Available for about a $20 donation at www.thepowermall.com.
- *Hijacking Catastrophe: 9/11, Fear & the Selling of American Empire.* Examines how a radical fringe of the Republican Party used the trauma of 9/11 to advance a pre-existing agenda to radically transform American foreign policy while rolling back civil liberties and social programs at home. Free online viewing at www.informationclearing house.info/article6895.htm.

- *Convoy of Death.* In Afghanistan, filmmaker Jamie Doran uncovered evidence of a massacre: Taliban prisoners of war suffocated in containers, shot in the desert under the watch of American troops. The film has been broadcast on national television all over the world and has been screened by the European parliament. Free viewing at www.informationclearinghouse.info/article3267.htm.
- *The Victor Is Not Asked if He Tells the Truth.* View online at www.informationclearinghouse.info/surfing.htm.

Relevant Online Lessons and Handouts

- "The Press and War: Do We Learn About the Issues by Reading the News?" by Susan Epstein at http://highschooljournalism.org/Teachers /Lesson_Plans/Detail.cfm?lessonplanid=267.
- "How to Detect Bias in the News," a handout by Newskit: A Consumers Guide to News Media, by The Learning Seed Company, available at: www.education-medias.ca/english/resources/educational/handouts /broadcast_news/bw_bias_in_the_news.cfm.
- The SMART Paradigm. The Constitutional Rights Foundation has developed the SMART paradigm to help students analyze and evaluate news pieces; posted online at www.crf-usa.org/Iraqwar_html /iraqwar_factfinders.html.

Alternative Media

- Alternative Radio, www.alternativeradio.org
- Alternet, www.alternet.org
- AirAmerica Radio, www.airamericaradio.com
- America for Sale, www.americaforsale.org
- Antiwar.com, www.antiwar.com
- Asia Times, www.atimes.com
- Collection of articles and reports by Robert Fisk, www.robert-fisk.com
- Common Dreams, www.commondreams.org
- CounterPunch, www.counterpunch.com
- Democracy Now: Radio and TV News, www.democracynow.org
- Der Spiegel (English online version), http://service.spiegel.de/cache /international/spiegel/0,1518,archiv,00.html
- Electronic Iraq, http://electroniciraq.net/

- FAIR: Fairness and Accuracy in Reporting, www.fair.org/index.php
- Free Speech TV Network, www.freespeech.org/fsitv/fscm2 /genx.php?name=home
- Hidden Agendas: The Films and Writing of John Pilger, www.johnpilger.com
- Information Clearing House, www.informationclearinghouse.info
- Independent Media Center, www.indymedia.org/en/index.shtml
- Le Monde Diplomatique (English online version), http: //mondediplo.com/
- Michael Moore, www.michaelmoore.com/index.php
- News Alternative, www.asia-stat.com/
- The Nation, www.thenation.com
- The Writings of Greg Palast, www.tbtmradio.com/geeklog /public_html/index.php
- The Memory Hole, www.thememoryhole.org/
- TruthOut, www.truthout.org
- whatreallyhappened.com
- Z Magazine, http://zmagsite.zmag.org/curTOC.htm

National and International Press Websites

- Worldwide News in English, www.thebigproject.co.uk/news/, provides links to online English versions of major newspapers around the world.

Media Awareness Resource Websites

- Media Awareness Network, http://www.media-awareness.ca/english /teachers/index.cfm
- PBS Parents [also for teachers] Media Awareness, www.pbs.org /parents/issuesadvice/media_awareness.html
- "The Merchants of Cool" PBS Report, www.pbs.org/wgbh/pages /frontline/shows/cool/>, is an eye-opener for teens
- Just Think, www.justthink.org/
- Don't Buy It: Get Media Smart, http://pbskids.org/dontbuyit /teachersguide.html
- Center for Media Literacy, www.medialit.org/default.html
- Northwest Media Literacy Center, www.mediathink.org/

If

If the media showed the graphic sights and sounds of the horror of war, would we continue to support future wars? Likely fearing the answer to the question, governments make sure that the reality of war is hidden from its citizens. When I was thinking about writing this section, I thought of a photo that captured the suffering so many children experience in war. Seeing a photo of a girl who just watched her parents get killed makes you want to shut your eyes and wish you never saw her. I want to rage against this senseless act of murder and shake those soldiers. I can hear her cries and screams even now as her parents' blood streaks her cheeks and covers her hands. E-mail me at chriscarlweber@earthlink and I will give you more information about this photo.

Journalists like Robert Fisk have repeatedly visited war zones in the Middle East and provided raw images, which are not for readers who are squeamish viewers. The following passages are from a newspaper article in which Fisk describes a visit to a Baghdad hospital in 2003.

> I'll leave out the description of the flies that have been clustering round the wounds in the Kindi emergency rooms, of the blood caked on the sheets, the blood still dripping from the wounds of those I talked to yesterday. All were civilians. All wanted to know why they had to suffer. All—save for the incandescent youth who ordered me to leave the little boy's bed—talked gently and quietly about their pain. No Iraqi government bus took me to the Kindi hospital. No doctor knew I was coming.
>
> . . . Then there was Safa Karim. She is 11 and she is dying. An American bomb fragment struck her in the stomach and she is bleeding internally, writhing on the bed with a massive bandage on her stomach and a tube down her nose and—somehow most terrible of all—a series of four dirty scarves that tie each of her wrists and ankles to the bed. She moans and thrashes on the bed, fighting pain and imprisonment at the same time. A relative said she is too ill to understand her fate. "She has been given 10 bottles of drugs and she has vomited them all up," he said.

Would we be so eager to support wars if we knew how horrible it was? Would we stand by watching more Safa Karims needlessly suffer? How many more innocent civilians would be slain if we witnessed their killings? Even if the mainstream media tells its side of the war story, the Internet provides us with a multitude of media websites from all over the world. It is up to us to arm ourselves with the truth and act upon it.

11

Speaking Out

The Right to Speak Out

Political dissidence in America has a long history. Our nation's independence began with voiced opposition, which prepared us for revolution. Every major cause—women's rights, racial integregation, and workers' rights—has achieved victory through Americans standing up and speaking out. Every war, including the Iraq War, has been criticized.

Michael Moore and Senator Robert Byrd were among those publicly protesting the Iraq War. Alongside them rang a powerful voice of sincerity and wisdom. This voice belonged to Charlotte Aldebron, a thirteen-year-old from Maine. After reading her speeches, I was astonished and pleasantly surprised that such insight and courage belonged to a teenager. Her actions made me feel ashamed because I could barely speak out against the war among my own colleagues, and yet here was Charlotte being a role model for all Americans. Please read her speech titled "What About the Iraqi Children?," located in Appendix A.

Jim Vacca's students spoke out on several issues in various ways. Reading his piece will show you how Vacca's students found their voices. Then you might support your students as they speak out on issues they care about and want changed.

> *The only thing necessary for the triumph of evil is for good people to do nothing.*
>
> —Edmund Burke

UP AGAINST THE WALL: MODELS OF ACTIVISM FROM *STUDENT WORKER* IN BOULDER, COLORADO

JIM VACCA

Teachers are given the charge to "open eyes" intentionally in the classroom. We divide up our expertise, develop lesson plans, design evaluations, conform to state standard diagnostics, and monitor lunchrooms. Students are assigned to us through complicated scheduling protocols; some students seek us out. I feel a responsibility to each of those students who enter my classroom at 7:30 A.M. We teach in the classroom and we teach with our lives, and when we learn with our students, then we begin to understand the value of education.

A spirit of critical dissent washed over many students. Boulder High *Student Worker* staff joined forces with that of another local high school, New Vista, and as an interschool venture published their own newspaper, *Thought Crime*, later renamed *Student Worker*. Their original statement resonated: "We are a group of open-minded youth, resisting the dominant and dominating culture, that is actively committed to bringing awareness and an alternative perspective to the issues and events that affect our collective future."

With the power of the pen they critiqued many aspects of student life. The kids interviewed Noam Chomsky, David Skaggs, and Howard Zinn. New Vista student Lucy Barnes asked Howard Zinn, professor emeritus at Boston University and author of *A People's History of the United States*, how to understand political unrest in a post-9/11 world. Zinn suggested, "To quell the sudden outbursts of prejudice we must put an end to war by hysteria. An atmosphere of fear has caused people to strike out irrationally, where an atmosphere of calm would allow people to act rationally and intelligently." He further added that in order to avert the threat of terrorism, "we must address the grievances behind terrorism." Students vigorously attacked homophobia, standardized testing as mandated through No Child Left Behind, sweatshop labor, military recruitment, and the Patriot Act.

Student Worker received its first spate of national attention when the Boulder High yearbook failed to include a picture of two girls kissing. *Student Worker,* in solidarity with the Gay/Straight Alliance, printed and distributed the picture and sponsored a "kiss-in" along Boulder Creek, attracting hundreds of students and the media. The tacit exclusion of gays and lesbians prompted *Student Worker's* first press release. The "kiss-in" would "demonstrate solidarity, from both heterosexual and homosexual students, with kids who must endure unfair treatment and policies because of their sexual orientation or perceived sexual orientation," read student organizer Tim Simons. An editorial from the *Daily Camera*, Boulder's newspaper, supported the students. "WE agree with the protestors. If parental permission is not required to publish a photograph of a girl and a guy kissing—or doing anything else that high schoolers do, whether controversial or not—then it is a blatant double standard to require it in same-sex smoochers."

The original organizers graduated, and *Student Worker* and its activist agenda diminished. In the following year, a skittish school board lost its nerve and failed to address legal threats against club activities in Boulder Valley brought on by the Heritage Foundation, which supported—with money and the threat of litigation—the formation of a Bible Club. In order to keep a Bible Club from establishing a pulpit in the public schools, the district temporarily pulled the plug on all clubs, mandating that student-initiated clubs could no longer advertise within the school or make public announcements. In effect, the *Student Worker* was bureaucratically silenced and went underground. Its spirit and energy were renewed by a new crop of students anxious to make their voices and concerns heard.

The political campaign of 2004 divided a nation and polarized its citizens. The election seemed more about a referendum on patriotism than setting goals for the future. Innuendo, name-calling, and character assassination poisoned local elections and bled into the national debate—a debate not about reasoned ideas but about volume.

My students saw this televised display as adults acting badly. *Student Worker* staff wanted an elected official to come talk with them, not at them. Weeks before the election, kids discussed how they wanted to respond, regardless of the outcome. They made a list of things that troubled them, and catalogued places where they experienced disequilibrium, including issues of Islam, global poverty, poor parenting, racism, and standardized testing.

They brainstormed everything on their minds. They brought up questions and ideas not addressed in their classrooms. They were creating curriculum.

They realized that they had more questions and concerns than answers. Feeling disconnected around these issues, they wanted to do something. They re-established themselves as a community, reviewed their history, discussed and debated, explored the idea of civil disobedience, thought about a postelection protest, but ultimately became energized over the prospect of a sitin—a take-over of the library at Boulder High School. Their original desire was to explode into action. I cautioned them about possible consequences, which ranged from work detail to suspension, to expulsion or possible arrest. Parents were not happy, the school administration was defensive, and the kids were "psyched." I was in constant communication with parents, who were invited to join the students in their planned protest. People were talking not just about what they thought but what they were going to do.

Student Worker staff negotiated with the school administration. By consensus spokespersons were chosen and made a rushed appointment to meet with Principal Ron Cabrera. They listed their concerns, argued why school was an appropriate venue for the protest, and with permission occupied the library. *Student Worker* leaders drafted a pledge that all kids had to sign before they were permitted into the library, modeled after Martin Luther King's Pledge of Non-Violent Resistance: all students would make the sleep-over protest drug free, alcohol free, and violence free, with separate sleeping sections for males and females. "We're taking a stand and letting people know how we feel. Protest is a legitimate forum for social change, " reflected Boulder High Junior Brian Martens.

The kids sang songs, did homework, read portions of King's "Letter from a Birmingham Jail," watched movies, planned future actions, and held two speaker forums with the one-hundred-plus participants. They also called and emailed local officials including Governor Bill Owens (who never responded), and set up their own internet blog. A few kids slept.

Students vowed they would not leave the library until they had an opportunity to speak with elected officials from both parties. They demanded to be taken seriously and did not want their concerns and energy trivialized.

At 5 A.M., the first news trucks arrived to cover a story of "regional interest" for the Denver metro area. At six o'clock, talk radio personalities were clogging the Boulder High phone lines. News of the "sit-in" hit Fox news through station affiliates in Denver. Before school opened, ABC, NBC, and CNN had reporters at Boulder High. At 7:30 A.M., Rep. Mark Udall's office called; he would meet with the kids at nine that morning. He noted: "Like any community, people want to be heard. I don't think it's any different if you're fifteen or fifty-five." Udall listened to the students and suggested ways of being effective change agents outside of the presidential election cycle.

Michael Moore featured the protest on his website. Brian Martens, one of the student activists who insisted on talking with Congressman Udall, reflected, "We want them to reassure us that out fears are misguided and that the government is doing everything within its power to prevent our futures from being destroyed."

Michael Moore summarized the student action in his weekly editorial: "Witness the Students at Boulder High School in Boulder, Colorado two days after the election. These kids can't even vote yet but that was not going to get in the way of expressing their outrage over what we adults had just done. . . . They told the media that they were protesting the election results and putting Bush on notice that there was no way they were going to allow the draft to come back. It was the most uplifting moment of the week."

If one is to support an emerging sense of concern and activism in students one must be willing to listen, not to merely act concerned, but to *be* concerned. The teacher who acts as an ally will let the students organize and argue, not design the organization and argument for them. The teacher/ally will act as a sounding board for their ideas. When students asked me about possible consequences for their actions, I suggested ways the administration and the community at large could respond. I let them follow their best instincts and supported them in thoughtful choices. When we expect the best from our students and give them the opportunity to express themselves, we lay the foundation to an education that directs their lives and blesses all with needed inspiration.

Jim Vacca teaches Language Arts at Boulder High School and is the faculty advisor for *Student Worker*. He has taught at the University of Colorado as a Clinical Professor in Education, worked as lead teacher in the Halcyon Adolescent Treatment Program, and mentored dozens of teachers in their classrooms. He encourages students to connect what they learn in school to how they choose to live in the world.

Lessons to Stir Activism

In the following piece, Ian McFeat suggests lessons that invite your students to the world of activism.

Activism Is Shown, Not Told

IAN MCFEAT

A colleague of mine once told me, "You can't force-feed your students to activism—it has to be nurtured amongst them; grown from their experiences; and shown, not told to them."

With that in mind, I looted some of the following lesson ideas to explain methods that help engage students as activists. My hope is that these lessons might compel students to move beyond criticism to become agents for change.

Trial Activity as Role-Play

"Role plays show, they don't tell," writes Bill Bigelow in the same-titled article in *Rethinking Schools*, Volume 1. There is a lot of truth to that statement. Role-plays show history, they don't lecture it, they don't throw it at students; they let students juggle it on their own, grapple with ideas and people. Ultimately, role-plays prompt students to change the world.

Trials offer a method of engaging students in events that change our world. And because of the multiple learning styles used during the trial activity, many reluctant learners excel given that their intelligences are valued. Trials flavor history with controversy, invigorate the senses, and allow students to step into the past as active participants. I generally find that trials are best used when there are multiple perspectives that need to be analyzed on a particular topic. Current events like Hurricane Katrina can also be used to analyze history in the making and spark students to action. (See article "Washin' Away, A Trial Activity Asks Who's Guilty for Katrina's Horrors," by Ian McFeat, *Rethinking Schools Online*, Volume 20 No. 2–Winter 2005/2006).

It is particularly important to debrief a role-play so that students might reflect on the lesson, which will give them ample opportunity to seek out answers to the problems we are left with when the role-play is finished.

Chalk Talks

Chalk Talks breathe democratic participation. I borrowed this lesson activity from the treasury of protocols developed by the Coalition of Essential Schools, www.essentialschools.org. This activity requires a long sheet of butcher paper, markers for every student, and a wall to tape up the paper. Students are prompted to respond to the question or statement circled in the middle of the paper. There is no talking during the activity, only written communication. Generally, I use this activity at the end of my units, usually as an assessment of students' learning. I have used the Chalk Talk to focus student creativity towards positive and productive solutions. For instance, during a unit entitled, "Schooling in America," I wrote, "So what? Now what?" as the prompt for the Chalk Talk. It was from this activity that students planned and implemented the first Learn-In on Equity at our school. Chalk Talks have a unique quality in that they provide access to students who might be reluctant to voice their opinions verbally. One student remarked that after all the conversation is gone, their words and ideas stay put. And this is the power of this protocol; the action is not forgotten and students are reminded daily when they look at the walls that they decided to change our world for the better.

Political Cartoons

As a start-up activity in my classroom I post political cartoons on the overhead and have students respond. A lesson idea in *Rethinking Globalization* describes an acronym used to help prompt students to action: S-H-O-W-D.

    S—(S)ee what you see.
    H—What's (H)appening to your feelings?
    O—Relate the cartoon to your (O)wn life.
    W—(W)hy do you think we face these problems?
    D—What do you think we should (D)o about them?

Students select a letter and respond to the cartoon. Sometimes I prompt students with only the last letter and ask them to write their thoughts down. As we share our ideas aloud, it becomes clear that activism is an essential part of our classroom community.

Dialogue Journals

Explained in detail by Linda Christensen in "Reading, Writing and Rising Up," a book of Rethinking Schools, dialogue journals provide students with concrete means of communication about texts that help them air frustrations, identify great writing, relate texts to their own lives, and help students move beyond the classroom to explain problems and create solutions.

Activism Through Music

When students begin to investigate and think critically about our world, one of the worries educators have is that students develop a cynicism about these problems. I have come across some powerful music that focuses this energy for change. Usually, topical songs provide great material for social activism amongst students, but some songs speaks more generally to this necessity for social change and activism. One powerful example, Ben Harper's "People Lead," from his 1995 album, "Fight for Your Mind,"directly challenges the idea that students need to wait for others to change the world. Instead, this song's catchy chorus entices students to "take the lead . . . or be led astray."

I have used this song with the Pointing Protocol (explained in detail at the Coalition of Essential Schools website) to link students with the importance of social activism. Students underline words, phrases, lines, or ideas that strike them and write notes in the margin. I usually prepare follow-up questions that focus the discussion toward activism. In the past, I have asked students how they plan to "take the lead" on the issue we are studying. (See Chapter Sixteen for a discussion of using protest music in the classroom.)

Activism in education is about teaching others outside our classrooms about issues studied. In my classroom, students create their own essays, short stories, poems, songs, dances, and other material related to each unit— performance seems a natural activity with which to share our work. We have held Poetry Slams and Teach-Ins on Katrina, the Iraq War, Schooling, and other topics. I would encourage you to find room to share student work from your classroom with your school community. Activism, even on a small scale, provides boundless opportunities for change in our world. I cannot think of a more worthy goal.

Ian McFeat, imcfeat@msn.com, teaches at Foss High School in Tacoma, Washington. His article "Tackling Tracking" appeared in the Summer 2005 issue of *Rethinking Schools*.

12

Who Are the Terrorists?

Digging Beneath the Surface

"Terrorist." Politicians and anchor people say this word all the time, but who are the terrorists? It's important for students to discuss this term and explore its possible meanings and scenarios. A "terrorist" is not as simple to know and comprehend as our politicians would have us believe. Bill Bigelow, a social studies teacher and author, provides teachers with valuable lessons to engage students in exploring the definitions of "terrorism" so that they can apply their understanding to current affairs.

As I read Bigelow's lessons that follow, I began asking myself additional questions about "terrorism." If a government terrorizes its own people with propaganda or by force, would that government be engaged in terrorism? Can a state, as well as a group, sponsor and engage in terrorism? What are the best ways to cope with terrorism? In his lessons, Bigelow gives teachers and students invaluable coping strategies: define "terrorism" and apply your knowledge to present-day political situations. Once you understand this beast, then you can deal with it more effectively.

WHOSE "TERRORISM"?

BILL BIGELOW

This classroom activity enlists students in defining terrorism and applying their definitions to world events. Shortly after the horrific Sept. 11th attacks on the World Trade Center and the Pentagon, President Bush announced them as acts of war, and proclaimed a "war on terrorism." But what exactly was the target of this war? What precisely did the president mean by terrorism? Despite uttering the words "terror," "terrorist," or "terrorism" 32 times in his Sept. 20th speech to the nation, he never once defined terrorism.

Teachers need to engage students in a deep critical reading of terms—"terrorism," "freedom," "patriotism," "our way of life"—that evoke vivid images but can be used for ambiguous ends. (See the handout titled "What Is Terrorism? Who Are the Terrorists?" following this article for definitions of "terrorism.")

Lesson on Terrorism

I wanted to design a lesson that would get students to surface the definitions of terrorism they carry around—albeit, most likely, unconsciously. And I wanted them to apply their definitions to a number of episodes, historical and contemporary, that involved some kind of violence or destruction. I didn't know for certain, but my hunch was that as students applied definitions consistently they might be able to call into question the "We're Good/They're Bad" dichotomies that have become more pronounced on the political landscape.

I wrote several "What Is Terrorism?" scenarios, but instead of using the actual names of countries involved I substituted made-up names. Given the widespread conflation of patriotism with support for U.S. government policies, I had no confidence that students would be able to label an action taken by their government as "terrorism" unless I attached pseudonyms to each country.

In the following scenario I used the example of U.S. support for the Nicaraguan contras in the 1980s. Tobian is the United States, Ambar is Nicaragua, and the country next door is Honduras.

"The government of Tobian is very unhappy with the government of Ambar, whose leaders came to power in a revolution that threw out the former Ambar dictator. Tobian decides to overthrow the new leaders of Ambar. They begin funding a guerrilla army that will attack Ambar from another country next door. So Tobian builds army bases in the next door country and allows the guerrilla army to use its bases. Almost all of the weapons and supplies of the guerrilla army are supplied by Tobian. The guerrillas generally try to avoid fighting the army of Ambar. Instead they attack clinics, schools, cooperative farms. Sometimes they mine the roads. Many, many civilians are killed and maimed by the Tobian-supported guerrillas. The guerrillas raid into Ambar and then retreat into the country next door where Tobian has military bases."

Three questions are included in the instructions for reflection and discussion after each situation. 1) Which, if any, of these activities should be considered "terrorism" according to your definition? 2) Who are the "terrorists"? 3) What more would you need to know to be more sure of your answer?

I knew that in such compressed scenarios lots of important details would be missing; hence, I included question number three to invite students to consider other details that might influence their decisions.

Other scenarios included Israeli soldiers taunting and shooting children in Palestinian refugee camps with the assistance of U.S. military aid; Indian farmers burning Monsanto-supplied, genetically modified cotton crops and threatening to destroy Monsanto offices; the 1998 U.S. cruise missile attack on Sudan's main pharmaceutical plant; and sanctions against Iraq that, according to U.N. reports, have killed as many as a half million children. The full list of situations can be found later in this chapter.

Defining Terrorism

As I was on leave the year I wrote this piece, my colleague, Sandra Childs, invited me into her Franklin High School classroom to teach this lesson to her 11th grade Global Studies students. I began by asking students to write down their own personal definitions of terrorism, keeping these questions in mind: Does terrorism need to involve the killing of many people or can it affect just one person? Can it involve simply the destruction of property, with no injuries? Can governments commit acts of terrorism, or is the term reserved only for people operating outside of governments? Must terrorism involve people of one country attacking citizens of another country? Does motive make a difference? Does terrorism need to be intentional?

Immediately following, I explained that in preparation for an activity, I'd like students to get into small groups and read their individual definitions to one another to see if they could build a consensus definition of terrorism. They could choose an exemplary definition from one member or, if they preferred, cobble one together from their separate definitions.

Some groups quickly agreed upon definitions; others would have spent the entire 83-minute class debating if Sandra and I had let them. In most cases, the definitions were simple, but thoughtful, for example, "Intentional acts that create terror, targeted towards a specific group, or innocent people. Not just directly, but indirectly."

I distributed the "What Is Terrorism?"situations to students, reviewed the instructions with them, and emphasized that all the scenarios were real. Their main task was to read each situation and to decide whether any of the actions described met their group's definition of "terrorism." I gave them permission to approach the situations in whatever order they liked.

Watching students attempt to apply their definitions, I was impressed by their eagerness to be consistent. As Sandra and I wandered from group to group, we heard students arguing over whether there was a distinction between oppression and terrorism. Most groups wanted more information on the motives of various actors. Some insisted that if a country supported terrorist acts in another country, then it, too, was a terrorist; others held that a supporting country could not be held fully responsible for the actions of the actual perpetrators—but if a country knew about terrorism enabled with its funds, and did nothing to prevent it, then it, too, could be considered guilty.

Although this activity was far too involved to be neatly contained in an 83-minute class, by the end many students came to important insights. One student said, "Ever since they announced that we were going to have a war on terrorism I have wondered who or what a terrorist is. And . . . it's suspicious that they still haven't defined terrorism." I asked students why they thought the U.S. government had failed to offer a clear definition of terrorism. One student said, "If you don't have any boundaries, then anyone can be a terrorist." Another said, "The U.S. government won't define terrorism because they don't want to be able to be considered terrorists."

These comments echoed Eqbal Ahmad's insight that countries that have no intention of being consistent will resist defining terms. One student wrote after the activity: "I also realized how many terrorism acts the U.S. has committed. When our government doesn't define terrorism, it makes me think that they just want a free shot to kill anyone they want." Wrote another student: "Bush *needs* to define terrorism in front of our nation before he does anything else, and then he needs to stick with the definition, not bend it to suit the U.S."

But then there was this student comment: "I, myself, am really tired of hearing about it. If I go to war, so what? I'll fight for my country. What does this have to do with global studies?" And this young man: "I feel if we don't get our revenge against these 'terrorists' it will diminish the trust of our nation towards our government."

These remarks reminded me of my class during the fall of 1990, after Iraq had invaded Kuwait and the United States was assembling its military attack force. Many students resisted critical analysis, sensing that critique eroded the "patriotic" unity then building in the country—that appending a "not so fast" onto the flag-waving interrupted a sense of collective purpose that felt good to many of them. At least that was how I read some students' resistance. During times of war, students may regard even the mildest critical examination of government policy as unpatriotic or even subversive. Nonetheless, I was impressed by how many students in Sandra's classes appeared eager to question their government's framing of key issues.

As we wrapped up in one class, Sandra asked a wonderful question: "What difference do you think it would make if students all over the country were having the discussion that we're having today?"

There were two quick answers before the bell rang: "I'd feel a lot better about the U.S.," and "I think we'd lose a lot of people who'd want to go fight for the country."

My interpretation: The more students understand about the exercise of U.S. power in the world—both military and economic—the less likely they are to want to extend it.

Economic Terrorism

After I'd used the "What Is Terrorism?" situations with Sandra's classes, I realized that, with the exception of sanctions, all of them were incidents of direct attacks on civilians or property. Did my examples narrow students' consideration of "terrorism"?

In her article "Solidarity Against All Forms of Terrorism," Indian environmentalist and scholar Vandana Shiva urges us to embrace a more expansive notion of terrorism. She asks us to consider "economic policies which push people into poverty and starvation as a form of terrorism," such as International Monetary Fund/World Bank–mandated structural adjustment programs that force governments to cut food and medical programs, with the full knowledge of the misery this will engender. In India, Shiva writes:

> Fifty million tribals who have been flooded out of their homes by dams over the past four decades were also victims of terrorism—they have faced the terror of technology and destructive development. . . . The whole world repeatedly watched the destruction of the World Trade Center towers, but the destruction of millions of sacred shrines and homes and farms by forces of injustice, greed, and globalization go unnoticed.

To help students consider whether some situations could be considered economic terrorism, I've added several new "What Is Terrorism?" scenarios. One deals with deaths in southern Africa from AIDS where, for instance, international banks have forced the Zambian government to pay annual debt service charges greater than spending on health and education *combined* and where, according to the United Nations, life expectancy will soon drop to *33 years*, a level not seen in the Western world since medieval times. Another new scenario focuses on transnational corporations that knowingly pay wages that are insufficient to sustain life.

Terrorism's Ghosts

The U.S. government is ill placed to lecture the world about terrorism, especially when it has never bothered to define it. Writing in the British daily *The Guardian*, Indian novelist Arundhati Roy offered the perspective of an individual who is on the receiving end of U.S. global power:

> The Sept. 11 attacks were a monstrous calling card from a world gone horribly wrong. The message may have been written by bin Laden (who knows?) and delivered by his couriers, but it could well have been signed by the ghosts of the victims of America's old wars. The

millions killed in Korea, Vietnam and Cambodia, the 17,500 killed when Israel—backed by the U.S.—invaded Lebanon in 1982, the 200,000 Iraqis killed in Operation Desert Storm, the thousands of Palestinians who have died fighting Israel's occupation of the West Bank. And the millions who died, in Yugoslavia, Somalia, Haiti, Chile, Nicaragua, El Salvador, the Dominican Republic, Panama, at the hands of all the terrorists, dictators, and genocidists whom the American government supported, trained, bankrolled, and supplied with arms. And this is far from being a comprehensive list.

It's not our role as teachers to climb on our soapbox to rail about U.S. foreign policy. And yet without an honest examination of events like those listed by Roy, how can we expect students to maintain any critical perspective on the U.S. "war against terrorism"? Let's clarify with students what precisely we mean by terrorism. And then let's encourage students to apply this definition to U.S. conduct in the world.

Underlying this curricular demand for consistency is the basic democratic, indeed human, premise that the lives of people from one nation are not worth more than the lives of people from another. A Pakistani university student, Nabil Ahmed, expressed this sentiment to the *Christian Science Monitor*: "There is only one way for America to be a friend of Islam. And that is if they consider our lives to be as precious as their own."

What Is Terrorism? Who Are the Terrorists? (Handout for Use with the Article "Whose Terrorism?" by Bill Bigelow)

Instructions

Based on the definitions of terrorism that your group came up with, and after reading each situation, discuss the following questions: 1. Which, if any, of these activities should be considered "terrorism" according to your definition? 2. Who are the "terrorists"? 3. What more would you need to know to be more sure of your answer? All the situations below are true, but the names of countries and peoples have been changed. It may help your group to make a diagram of some of the situations.

Situations

1. Soldiers from the country of Marak surround a refugee camp made up of people from the country of Bragan. The refugee camp is crowded and the people there are extremely poor. Most of the Bragan people in the camp hate the army of Marak, believing that Marak had invaded

Bragan, had taken all the best land and resources for themselves, and treat people from Bragan very poorly. Young men in the refugee camp sometimes fire guns at the soldiers.

According to an eyewitness, a reporter from the *New York Times,* Marak soldiers use loudspeakers to call insults into the refugee camp—in the Bragan language. Over the loudspeakers, soldiers shout obscenities and things like "son of a whore!" They dare young Bragan boys—sometimes as young as 10 or 11—to come near the electric fence separating the refugee camp from a wealthy settlement of Marak citizens. When the boys and young men go near the fence to throw stones or yell at the Marak soldiers, the soldiers use silencers and fire on them with live ammunition, often killing or maiming them. In an article, the *New York Times* reporter expressed horror at what he witnessed. He wrote: "Children have been shot in other conflicts I have covered—death squads gunned them down in El Salvador and Guatemala, mothers with infants were lined up and massacred in Algeria, and Serb snipers put children in their sights and watched them crumple onto the pavement in Sarajevo—but I have never before watched soldiers entice children like mice into a trap and murder them for sport." The Marak government clearly knows about the behavior of their soldiers and does nothing to stop them. Indeed, Marak soldiers so regularly taunt citizens of Bragan, that this behavior appears to be the policy of the Marak government. One additional fact: Every year, Marak is given enormous amounts of money and military equipment by the country of Bolaire, which is aware of how these are used by Marak.

2. Farmers from the country of Belveron are angry at their own government and at a corporation from the country of Paradar. The Belveron government has allowed the Paradar corporation to plant "test" crops of genetically engineered cotton. The genetically engineered crops produce their own pesticide. Many Belveron farmers worry that the genetically engineered crops will pollute their crops—as has happened in other countries—and will create a breed of super-pests that will be immune to chemical pesticides and to the organic pest control methods many poor farmers use. Without growing cotton, the farmers have no way to feed their families. Belveron farmers also believe the Paradar Corporation does not really care about them, but only for their own profit. They believe the corporation wants to get Belveron farmers "addicted" to genetically engineered cotton seeds—which the corporation has patented—in order to have a monopoly. Belveron farmers further point out the corporation has not told them that the "tests" on

their land may be risky, and could pollute their non–genetically engineered cotton crops.

Belveron farmers have announced that they will burn all the genetically engineered cotton crops to the ground. They hope to drive the Paradar Corporation out of Belveron. Belveron farmers have also threatened to destroy the offices of the Paradar Corporation.

3. The army of Kalimo has invaded the country of Iona, next door. There are a number of refugee camps in Iona with thousands of people living in them. The refugees themselves lost their homes many years before—some in wars with Kalimo, others forced out by Kalimo. The area around the refugee camps is controlled by the Kalimo army. The commander of the Kalimo army sealed off the refugee camps and allowed militias from Iona, who are hostile to the refugees, to enter two refugee camps and slaughter hundreds of people. The killing lasted 40 hours. At least 1,800 people were murdered, perhaps more. One additional fact: The army of Kalimo receives a great deal of military aid from the country of Terramar. Terramar learned of the massacre of the refugees, but did not halt military aid to Kalimo.

4. A corporation based in the country of Menin has a chemical factory located in the much poorer country of Pungor. One night, huge amounts of poisonous gases from the factory begin to spew out into the area around the factory. Nobody outside the factory was warned because someone in the company had turned off the safety siren. Not until the gas was upon residents in their beds, searing their eyes and filling their mouths and lungs, did the communities surrounding the factory know of their danger. According to one report: "Gasping for breath and near blind, people stampeded into narrow alleys. In the mayhem children were torn from the hands of their mothers, never to see them again. Those who still could were screaming. Some were wracked with seizures and fell under trampling feet. Some, stumbling in a sea of gas, their lungs on fire, were drowned in their own bodily fluids." No one knows how many people died, but perhaps as many as 6,000 that night and in the years after, more than 10,000.

The corporation had begun a cost-cutting drive prior to the disaster: lowering training periods for operatives, using low-cost materials, adopting hazardous operating procedures, and cutting the number of operatives in half. A confidential company audit prior to the accident identified 61 hazards. Nothing was done.

After the tragedy, the corporation concentrated on avoiding liability, sending in its legal team days before a medical team. Company officials lied about the poisonous nature of the chemicals at the plant. To this day, the corporation refuses to disclose medical information on the leaked gases, maintaining it to be a "trade secret." The company paid some victims' families, on average, less than $350—a total loss of 48 cents per share of company stock.

Conditions in this Pungor community are still hazardous, soil and water are still heavily contaminated. Mercury has been found at between 20,000 to 6 million times the expected levels. The rate of stillborn infants there is three times the national average of Pungor; infant mortality is twice as high.

5. The government of Tobian is very unhappy with the government of Ambar, whose leaders came to power in a revolution that threw out the former Ambar dictator. Tobian decides to overthrow the new leaders of Ambar. They begin funding a guerrilla army that will attack Ambar from another country next door. So Tobian builds army bases in the next-door country and allows the guerrilla army to use its bases. Almost all of the weapons and supplies of the guerrilla army are supplied by Tobian. The guerrillas generally try to avoid fighting the army of Ambar. Instead they attack clinics, schools, cooperative farms. Sometimes they mine the roads. Many, many civilians are killed and maimed by the Tobian-supported guerrillas. The guerrillas raid into Ambar and then retreat into the country next door where Tobian has military bases.

6. Simultaneously, the embassies of the country of Anza in two other countries were bombed. In one country, 213 people were killed and over 1,000 injured; in the other, 11 people were killed and at least 70 injured. In retaliation, Anza launched missiles at the capital city of Baltus, destroying a pharmaceutical factory and injuring at least 10 people, and killing one. Anza claimed this factory manufactured chemicals that could be used to make VX nerve gas—although Anza offered no substantial proof of this claim. Anza also claimed that a prominent individual who they link to the embassy bombings was connected to the pharmaceutical factory, although they provided no evidence of that claim, either—and a great deal of evidence exists to prove that there is no link. Baltus pointed out that two years earlier they expelled the prominent individual, and vigorously denied that the pharmaceutical plant was producing nerve gas agents. They said that this was an important factory, producing 70 percent of the needed medicines for the people of Baltus—including vital medicines to treat malaria and tuberculosis. They allowed journalists and other diplomats to visit the factory to verify that no chemical weapons were being

produced. Journalists and other visitors agreed that the destroyed factory appeared to be producing only medicines. It is not known how many people died in Baltus for lack of the medicines produced in that factory. Anza blocked the United Nations from launching the investigation demanded by Baltus.

7. At least one million people in the country of Lukin are infected with HIV/AIDS. Between 1991 and 2001, 700,000 people died of AIDS in Lukin. Currently, about 300 people die each day of AIDS-related causes. Largely because of the HIV/AIDS crisis, life expectancy in Lukin is expected to drop from 43 to 33 years, a level last experienced in Europe in medieval times. AIDS could be controlled with a combination of drugs, frequently called a drug "cocktail," including AZT. However, given current drug prices, this could cost as much as $18,000 a year per patient.

   This year, Lukin will pay $174 million in *interest payments* on its debt—mostly to two large international banks. This debt was incurred many years ago, by a different government than the current one. The loans were pushed by banks with huge amounts of money to lend because oil-producing countries had deposited so much revenue into these banks. As one observer put it, "The banks were hot to get in. All the banks . . . stepped forward. They showed no foresight. They didn't do any credit analysis. It was wild." Loans benefited mostly bankers and the rich of Lukin. However, most people in Lukin are poor—the gross national product (GNP) per capita is $350. The $174 million in interest payments is more money than Lukin will spend on health care and education *combined.* Money that could pay for AIDS prevention and therapies for people with AIDS instead is being sent to banks in so-called developed countries.

   The international banks know about the dire health situation in Lukin. They allowed Lukin to postpone some debts—but only after Lukin agreed to certain conditions set by the banks giving the banks greater control over Lukin's economy; for example, requiring Lukin to sell its national bank to private investors. Still, so long as the banks force Lukin to pay interest on its debts, there is no way Lukin can deal with the AIDS crisis. Three hundred people a day continue to die.

8. Led by the country of Lomandia, the United Nations waged a war against the country of Moretta, saying that Moretta illegally invaded another nearby country. After Moretta's army was defeated and removed from the country they'd invaded, Lomandia pushed for "sanctions" against Moretta, until Moretta proves it is not engaged in

a program to produce "weapons of mass destruction," like nuclear bombs or poison gas. The sanctions meant that Moretta was not allowed to buy or sell almost anything from other countries in the world. Moretta cannot get spare parts to repair water purification plants damaged by bombing during the war. It cannot get medicines and spare parts for medical equipment. Moretta claims it allowed inspections from the United Nations, but Lomandia says that it has not. According to the United Nations perhaps a half million children have died as a result of the sanctions. Documents from Lomandia show that it knew that Moretta civilians were dying as a result of water-born diseases. When asked in a television interview about the reports of massive numbers of civilian deaths—perhaps as many as a million people over several years—a high government official from Lomandia said: "It's worth it."

9. Bartavia is considered by many to be one of the most repressive countries in the world, especially if you are not white. Only whites can vote, only whites can travel freely, only whites can live where they like. Most whites live comfortably, even luxuriously. Conditions for people who are not white are some of the worst in the world. Bartavia imprisons people who organize for change. Torture is widespread. Over the years, there have been numerous massacres of non-white Bartavia civilians—sometimes of young children. The main organizations working for change in Bartavia have asked the world not to invest money in Bartavia and not to have economic or cultural relations with the country until it commits itself to change. Nonetheless, many countries continue to do business with Bartavia. One in particular, Sarino, has allowed its corporations to increase their investments in Bartavia from $150 million to $2.5 billion—all this during a period of tremendous violence and discrimination. Who knows how many thousands of people have been killed—through guns or poverty—as a result of Sarino's actions?

10. The Sport-King Corporation produces athletic equipment sold all over the world. Although its headquarters is in the country of Morcosas, its products are manufactured in other countries. Sport-King contracts with subcontractors to make its products. Over 500,000 people, mostly women, work for these subcontractors in poor countries.

Sport-King has a "Code of Conduct" which is supposed to ensure that workers are not mistreated by Sport-King's subcontractors. For example, no child laborers are supposed to be hired, no prisoners may be used as workers, workers may not be forced to work more than 60 hours a week, etc. Sport-King's "Code of Conduct" specifies that workers must be paid a country's "minimum wage." However, it does not say that this minimum wage needs to be a *living* wage. Even poor-country governments admit the minimum wage is not enough for people to live on. Sport-King says it pays the legal wage, but it knows that not all its workers can survive on this wage.

Companies like Sport-King locate factories in countries that don't allow unions, that outlaw strikes, and that jail workers who demand higher pay and better conditions. In fact, Sport-King chooses to locate its factories in some of the most repressive countries in the world. Human rights groups argue that companies like Sport-King knowingly locate factories in very repressive places so workers can more easily be controlled and exploited. These human rights groups argue that companies like Sport-King could easily afford to pay their workers a living wage, but because this would come out of their enormous profits they choose not to.

What Is Terrorism? Who Are the Terrorists?

Who's Who

Situation 1: The country of Marak is Israel, Bragan is Palestine, Bolaire is the United States. This particular example is taken from "A Gaza Diary" by Chris Hedges, in the October 2001 *Harpers.*

Situation 2: The country of Belveron is India. Paradar is the United States. The corporation is Monsanto.

Situation 3: Kalimo is Israel, Iona is Lebanon, Terramar is the United States, the refugees are Palestinian. The camps were Sabra and Shatila in 1982. The militia was Christian Phalangist.

Situation 4: The country of Menin is the United States, Pungor is India. The corporation was Union Carbide, in Bhopal, India. The year was 1985.

Situation 5: The country of Tobian is the United States. Ambar is Nicaragua. The country next door is Honduras. The time is the 1980s during the U.S.-sponsored contra war.

Situation 6: The country of Anza is the United States. Baltus is Sudan. The countries where the U.S. embassies were bombed are Kenya and Tanzania. The prominent individual mentioned is Osama bin Laden.

Situation 7: The country of Lukin is Zambia. The banks are the International Monetary Fund and the World Bank.

Situation 8: The country of Lomandia is the United States. Moretta is Iraq. The U.S. official quoted was Secretary of State Madeleine Albright on *60 Minutes,* interviewed by Leslie Stahl.

Situation 9: The country of Bartavia is South Africa during apartheid. Sarino is the United States.

Situation 10: Sport-King is Nike, although it could be many transnational corporations. The country of Morcosas is the United States.

Bill Bigelow (bbpdx@aol.com) has taught social studies in Portland, Oregon, since 1978. He is an editor of *Rethinking Schools* magazine (www.rethinkingschools.org), and he co-edited *Rethinking Columbus: The Next Five Hundred Years* and *Rethinking Globalization: Teaching for Justice in an Unjust World.* His latest book is *The Line Between Us: Teaching About the Border and Mexican Immigration.* "Whose Terrorism?" first appeared in *Rethinking Schools* magazine, Winter 2001/2002, and is reprinted here by permission of Rethinking Schools.

Rethinking Schools, www.rethinkingschools.org, is a nonprofit, independent publisher of educational materials, including books and a quarterly magazine. They advocate the reform of elementary and secondary education, with a strong emphasis on issues of equity and social justice.

Additional Resources and Activities Suggested by Chris Weber

- *Whose Wars? Teaching About the Iraq War and the War on Terrorism* is a collection of the best articles from *Rethinking Schools* on these issues, from www.rethinkingschools.org.
- Other teaching materials are available from Teaching for Change, www.teachingforchange.org.

Films About Terrorism

- *Fahrenheit 9/11* by Michael Moore
  A teacher's guide for *Fahrenheit 9/11* can be downloaded at www.michaelmoore.com/books-films/fahrenheit911/teachersguide/. The lessons and activities in this guide are designed to help students develop a critical analytical ability, historical perspective, and applied math skills that will open their minds beyond the current issues covered. The individual units may easily be adapted to many levels and taught across the curriculum.
- *The Power of Nightmares—Part III—The Shadows in the Cave. The Power of Nightmares* assesses whether the threat from a hidden and organized terrorist network is an illusion. Go to http://207.44.245.159/video1040.htm.

- *Hijacking Catastrophe 9/11, Fear, and the Selling of American Empire.* *Hijacking Catastrophe* provides a thoughtful explanation of the modern American empire. Go to www.informationclearinghouse.info /article6895.htm. Other powerful videos are available at www.informationclearinghouse.info.

- *Little Terrorist* (short film). Go to www.lff.org.uk/films_print.php ?FilmID=355 to view the above film.

13

Teaching Peace: One Student at a Time

Frodo Baggins: I can't do this Sam.

Sam Gamgee: I know. It's all wrong. By rights we shouldn't even be here. But we are. It's like in the great stories, Mr. Frodo. The ones that really mattered. Full of darkness and danger, they were. And sometimes you didn't want to know the end. Because how could the end be happy? How could the world go back to the way it was when so much bad had happened? But in the end, it's only a passing thing, this shadow. Even darkness must pass. A new day will come. And when the sun shines it will shine out the clearer. Those were the stories that stayed with you. That meant something, even if you were too small to understand why. But I think, Mr. Frodo, I do understand. I know now. Folk in those stories had lots of chances of turning back, only they didn't. They kept going. Because they were holding on to something.

Frodo: What are we holding on to Sam?

Sam: That there's some good in this world, Mr. Frodo . . . and it's worth fighting for.

—Lord of the Rings: The Two Towers

If We Do This

The preceding quote is what this book is all about—the good we fight for and teach our students to live for. Peace is part of this good and worth actively struggling for each day. After I read Katherine R. Morgan's article, I knew her ideas needed to be shared. What better way to learn about student activism than with a lesson whose underlying theme is teaching peace—one student at a time? If we do that, we can make a difference in our students' lives and in our own.

TEACHING PEACE: ONE STUDENT AT A TIME

KATHERINE R. MORGAN

"Peace isn't just a word, it's a feeling; it's feeling safe and it's not just not having war, but having happiness within yourself. You cannot have peace with others until you can have peace with yourself." This student's struggle to define peace mirrored my own, as I tried to create a semester-long high school English elective that wouldn't just be about the absence of war. I had a summer to contemplate the syllabus, and I procrastinated on its design until early August.

I finally brainstormed essential questions we could explore in six three-week units. Though this was a productive exercise, I came up with six questions/topics of inquiry I realized we couldn't possibly cover in the time frame available:

- Toward a definition of peace: Is peace possible? What are the conditions that reduce or enhance the possibilities of peace?
- What do various religious/philosophical systems say about peace?
- Must we have war in order to have peace?
- Who are, and have been, the major spokespersons for peace?
- Does our society take peace for granted? Are we a peaceful society?
- How do literature, art, music, film, and photography present peace?

As my vision for the course evolved, I realized it would be important to begin as close to home as possible, and move toward a more global idea of peace. My experience has been that, in general, adolescents don't lead very peaceful lives, and perhaps the place to start was with a discussion of peace in our classroom and in their lives. On the first day, we grappled with the questions: How can our classroom be a model of peaceful interaction? What should it look like? Why study peace? How can we study peace? Their ideas about achieving a peaceful classroom set the stage for understanding many of the concepts which, if applied in the world, would lead to peace:

- sharing feelings/resources/information
- getting and giving positive feedback
- being open-minded
- respecting everyone
- thinking before speaking
- using good listening skills—not interrupting, absorbing what people say, being honest (speaking your mind), and being forgiving (not jumping to conclusions).

How simple it seems when it's spelled out like this! I wondered if we could create a classroom in which we could consistently implement these ideas, and how I could help students connect these concepts to national and international issues. I began by asking them how we could study peace in a way that would be meaningful. Their central ideas were not far from mine:

- study Gandhi and Mother Teresa (and other Nobel Peace Prize winners)
- study violence and what it stems from (the only topic not on my list)
- study past nonviolent protests and groups that promote nonviolence
- study countries that appear to be more peaceful than we are
- study philosophies of peace
- study literature, music, and art

During the first week I asked them to examine their own lives through a questionnaire I devised. After we shared responses, they used it to interview a parent. They focused first on their definition of peace, then what they "did" when they were peaceful. I asked about the level of conflict in their lives and how they managed it. Finally, I wanted to know if they thought their community, their state, and their nation were peaceful. As we shared answers in class discussion, we uncovered several interesting points. Most students thought their days were "peaceful, but hectic." They had conflict with family members (mostly their parents); tended to ignore conflict and hope it would go away; saw their family and community as peaceful; were unaware of whether or not their state was peaceful, and overwhelmingly, said the nation was not peaceful.

When I asked "Do you think there is a connection between peace in your life and 'world peace'?," answers ran the gamut from "No, I don't think a single individual has much power with peace. Evilness [sic] and destruction and hatred can be started by one person, but peace doesn't seem to work that easy [sic]" to the other end of the spectrum, "I would have to say 'yes,' because I think that everyone's self-peace adds up to world peace. If we want to achieve world peace then we have to do it one person at a time. World peace isn't just most people, it means everyone. So I think everyone contributes to it." We could have spent the rest of the semester discussing the range of views expressed on these subjects alone, and we returned many times to these topics.

Many students were skeptical that peace in their own lives had any effect on world peace. To further explore the concept we read *Being Peace* by Thich Nhat Hanh. We learned many ways to be peaceful and to spread peace to others. My favorite quote from that book is one I used frequently throughout the first few weeks of class: "Let peace begin with me. Let me begin with peace."

This year, we had a graphic illustration of how that works in reality. A student brought in an article about the International Day of Peace, September 21. The class wanted to mark that day in some way. We made a huge banner proclaiming the day and hung it in the cafeteria. We arranged for the school community to observe a moment of silence at noon to think about peace. After we hung the banner, others got involved. Social studies classes made paper patchwork quilts and a teacher hung a peace flag with handouts for students focusing on conflict resolution. World Language students made banners in French and Spanish proclaiming the International Day of Peace and invited students to write their thoughts about peace. Two students passed out white ribbons for armbands and nearly every student and faculty member wore their white ribbons that day. For my students, the concept that "peace begins with me" took on new meaning.

At the end of the class, one student wrote, "I used to think that the only way peace would be possible would be to rally behind our government to change. Now, I have realized that while this is important, it is not the only thing that we should be doing. We all need to step out from behind our government and make individual efforts to make connections with other individuals from the global community. Once we take the creation of peace back into our own hands, peace will finally become a possibility." I like to think that each of my students left the class with the idea that they can take the creation of peace back into their own hands, and that gradually, one student at a time, we can create a more peaceful world.

Katherine R. Morgan teaches English and Peace Studies at Oyster River High School, Durham, NH. She is a recent recipient of the U.S.–Eurasian Teaching Excellence Award given by the American Council on Education, which allowed her to spend three weeks in Ukraine as a Teacher-Diplomat. Her publications include *My Ever Dear Daughter, My Own Dear Mother* (University of Iowa 1996) and *Writing Process Revisited: Sharing Our Stories* (NCTE 1997). She is currently working on a novel for middle grade readers.

Portions of this article originally appeared in *The Change Agent*, Issue 21, September 2005. Published by the New England Literacy Resource Center at World Education in Boston, MA, at www.nelrc.org/changeagent. Reprinted by permission of the author and publisher.

Peace Begins with Us, by Chris Weber

Peace is in our hands, not our government's. One of Morgan's students suggested a course for peace building through personal connections made between individuals, rather than organizations and politicians. On a personal note, I worked with Japanese professors and teachers on a literary project for several years. My students helped tsunami victims and Ugandan refugees in various ways. When I trek in the Himalayas or Andes, I pass out school supplies along with a smile. Each one of us can establish person-to-person relationships with people in other countries, which will be mightier than any nuclear weapons arsenal we have. Let peace begin with us.

14

Where Peace Lives—in Our Hearts

Exploring the Issue of Peace

Albert Camus wrote, "We used to wonder where war lived, what it was that made it so vile. And now we realize that we know where it lives ... inside ourselves." The same can be said for peace, but then, what is peace? How can students bring peace to themselves and to others? What is violence? What is active nonviolence? These questions and more are explored within the following lessons by Leah Wells (abridged here but appearing in their entirety at http://72.14.207.104/custom?q=cache:W1Y57DxFW0MJ:www .wagingpeace.org/menu/programs/youth-outreach/peace-ed-book/ teachingpeace.pdf+personal+peacemaking+leah+c+wells&hl=en&gl=us& ct=clnk&cd=9&ie=UTF-8). Copyright Nuclear Age Peace Foundation 2003. Reprinted with permission.

By exploring these questions, students can learn about peace and how to be at peace with themselves—the first step of peacemakers.

PERSONAL PEACEMAKING

LEAH C. WELLS

The course begins by thinking about personal nonviolence: What is closer to us than our bodies and spirits? We explore the most prevalent myths about nonviolence: that its practitioners are doormats, letting people walk all over them, and that the only options available when confronted with violence are fight or flight, kill or be killed.

Are there other options? What are they? Is nonviolence merely passive? Students are often skeptical about the potential of nonviolence "working." This is a good thing. If they buy into what we're saying on the first day, then we have some real rethinking to do about what we're teaching. The essence of learning about peacemaking is the tangible struggle—the psychological struggle to understand the world in a new context and to personalize the information in a meaningful way.

Crucial Skepticism

A lot of students—many football players, many gang members, many who support war and who believe in "an eye for an eye"—have tough exteriors. Teaching a course on nonviolence in the United States to an audience of high school students groomed on MTV and X-treme reality shows by beginning the semester with a rational discussion of the merits of nonviolence is laughable. What happens first in class is a great amount of doubt; students rarely believe it's going to work. They have their personal guards up and their educational filters on. This is why teaching nonviolently is so important. One can't teach about nonviolence without teaching through nonviolence.

Students are not always easy converts to nonviolence because they lack the historical and experiential evidence that it can work; nonviolence requires vision and patience—a lost value in modern society. Students are exceptionally impatient. They have grown up in a fast food, fast talk, easy come, easy go culture requiring 30-second soundbites and flashy images to capture their attention. Often nonviolence does not work like this, but in subtle ways and in ways many people might not consider "successful" by conventional standards.

At first I was intimidated by the resistance I encountered by some students. As the peacemaking class continued, however, I realized the class was not only about content and giving evidence of when and where and how nonviolence operates, but also teaching the content in a nonviolent manner. Essentially, the patience I want my students to understand, I must also employ. More than once I drew optimism from remembering mentors whose patience and skill made the material come to life. I began to lean on teachings which helped me make sense of the nuances of nonviolence.

Figuring Out Violence and Nonviolence

Violence has a very simple dynamic. Jim Lawson, pastor emeritus of the Holman United Methodist Church and an architect of the civil rights movement, says the "might makes right" polarity of violence is simplistic because it only takes the physically stronger person to make the other say "uncle." Violence says, "I'm bigger; I'm stronger. I have more power, more money, more weapons, more strength, more influence. I can make you do what I want because you fear me." Violence is intimidation and coercion, depriving people of free will and their conscious choice. Violence is isolation and separation, making people feel alone and secluded. Violence capriciously and systematically segregates people. Violence creates the "us versus them" situation where people can learn to hate and fight and go to war because of artificial categories that power holders claim makes one group better than another.

Put into relevant terms for students, this begins to make sense. Ask a sophomore how various groups or "cliques" use their power and influence to make other students feel inferior. Ask students if everyone gets invited to parties, if everyone is in the "cool" crowd, if everyone gets treated equally. More than likely, it will be readily evident to students how the dynamics of violence works.

Making the concepts of violence and nonviolence relevant is the key to bringing students onboard for the semester.

Nonviolence is a multitude of options, not just a "fight or flight" one-or-the-other choice like violence. It requires, at the very least, creativity. It's tough to conceptualize, though, because there's no one right answer. The difference between nonviolence and violence is like the difference between an essay exam and a multiple-choice test.

One of my students once wrote, "Nonviolence is organized and constructive, and the main point is to send a message or resolve something. It is positive and purposeful. Nonviolence is not being passive, though, not letting people walk all over you. Nonviolence is about standing up for justice, or laying down for it if that is your form of protesting, but certainly not standing back."

A friend of mine said that "peace is an inside job." That is really the message of the first part of the class—to build a classroom culture where personal peacemaking is taught, experienced, and lived.

Another student told the class that "you yourself need to be at peace, because when you are at peace with yourself, you can start spreading peace elsewhere."

Hot and Cold Violence

It's important to give students a language to talk about violence, to facilitate their becoming more articulate in how they speak and think about their lives and the world. Giving the meaning of violence more finesse helps students refine its meaning, making the scope of what can be considered violent much more vast. Colman McCarthy first used these terms to describe a difference in scale and visibility which distinguishes different kinds of violence.

Hot violence is the visceral response which comes from overt acts of violence—a fistfight, the bloody uncensored scenes of war, the twin towers of the World Trade Center collapsing. Hot violence—rapes, stabbings, murder—makes the front pages of the newspaper.

Cold violence, on the other hand, is much more subtle and pervasive. It is the undercurrent, the steady, institutionalized oppression. Cold violence is homelessness, joblessness, malnutrition, and poverty—so much like static components of modern life that people rarely question its origins or its persistence. The cold violence of September 11 was that on that day, as happens every day, more than 40,000 people worldwide died of hunger-related illnesses.

Many students come to class thinking that humans have a genetic predisposition toward violence. Surrounded by violent images, conflict, structures that disallow their investigating nonviolent options, many students believe that nonviolence doesn't work.

The goal of lessons on nonviolence is not to convince students of anything other than believing in themselves and their power to learn and think critically. One quote by Martin Luther King, Jr. aptly summarizes this goal: "The arc of the universe is long but it bends toward justice." If my students don't understand what nonviolence is about at the end of 13 weeks, I don't feel defeated. How can I expect to put a dent in my students' lifetimes of experience in an extraordinarily violent world? At the very least, I feel grateful they stayed with the class and began to think critically about the issue of nonviolence, regardless of whether or not they accept it into their lives.

Most importantly, the goal of the class is not to create a plethora of disciples regurgitating the teacher's beliefs; the peace teacher is the neutral facilitator, allowing students to find their voices, making them probe deeper into their assumptions, backgrounds, and operating principles. The peace teacher must be vigilant not to indoctrinate but rather foster true learning, cooperation, and creativity.

Quotes to Explore

"If we believe that active nonviolence is an effective alternative to flight or fight in other areas of life, we need to explore how we can respond nonviolently in this most critical of all personal dangers, when an assault occurs. Here are some true stories about people who were not experienced in nonviolence, not committed to ahimsa, but who did just the right nonviolent thing at the right time."—Gerard A. Vanderhaar

- How would you explain the idea of "fight or flight"? Are these the only two options for a person faced with a violent situation?
- Does "fight" mean "kill"? Can you fight someone nonviolently? How might you protect yourself and the other person in a fight, if you choose this option?

- Does "flight" mean "run away" only? How are people who choose this option often labeled? Why might this label be inaccurate or unfair?
- If you were to be attacked, what are other options besides fighting back with a willingness to injure or even kill your attacker? Do you know of personal evidence where doing something other than fighting back has worked to stave off an attack?

"Most importantly, one comes to realize that the 'end' does not justify the 'means': we get what we do, not what we hope for or intend. You cannot improve a man through punishment, nor can you bring peace through war or brotherhood through brutalization."—Edward Guinan

- Where does the concept of "ends and means" come from? Where throughout history have people chosen just or unjust means to arrive at their desired end?
- If we want to have a just and fair ending, must we use just and fair methods to reach our goals? Can you have a just ending if you use unjust means? Think of some examples to support your opinion.
- What do we have to show for our efforts if we use less than honorable means to reach our goals, and then fail to reach them? What remains? Is it "the thought that counts" or do we need a tangible result?
- How do you decide what means to use to reach the desired end?

"We have been too willing to discuss violence in terms of ghetto upris- ings, student unrest, street thievery, and trashing, and have been unwilling to direct our attention to the more pathological types of violence that are ac- ceptable—the types that daily crush the humanity and life from untold mil- lions of brothers and sisters."—Edward Guinan

- How else can we view violence other than the above definitions?
- What is hot and cold violence? What are examples of each from your personal life? From your local community? From your country? From the world?
- Why is it necessary to make the distinction between the different types of violence?
- Why do we tend to only hear about hot violence?

"Nonviolence means taking the responsibility for aiding the direction of human communication and brotherhood. Nonviolence means an active opposition to those acts and attitudes that demean and brutalize another and it means an active support of those values and expressions that foster human solidarity."—Edward Guinan

- What is nonviolence?
- Why is creativity such an integral part of nonviolence?
- How would you explain nonviolence to a skeptic?
- What are the physical, emotional, and societal risks that a person takes in practicing nonviolence?
- Why don't more people know about and practice nonviolence? Can it be a way of life? How might it become integrated into a person's daily life? Into societal institutions? Into global policies?

"While it is indisputable that wars have been fought, the fact that they seem to dominate our history may say more about how history is presented than about what actually happened."—Alfie Kohn

- Why can we recall more about our history in wars than our history in peace? Why is war seen as more dynamic than peace?
- Is peace more than the absence of war? Why can we define what "a war" is but have difficulty defining what "a peace" is? What is peace?
- Who writes history? Who controls the narrative of what happened and how it is presented? Is history written by the winners or the losers?
- Does it matter from whose perspective history is written? How are people and stories included or excluded depending on who is doing the telling?

"The story of the human race is characterized by efforts to get along much more than by violent disputes, although it's the latter that makes the history books. Violence is actually exceptional. The human race has survived because of cooperation, not aggression."—Gerard A. Vanderhaar

- Why has nonviolence been systematically written out of textbooks and school curriculum?
- What might administrators and teachers think about proposing "math day" in the same way they propose "peace day"? How have we segregated peacemaking, making it a special occasion rather than a way of life? Could you learn everything you needed to learn about math if teachers only taught it once a year?
- How can concepts of peacemaking be integrated into every subject matter in school? How can the curriculum be amended to incorporate more information about peace and nonviolence?

"Breathing in, I calm my body. Breathing out, I smile. Dwelling in the present moment, I know this is a wonderful moment."—Thich Nhat Hanh

- Thich Nhat Hanh, a Buddhist monk from Vietnam, writes about breathing being the link between our mind and our body. Do you encounter times when your mind is thinking one thing and your body is doing another? Is it important for our mind and body to be unified? How does it feel to be "torn" between what you are thinking and what you are doing? What do you do when this happens?

- What if classes in school began by conscientious breathing? What problems do you think might be averted if teachers and students took the time to breathe together? What happens when people forget to breathe?

- Have you ever been told to "clear your mind" and erase your thoughts? Because many people find this difficult, how might breathing "in and out" and naming those breaths be helpful?

"In my tradition, we use the temple bells to remind us to come back to the present moment. Every time we hear the bell, we stop talking, stop our thinking, and return to ourselves, breathing in and out, and smiling."—Thich Nhat Hanh

- Where do you hear bells throughout the day? Make a list of the instances and write or say how you feel about each bell. Summarize how you feel when you hear them.

- Do bells evoke a positive or negative feeling for Thich Nhat Hanh? Why?

Experiential Lesson Plans

Peacemaker Pop Quiz

Objective: A beginning-of-the-semester exercise to help students orient themselves in their world and familiarize themselves with vocabulary like conflict, violence, and nonviolence, which they will be using throughout the semester.

The exercise begins with a pop quiz about prominent figures in the world. (I usually promise an automatic "A" to students who get all 10 answers correct, as an incentive.) On a piece of paper, students write their answers to the following prompts: Who are:

1. Stonewall Jackson
2. Thomas Jefferson
3. Arnold Schwarzenegger
4. Ronald Reagan

5. Woodrow Wilson

6. Dorothy Day

7. Jeanette Rankin

8. A.J. Muste

9. Mairead Maguire

10. Mkhuseli Jack

After reading all the names, ask students to identify each person. The first five should be easy. The last five get tougher. You may use these suggested people or substitute your own favorite famous characters in this list.

The following questions are helpful to ask after reading and debriefing the answers to this list:

- Why are the first five people very familiar to us?
- What contributions to our world do they have in common?
- Why are we unfamiliar with the last five people on the list?
- Are their contributions less important?
- Why have nonviolent leaders been written out of history?
- Create your own list.

Following a discussion of these questions, consider reading aloud in class "If We Listen Well" by Edward Guinan from the *Solutions to Violence* textbook. This essay segues into the next lesson plan, which explores definitions of the terms "conflict," "violence," and "nonviolence."

Nonviolence Grid

Objective: Provide a forum for safe self-expression and the opportunity to experience differences in opinion.

Time: 30–40 minutes, plus time to process and debrief.

Rules: Agree to talk one person at a time and not to use personal insults even if you strongly disagree with someone's opinion.

The Nonviolence Grid is a technique used by the Fellowship of Reconciliation in the Peacemaker Training Institute. This exercise allows students to explore their feelings toward various social issues while physically moving throughout the room, experiencing their opinions in spatial proximity to their classmates. The game begins by placing four large cards on the ground in the cardinal directions (N, S, E, W). The North and East cards have large "plus" symbols, and the West and South cards have "minus" symbols on them. The North/South axis represents "better for society" and "worse for society" at each extreme and the East/West axis similarly represents "more violent" and "less violent."

Move desks to the periphery of the classroom so there is room to move. Students stand in the middle of the room at the start. The teacher may move around, but should refrain from participation. The teacher reads the following "opinion statements" and students move in the room to the place on the grid which best fits their feelings toward the statement. The teacher asks various students to justify why they are standing where they are. The teacher may spend between three and five minutes on each question, and students are allowed to move if they change their minds. Students may volunteer their answers or the teacher may call on them to answer.

The following questions are samples, but teachers are encouraged to invent others, especially ones which are relevant or more age-appropriate in their classrooms and/or schools:

- Is arming airline pilots better or worse for society, more or less violent?
- Is arming school teachers better or worse for society, more or less violent?
- Is sacrificing some of our rights to privacy in order to combat violence like terrorism better or worse for society, more or less violent?
- Is attacking someone before they have the chance to attack you better or worse for society, more or less violent?
- Is not eating meat better or worse for society, more or less violent?
- Is participating in a march/boycott better or worse for society, more or less violent?
- Is telling a "little white lie" better or worse for society, more or less violent?
- Is traveling to another country better or worse for society, more or less violent?
- Is speaking up for someone who needs help better or worse for society, more or less violent?
- Is using racial slurs or gender-biased language better or worse for society, more or less violent?
- Is only associating with people of your own age/race/social class/etc. better or worse for society, more or less violent?
- Create your own questions.

Processing the Game

Since this game requires a great deal of physical and verbal participation, it is important to remember that some students process learning very differently. A written response from the students may be assigned, as well as oral discussion of the following questions:

1. How did you feel about having other people know literally where you stand on different issues?
2. How did it feel to see that everyone did not agree on the answers?
3. What do you think this game represents in a larger society?
4. Should everyone agree on the answers to these questions?
5. What was difficult about this game?
6. What did you learn about yourself in this game?
7. What did you learn about your classmates in this game?
8. Are there any situations where the outcome is not clear-cut and well defined?
9. Create your own questions.

Exploring Interconnectedness

Objective: Helping students understand the idea of interconnectedness, and that the conflict they encounter in their lives is relevant to the conflict occurring in their community, country, and world. Students should explore the idea that conflict is universal and that nonviolence is accessible to people of all ages, races, religions, etc.

On the chalkboard, write the word "conflict." Students should generate a working definition of what conflict means, what it sounds like, what it feels like, where it happens, and any other relevant contributions for creating a written description of what this word means. Hint: Many times, students will respond with negative comments about conflict. Try to prime them with a question about whether or not conflict can be positive as well. Colman McCarthy, founder of the Center for Teaching Peace, says that conflict is a neutral word that just means "something has to change."

After brainstorming the definition, move to defining "violence." Ask students if the two words are interchangeable or if they mean different things. One important point to make is that no one is exempt from conflict; you can do this by asking if anyone is currently experiencing any kind of conflict, or if anyone has ever experienced any kind of conflict.

Finally, write the word "nonviolence" on the chalkboard. Ask students what they first think of when they see this word. Many times students will respond by saying, "It's the opposite of violence." Others will equate nonviolence with passivity. Sometimes students are perplexed by this word, and it is helpful to start with a dictionary definition. One important element which helps to delineate the difference between violence and nonviolence is that the dynamics of violence are very simple: one force overpowering another. Nonviolence, on the other hand, inherently invites creativity and responding with solutions "outside the box."

The final element to this exercise involves a spiraling diagram. Start by labeling a point on the chalkboard with the word "me." What kinds of conflict and/or violence can an individual personally experience? Common answers are conflict within oneself and with parents, friends, teachers, significant others, coaches, bosses, etc. Write responses on the board, and once that list is exhausted, draw a spiral around those words. Label another point "my community." Where does violence occur in the community? At school? In the neighborhood? With the police or other local authorities? Are there instances of environmental violence or conflict in the area? Are there particular issues which involve community conflict? Interesting responses have been road rage, pollution, domestic violence, gang activity, and police brutality, but by no means is this list comprehensive.

Draw another spiral around those responses. Label another point "my country." Where is there violence in the country? What kinds of situations—child labor, poverty, freedom of speech and assembly, weapons-making, and homelessness—can students identify as being conflicts within their country? Finally, draw the final spiral around these responses. Mark a point labeled "my world." Have students list conflicts or instances of violence transpiring across the globe. Students often list conflicts in terms of wars, where violence is actively occurring. Encourage them to think about what wars mean for the people involved. This part of the exercise should provide the final visual component for students to recognize that the conflicts they experience on a personal level spiral outward to a global level.

Resources (Books and Websites)

- *All of One Peace* by Colman McCarthy
- *Peace Is Every Step* by Thich Nhat Hanh
- Alternatives to Violence Project: www.avpusa.org
- California Association of Student Councils (leadership training): www.casc.net

- Common Dreams News Source at www.commondreams.org
- C-Span video of Colman McCarthy: Service Learning, August 2001 at Georgetown University Institute for Peace and Justice at www.ipj-ppj.org/
- The Fellowship of Reconciliation Peacemaker Training Institute at www.forusa.org
- The Nonviolence Web at www.nonviolence.org
- Website for Alfie Kohn at www.alfiekohn.org

The Nuclear Age Peace Foundation

"Personal Peacemaking" is a chapter in *Teaching Peace: A Guide for the Classroom and Everyday Life* by Leah C. Wells, published by the Nuclear Age Peace Foundation in 2003. David Krieger, president of the Nuclear Age Peace Foundation, kindly gave permission to reprint "Personal Peacemaking."

The Nuclear Age Peace Foundation, on the web at www.wagingpeace.org, and www.nuclearfiles.org, initiates and supports worldwide efforts to abolish nuclear weapons, to strengthen international law and institutions, and to inspire and empower youth to create a more peaceful world. It sponsors two annual writing contests, which will be of interest to your students:

- The Swackhamer Peace Essay Contest is an annual international high school essay contest answering topical questions related to global peace and security at www.wagingpeace.org/menu/programs/awards-&-contests/swack contest/index.htm.
- The Barbara Mandigo Kelly Peace Poetry Awards is an annual series of awards to encourage poets to explore and illuminate positive visions of peace and the human spirit. The Poetry Awards include three age categories: Adult, Youth 13–18, and Youth 12 & Under at www.wagingpeace.org/menu/programs/awards-&-contests/bmk-contest/index.htm.

Related Resources Suggested by Chris Weber

- Free the Children, www.freethechildren.com, is an international network of children helping children at local, national, and international levels through representation, leadership, and action.
- PeaceEd.org, www.peaceed.org/, is a resource for an active growing network of individuals and groups to share information; build

community and connections; and support local, regional, and national efforts to address the roots of violence by educating for a culture of peace.

- PeaceJam, www.peacejam.org, is an international education program built around leading Nobel Peace Laureates who work personally with youth to pass on the spirit, skills, and wisdom they embody.

15

Students' Perspectives on Teaching Peace

Students' Advice to Teachers

So far, you have read chapters written by adults. In this chapter, students will do much of the talking. Why? Whenever I present at national or state conventions, students accompany me. Afterwards, teachers thank me for having students share their viewpoints as only they can. In this chapter, students will tell you about their desires and what they want and need from teachers. They will give advice so you can build more meaningful classes as you explore peace together with your students.

> I like to wash,
> By way of experiment,
> The dust of this world
> In the droplets of dew.
>
> —Basho

A WORD FROM THE TEACHER

SHANA MAZIARZ, PEACE STUDIES TEACHER,
THE WOOLMAN SEMESTER

I have finally settled into the realization that teaching is my activism. I believe that violence is the result of inarticulateness. The fact that we live in a violent society born out of violence, and at times resolved to this path, speaks volumes about our collective inability to speak and to listen. At its best, education allows us to find a home in ourselves, and consequently in the world; it allows us to find our truth, and thus, our words. At my best, I get out of the way and listen to what my students have to say.

This chapter is a project toward actively making peace. In preparing for this publication, my eight students had to find their public voices. Writing this was not easy for them. Whenever we use our voice in the service of our truth, we risk being misunderstood, ignored, abused. This chapter represents a process of learning to speak one's mind, and at the same time consider another's perspective. I have a great deal of trust in and respect for my students and am constantly on the edge of my seat. And while that means they may not have said exactly what I would have said in the following pages, I am listening.

Student Perspectives

We are passionate. We strive to create change and reach a deeper understanding of our history and present reality. Our motivation and drive to become active in creating peace comes from a longing for mental and spiritual liberation. We realize that nothing exists in a vacuum, and in order to place peace in context, we have committed ourselves to bear witness to the current global state of affairs. We hope that in learning from others, we can become resources of knowledge. The mentors in our lives fill the roles we are working to assume. We are constantly in the process of realizing the importance of our responsibility as the next generation.

This chapter will help teachers understand our points of view as students, and what we want to experience in the classroom. If the environment in the classroom is honest, unrestricted, and authentic, then healthy relationships will form, and ultimately, a positive atmosphere. When we have a meaningful class, we are more likely to take what we learned with us into the world, and to incorporate it into our lives. In the process of discovering peace, we need to feel we are co-creators of our education.

One of the most important parts of bringing peace into the learning environment is the dialogue between student and teacher. As students, we would like to share our experiences of discovering truth and peace within ourselves, and advocate some methods that can be used to create a stronger learning environment.

Jacob Ballin, Jesse Bradford, Cassidy Gardner, Mallory Marshall, Alison Mohr, Vayu Morrissey, Rebecca Sullivan, and Bonnie Webster are students at The Woolman Semester, a semester studies program for high school juniors, seniors, and postgraduates focused on exploring issues of peace, justice, and sustainability that is located in Nevada City, CA. For more information about The Woolman Semester, please visit www.woolman.org.

MY GUN CARRIES HIS BULLETS

Cassidy Gardner

Each bullet tells a different story
But he cannot remember
His eyes are blank with emotion

Knees shook from confusion
He says he is dying for me
He says it is because she says he says
He has no story
Pages are blank
But carry weight
He is dying in the face of our enemy
But so am I
My enemy is his story
His is lying on the ground
The main difference?
I keep my bullets in my mouth

KEEPING PEACE ALIVE: RESISTING THE URGE TO TEACH PEACE AS HISTORY

Jesse Bradford

It has been said that those who do not learn history are doomed to repeat it. I would add that those who *only* learn history are doomed to do nothing. In bringing the subject of peace into a classroom, it is easy to fall back on the great peacemakers of the past and therefore disengage your students from the ways they can create change in their communities, and in the world. Peace is not an event that happened once, or even a few times. Peace is an ongoing process that can involve everyone, and therefore, should be taught in an active, progressive, and engaging way.

Perhaps you could teach students about peaceful marches during the black freedom struggle of the 1960s, but then take them to a peace march and let them decide for themselves whether or not marches are still effective today. Teach them about how Gandhi spoke truth to power and wrote letters to governmental representatives, but then allow the students to write letters themselves, and send them. Teach them about how Henry David Thoreau spent a night in jail for refusing to pay taxes to a government involved in a war, but then let them read his own words in *Civil Disobedience*, and ask them to go home and talk to their parents about why *they* pay taxes.

The need to teach students the history of peace is obvious, but should not be the only goal of the teacher. Without knowing who Gandhi was, or what Martin Luther King Jr. did, or why Cesar Chavez is important, students will lack a foundation of knowledge that will help them in their journey toward activism. Teach your students about the past and ask them to creatively use that knowledge to work on a problem that is important to them. Students will realize that links to the past are key, but that dialogue with the present is the critical step toward creating peace in the world.

MAKING PEACE PERSONAL

Mallory Marshall

Becoming an active peacemaker is not about having long hair, flashing the peace sign, and wearing hemp clothing. It is important to explore with students what stereotypes are associated with peace. Ask students why they feel there are stereotypes connected with peace activists. Engage students with questions that allow them to express their personal thoughts and feelings about peace. In this way students can make peace something personal. Questions to generate dialogue could include: What does peace mean to you? What is the true purpose of activism? What does it mean to be an active peacemaker? How can you incorporate peace into your everyday life? Engaging in open dialogue will help students to think of different ways to look at peace and how it relates to them personally.

Beyond classroom discussions, volunteering in the community is one way for students to incorporate peace into their lives. When students create a personal relationship with people through volunteering, peace becomes clearer.

Peace became personal for me last summer, while volunteering with a children's program. Swimming with Michael was an experience I will always remember. When he swam in the water, he was so full of energy and life. He was having so much fun jumping in and out of the water. I will never forget the look in his eyes while we swam; they seemed to sparkle with pure joy and delight. After spending time with Michael, I realized how precious life is and how I need to live in the moment and to be passionate about what I do with my life. I learned so much from that one afternoon with Michael, and I will always carry that experience with me.

It is through my own experiences that I change my thoughts and life. There is no one path to peace. Each person must take their own personal journey to find what peace means to them.

IT'S ALL ABOUT THE RELATIONSHIP

Vayu Morrissey

It is important to bring attention and intention to our everyday relationships with other human beings. You have the opportunity to develop hundreds of powerful relationships. The teachers who have had an influence on me, whom I will never forget, are the ones who were willing to positively engage in order to establish a real relationship with me. We all long to be seen and understood and to know that someone will take the time to do this, makes me feel valuable. It is often through our relationships that we recognize our own sense of worth, and this is what allows us to take risks with our lives.

The purpose of my writing is to serve as a strong reminder that as someone who is older, and has more experience, and most importantly, a different perspective on things, you have an opportunity to pass on wisdom, knowledge, and positive guidance, but also to establish a reciprocal relationship. Make the effort to see your students as human beings, with feelings and needs, with something to offer that nobody else can. Changing the way you view your relationship will change the way you feel about your role not only as a teacher, but as a person, affecting and being affected by the lives of other human beings. Be that reaffirming and strengthening force in the lives of your students. You can make a profound difference simply by recognizing the humanity in each of your students. When teachers engage in this way, they effectively become active peacemakers, giving students the foundation to do the same.

CONNECTING THROUGH THE WRITTEN WORD

Rebecca Sullivan

Often students learn about peace through personal discovery, potentially making their thoughts uncomfortable to share with the class. Students may be intimidated by what others are saying but still have something to share. Having a journal gives them a chance to explain what they think without confronting the entire class. A few weeks ago I was frustrated with a teacher, and wrote in my journal to collect my thoughts. When I confronted her, I felt confident that I was not going to blow up because I knew exactly what I wanted to say. There are many ways that teachers can adjust their lesson plans and learning methods so everyone feels included.

Another idea is to have an online chat room where students and teachers can help each other and dialogue outside of class. A chat room can also help students learn more about each other, by providing a safe place to share. When students are intimidated by hard topics, nontraditional ways of communication, such as journaling, can help students figure out what they are feeling, and how to express it. The creative use of writing can allow relationships and learning to extend outside the limitations of the classroom.

THE ROLE OF THE TEACHER

Alison Mohr

I have had teachers who, with the best of intentions, infused their bias into the structure of the class. I understand that bias is inevitable, but unexamined bias can have harmful affects on the learning environment. Whether or not I agree with the bias, it affects how I feel about the class. Most often bias becomes problematic when it is subconscious, and therefore, ignored. Covertly biased teaching makes me feel mistrusted and manipulated; it is as if my teacher does not trust me to have valid opinions.

Some teachers notice and wish to suppress their biases. They attempt to conceal their opinions, ostensibly to allow their students to feel comfortable speaking their minds. However, in order for students to be engaged in the learning process, the teacher must be as well. Part of a teacher's job is to learn with their students. The first step is to accept that they, like everyone else, will never be complete, and as a result, to have the courage to look critically at their teaching and allow it to evolve. This also requires teachers to be open about their biases and opinions. You walk a fine line as a teacher. Examine how your power influences the learning experience. Part of that is exploring when to teach the class and when to let the class teach itself.

GETTING BEYOND THE STATUS QUO

Cassidy Gardner

Forming a culture of peace essentially requires teachers to look critically at how they might unintentionally make inaccurate assumptions about their students. Race, political background, gender, physical appearance, and learning abilities have all caused teachers to consciously or subconsciously categorize their students. This ultimately can affect students' educational processes and how they feel about themselves. For example, a student with a more conservative viewpoint may be pushed out of a discussion revolving around the ideals of peace. Everyone wants peace, though not everyone believes it can be achieved in the same ways. By not letting certain students speak, the teacher diminishes the opportunity for other students to arrive at new conclusions. This is a very live issue and one that I have witnessed personally. A friend of mine who had just moved to America had a unique way of expressing herself, mostly through story. She raised her hand often, though was rarely called on. Many of her teachers thought she wasn't learning because she expressed her personal knowledge through her own experiences, rather than reiterating the teachers' or books' words. She was a very bright student and had a lot to offer, and without her voice, others were missing out on her unique way of viewing life. Teachers should constantly make the effort to amplify all student voices. Peace requires multiple perspectives and is a process in which everyone must be accounted for.

CARRYING PEACE INTO THE CLASSROOM AND BEYOND: PROVIDING MORE CONTEXT

Bonnie Webster

Students have to open themselves up to their own ideals before they can begin to absorb lessons around topics as complex as peace. It's easy to fall into the trap of just lecturing or having class discussions about peace-related issues. However, without developing personal and collective definitions of peace, it's usually unproductive to the students. To nurture a peace-learning atmosphere, be sure to include respect, honesty, and joy in your teaching and classroom setting. Honesty should not make you more brutal; joy doesn't mean you always have to be happy; and respect doesn't mean you let students get away with things.

Know your definition of peace and your personal joys, so you may dive deeper into this conversation of peace with your students. Class discussions are one way to give students personal insight, but something more is required. You have an obligation to be as Socratic as possible and encourage students to find deeper answers. Students have to be constantly involved and invested in the peace-based relationship you are building with them. A one-sided conversation defeats the purpose of a lesson of peace. Remember that everyone in the classroom is a teacher and should be treated as such; that is the true atmosphere of peace.

In Their Own Words, by Chris Weber

In their own words, these students are saying what Ghandi said: our hope for peace begins with young people. These young authors are also telling us that we need to listen to our students and work with them. Morever, the most important thing that I can ever do for my students is to show them that I care deeply about them and their learning.

$$\underline{16}$$

Speaking Out Through Protest Music

When a situation is dire enough, you'll do anything to effect a change and brave any consequences. I thought at one point, I can take a chance of alienating or worrying (that's the way I thought of it), you know, some of the people listening to my music. I can take that chance because I would do anything rather than go on being a success and make a lot of money, and live a privileged life here in the United States while we decimate the people of another country.

—Jackson Browne

Never Too Young to Sing

After I finished singing a Dylan song to my class, Sebastian, a third grade girl, asked, "Do you know 'Blowing in the Wind?' That's my favorite." Music can show students of all ages a powerful way of exploring and delivering messages about social issues, such as war, the environment, and civil rights. By studying lyrics, students can learn how songwriters incorporate messages into their songs. They can also feel the timeless impact of lyrics as relevant today as when they were first sung. Jackson Browne's "Lives in the Balance," written in 1986, could easily have been written now:

> . . . You might ask what it takes to remember
> When you know that you've seen it before
> Where a government lies to a people
> And a country is drifting to war. . . .
>
> They sell us the President the same way
> They sell us our clothes and our cars
> They sell us every thing from youth to religion
> The same time they sell us our wars
> I want to know who the men in the shadows are

I want to hear somebody asking them why
They can be counted on to tell us who our enemies are
But they're never the ones to fight or to die. . . .
(© Swallow Turn Music 1986. Reprinted with permission.)

A powerful animated editorial by Andrew Thomas is set to Jackson Browne's solo acoustic version of the 1986 classic "Lives in the Balance." This must-see video can be viewed for free at: www.therandirhodesshow.com/live/node/2983 or www.jacksonbrowne.com/.

When I pick up my guitar and sing, students are right with me. Nothing beats a live classroom performance, except having students sing along with you. Moreover, you can encourage them to write their own songs.

Music Can Be a Powerful Opening to Students of All Ages

BOB PETERSON

Songs, like poetry, are an important component of my teaching. The lyrical metaphors, rhythms, and stories in many songs motivate and educate students. It's amazing what my fifth graders remember from a song, as compared to what they forget from my talking.

I introduce a "song of the week" each Monday and students put a copy in their three-ring binder with the rest of my alternative curriculum. We start each morning with the song, and usually within a day or two the children are singing along—regardless of musical genre. Sometimes I use a song to introduce a unit of study, other times a particular point in a lesson.

At a recent anti-war rally I heard a song I thought would work well with my students. I also searched the web and found a number of songs that could help teachers approach this subject. The growing quantity of such songs is a tribute to the many artists who are performing at numerous anti-war rallies around the world.

The lyrics of virtually any song can be found on the web with a bit of "googling." Finding a free (and legal) MP3 download is a bit harder—but worth the effort. (Don't be intimidated about downloading a song or burning a CD—any teenager can help you.) Several websites have collections of anti-war music. One is the United Kingdom–based Peace Not War organization, which has published a two-disc CD, "Peace Not War." You can hear the songs and read the lyrics at www.peace-not-war.org. Another site is the Chicago-based Voices in the Wilderness, which has put out a CD called "Stoking the Fires of Resistance." Some songs and lyrics from that CD are available through www.fbirecords.com/stokingthefires.htm#songs.

Public libraries are another decent source for CDs—especially with online searchable catalogs—although generally those are for older ones. I prefer to have a copy of the songs I use on a CD, either one that I've purchased, downloaded, or copied.

The first song I used with my students about Iraq was "Not in My Name," by John McCutcheon, in which he sings, "But in Hiroshima, New York, or in Baghdad, it's the innocent who die for the crime." One verse also criticizes capital punishment, but the chorus is the most powerful, a simple "Not in my name." As part of our discussion, we read the "Pledge of Resistance" from the Not in Our Name website and looked at a full-page newspaper ad by the same group. The pledge is available in 19 different languages at www.notinourname.net/pledge_about.html.

Sandra Baran's "Wake Up," performed by Voices and Minna Bromberg, has a powerful and lively refrain—"Wake up! The children are dying, the children of Iraq!"—that catches the energy of my students. Key phrases encourage further inquiry like, "The Gulf War did not end as reported. It still goes on these many years."

I've used other songs that speak more generally about issues of global justice. An annotated listing of those songs is in the resource section of the book Bill Bigelow and I co-edited, *Rethinking Globalization: Teaching for Justice in an Unjust World*, also available online at www.rethinkingschools.org /publication/rg/rgresour.shtml.

Below is a sampling of some of the songs I think are most useful in the classroom. Please email additional suggestions so we can periodically update this list, which is being simultaneously published on the Rethinking Schools website.

- "Ashcroft's Army" by John McCutcheon—a funny, but tragic song about how civil rights in the U.S. are being eroded. Lyrics and free MP3 download available at: www.folkmusic.com/t_mp3.htm.

- "Bomb da World" by Michael Franti and Spearhead, a rapper who records on his own Boo Boo Wax imprint. The chorus goes, "You can bomb the world to pieces, but you can't bomb it into peace."

- "Bombs over Baghdad" by John Trudell. ("AKA Graffiti Man" CD, Rykodisc, 1992.) An angry anti-war poem/song from a longtime Native-American activist.

- "Jacob's Ladder" (Not in My Name) by Chumbawamba (who played it at the January 18, 2003 protest in Washington, DC). Lyrics at www.geocities.com/SunsetStrip/Basement/8448/index.html. Free download at www.chumba.com.

- "Masters of War" by Bob Dylan. ("Freewheelin' Bob Dylan" CD, Columbia, 1963.) This song was written at the beginning of U.S. involvement in Vietnam but speaks to the broad issue of investment in instruments of death and destruction versus human needs.
- "Not in My Name" by John McCutcheon. ("The Greatest Show Never Told" CD, Redhouse, 2002.)
- "Paz y Libertad" by José-Luis Orozco. ("Rainbow Sign" CD, Rounder, 1992.) An easy bilingual ballad that calls for peace and freedom in the world. Great for young children as well as upper elementary.
- "The Price of Oil" by Billy Bragg. Free MP3 download available at www.billybragg.co.uk/multimedia/price_of_oil.mp3. A powerful song that traces the war on Iraq, U.S. support of Pinochet, and the rigged Florida election to the "price of oil." Includes mild profanity.
- "Self-Evident" by Ani DiFranco. A song/poem/rap that covers lots of territory with very powerful lyrics including: "We hold these truths to be self-evident:/# 1 george w. bush is not president/# 2 america is not a true democracy/#3 the media is not fooling me." Available at www.peace-not-war.org/Music/AniDiFranco/.
- "Wake Up," written by Sandra Baran and performed by Voices and Minna Bromberg. ("Stoking the Fires of Resistance" CD.) See description above.
- "We're the Cops of the World" by Phil Ochs. ("There But for Fortune" CD, Elektra Asylum Records, 1989.) A Vietnam war–era song that criticizes how the U.S. military has secured the world for U.S. business—"The name for our profits is democracy."

Bob Peterson, repmilw@aol.com, teaches fifth grade at La Escuela Fratney in Milwaukee and is an editor of *Rethinking Schools,* www.rethinkingschools.org. "Music Can Be a Powerful Opening to Students of All Ages" first appeared in *Rethinking Schools* magazine, Winter, 2001/2002 and is reprinted here by permission of Rethinking Schools.

Web Resources

- Anti War Songs, à la Carte © with links to legal downloads and lyrics, www.lacarte.org/songs/anti-war/
- No Bravery, a music video at www.informationclearinghouse.info /article11799.htm
- Protest Songs site at www.sfheart.com/protest/index1.html
- Znet's Selected Anti War Songs, www.zmag.org/Songs/songarchive.htm

Living with War

When Neil Young's album *Living with War* first streamed on the Internet, I listened to it over and over again. While its powerful message and music has inspired me during this book's final stages, I feel Mr. Young's example of speaking out is one to follow. "Living with War" serves as an example of the protest song as a vehicle for political expression. Its lyrics will be excellent kernels for classroom discussion.

Like Neil Young said, ". . . this is about exchanging ideas . . . it's about getting a message out. It's about empowering people by giving them a voice. I know not everyone believes what I say is what they think. But like I said before . . . red and blue is not black and white. We're all together. It's a record about unification." —Neil Young (Apr 18, 2006)

If enough people start speaking out like Neil Young, maybe his next album will be titled *Living with Peace*.

Appendix A

What About the Iraqi Children?
Charlotte Aldebron

March 6, 2003

(The following is a transcript of a speech given by Charlotte, then thirteen years old, at a peace rally in Maine.)

When people think about bombing Iraq, they see a picture in their heads of Saddam Hussein in a military uniform, or maybe soldiers with big black mustaches carrying guns, or the mosaic of George Bush Senior on the lobby floor of the Al-Rashid Hotel with the word "criminal." But guess what? More than half of Iraq's twenty-four million people are children under the age of fifteen. That's twelve million kids. Kids like me. Well, I'm almost thirteen, so some are a little older, and some a lot younger, some boys instead of girls, some with brown hair, not red. But kids who are pretty much like me just the same. So take a look at me—a good long look. Because I am what you should see in your head when you think about bombing Iraq. I am what you are going to destroy.

If I am lucky, I will be killed instantly, like the three hundred children murdered by your "smart" bombs in a Baghdad bomb shelter on February 16, 1991. The blast caused a fire so intense that it flash-burned outlines of those children and their mothers on the walls; you can still peel strips of blackened skin—souvenirs of your victory—from the stones.

But maybe I won't be lucky and I'll die slowly, like fourteen-year-old Ali Faisal, who right now is in the "death ward" of the Baghdad children's hospital. He has malignant lymphoma—cancer—caused by the depleted uranium in your Gulf War missiles. Or maybe I will die painfully and needlessly like eighteen-month-old Mustafa, whose vital organs are being devoured by sand-fly parasites. I know it's hard to believe, but Mustafa could be totally cured with just $25 worth of medicine, but there is none of this medicine because of your sanctions.

Or maybe I won't die at all but will live for years with the psychological damage that you can't see from the outside, like Salman Mohammed, who even now can't forget the terror he lived through with his little sisters when you bombed Iraq in 1991. Salman's father made the whole family sleep in the same room so that they would all survive together, or die together. He still has nightmares about the air-raid sirens.

Or maybe I will be orphaned like Ali, who was three when you killed his father in the Gulf War. Ali scraped at the dirt covering his father's grave every day for three years calling out to him, "It's all right Daddy, you can come out now, the men who put you here have gone away." Well, Ali, you're wrong. It looks like those men are coming back.

Or maybe I will make it in one piece, like Luay Majed, who remembers that the Gulf War meant he didn't have to go to school and could stay up as late as he wanted. But today, with no education, he tries to live by selling newspapers on the street.

Imagine that these are your children—or nieces or nephews or neighbors. Imagine your son screaming from the agony of a severed limb, but you can't do anything to ease the pain or comfort him. Imagine your daughter crying out from under the rubble of a collapsed building, but you can't get to her. Imagine your children wandering the streets, hungry and alone, after having watched you die before their eyes.

This is not an adventure movie or a fantasy or a video game. This is reality for children in Iraq. Recently, an international group of researchers went to Iraq to find out how children there are being affected by the possibility of war. Half the children they talked to said they saw no point in living any more. Even really young kids knew about war and worried about it. One five-year-old, Assem, described it as "guns and bombs and the air will be cold and hot and we will burn very much." Ten-year-old Aesar had a message for President Bush: he wanted him to know that "A lot of Iraqi children will die. You will see it on TV and then you will regret."

Back in elementary school I was taught to solve problems with other kids not by hitting or name-calling, but by talking and using "I" messages. The idea of an "I" message was to make the other person understand how bad his or her actions made you feel, so that the person would sympathize with you and stop it. Now I am going to give you an "I" message. Only it's going to be a "We" message. "We" as in all the children in Iraq who are waiting helplessly for something bad to happen. "We" as in the children of the world who don't make any of the decisions but have to suffer all the consequences. "We" as in those whose voices are too small and too far away to be heard.

We feel scared when we don't know if we'll live another day.

We feel angry when people want to kill us or injure us or steal our future.

We feel sad because all we want is a mom and a dad who we know will be there the next day.

And, finally, we feel confused—because we don't even know what we did wrong.

Appendix B

Cultivating Habits of Social Justice and the SOA
Jean Daigneau

St. Patrick School (Kent, Ohio) middle school teacher Susanne Brych encourages her students to develop habits of social activism, by providing opportunities for reflection, discussion, and action surrounding social justice issues incorporated into her English, social studies, and religion classes. Brych does not spoon-feed her students to take a stand. Rather, she believes "they must be guided . . . to decide for themselves if they want to do something. Usually it takes just providing information."

One issue addressed is the movement to close the School of the Americas (SOA), renamed the Western Hemisphere Institute for Security Cooperation, in Fort Benning, Georgia, established in 1946. Many of the school's 60,000 graduates have been positively linked to thousands of deaths in Latin America.

Brych presents the topic as something "that impacts the lives of people not far from here, but that utilizes our tax dollars." Students watch videos on the SOA and Central America and the movie *Romero*. The class discusses freedoms we often take for granted—the right to vote or to live without fear because of political beliefs.

Students discuss their feelings—pro and con—about what is taught at the SOA, whether funding the school is a wise use of the country's financial resources, and whether there's a connection between the SOA and human rights violations in Latin America, among other things.

Some parents thank Brych for bringing this issue to the forefront, but others call or write opposing her views. She addresses these viewpoints with her students, emphasizing that she is not condemning military personnel in this country, which parents often assume.

Students discuss their responsibilities concerning social justice issues. Interested students brainstorm ways they can act, including writing to government representatives and local newspapers, educating their peers and families, boycotting corporations promoting sweatshops or engaging in unfair labor practices, and joining the nonviolent vigil at Fort Benning in November.

The project culminates with letters written to government leaders and incorporates instruction on how to address and formulate such correspondence. Students share and discuss responses they receive along with letters published in local newspapers. Participation is strictly optional.

Brych urges her students to act, regardless of their position on an issue. "It's so important for young people to lead movements because it gives them a feeling of empowerment. . . . Instead of complaining or waiting for someone else to take action, they know they can do it. They are that someone."

"The young are our future; they have fresh ideas, see things differently, are enthusiastic. We develop habits for every other aspect of our lives. The habit of social activism should be cultivated as well."

Eighth-grader Christopher Biats echoes these sentiments. "If kids start young to do things, they'll realize that they can actually do something by themselves. One person can make a difference because he can change the opinion of others by sharing his ideas."

Jean Daigneau works at St. Patrick School. She's also a children's writer and the Regional Advisor for the Northern Ohio Society of Children's Bookwriters and Illustrators.

Resources

School of Assassins. Maryknoll, New York: Maryknoll World Productions 1995.

SOA: Guns and Greed. Maryknoll, New York: Maryknoll World Productions 2001.

Appendix C

Drain the Swamp and There Will Be No More Mosquitoes: By Attacking Iraq, the U.S. Will Invite a New Wave of Terrorist Attacks
Noam Chomsky

September 11 shocked many Americans into an awareness that they had better pay much closer attention to what the U.S. government does in the world and how it is perceived. Many issues have been opened for discussion that were not on the agenda before. That's all to the good.

It is also the merest sanity, if we hope to reduce the likelihood of future atrocities. It may be comforting to pretend that our enemies "hate our freedoms," as President Bush stated, but it is hardly wise to ignore the real world, which conveys different lessons.

The president is not the first to ask: "Why do they hate us?" In a staff discussion forty-four years ago, President Eisenhower described "the campaign of hatred against us [in the Arab world], not by the governments but by the people." His National Security Council outlined the basic reasons: the U.S. supports corrupt and oppressive governments and is "opposing political or economic progress" because of its interest in controlling the oil resources of the region.

Post–September 11 surveys in the Arab world reveal that the same reasons hold today, compounded with resentment over specific policies. Strikingly, that is even true of privileged, western-oriented sectors in the region.

To cite just one recent example: in the August 1 issue of *Far Eastern Economic Review*, the internationally recognized regional specialist Ahmed Rashid writes that in Pakistan "there is growing anger that U.S. support is allowing [Musharraf's] military regime to delay the promise of democracy."

Today we do ourselves few favors by choosing to believe that "they hate us" and "hate our freedoms." On the contrary, these are attitudes of people who like Americans and admire much about the U.S., including its freedoms. What they hate is official policies that deny them the freedoms to which they too aspire.

For such reasons, the post–September 11 rantings of Osama bin Laden—for example, about U.S. support for corrupt and brutal regimes, or about the U.S. "invasion" of Saudi Arabia—have a certain resonance, even among those who despise and fear him. From resentment, anger, and frustration, terrorist bands hope to draw support and recruits.

We should also be aware that much of the world regards Washington as a terrorist regime. In recent years, the U.S. has taken or backed actions in Colombia, Nicaragua, Panama, Sudan, and Turkey, to name a few, that meet official U.S. definitions of "terrorism"—that is, when Americans apply the term to enemies.

In the most sober establishment journal, *Foreign Affairs*, Samuel Huntington wrote in 1999: "While the U.S. regularly denounces various countries as 'rogue states,' in the eyes of many countries it is becoming the rogue superpower . . . the single greatest external threat to their societies."

Such perceptions are not changed by the fact that, on September 11, for the first time, a western country was subjected on home soil to a horrendous terrorist attack of a kind all too familiar to victims of western power. The attack goes far beyond what's sometimes called the "retail terror" of the IRA, FLN, or Red Brigades.

The September 11 terrorism elicited harsh condemnation throughout the world and an outpouring of sympathy for the innocent victims. But with qualifications.

An international Gallup poll in late September found little support for "a military attack" by the U.S. in Afghanistan. In Latin America, the region with the most experience of U.S. intervention, support ranged from 2 percent in Mexico to 16 percent in Panama.

The current "campaign of hatred" in the Arab world is, of course, also fuelled by U.S. policies toward Israel-Palestine and Iraq. The U.S. has provided the crucial support for Israel's harsh military occupation, now in its 35th year.

One way for the U.S. to lessen Israeli-Palestinian tensions would be to stop refusing to join the long-standing international consensus that calls for recognition of the right of all states in the region to live in peace and security, including a Palestinian state in the currently occupied territories (perhaps with minor and mutual border adjustments).

In Iraq, a decade of harsh sanctions under U.S. pressure has strengthened Saddam Hussein while leading to the death of hundreds of thousands of Iraqis—perhaps more people "than have been slain by all so-called weapons of mass destruction throughout history," military analysts John and Karl Mueller wrote in *Foreign Affairs* in 1999.

Washington's present justifications to attack Iraq have far less credibility than when President Bush Sr. was welcoming Saddam as an ally and a trading partner after he had committed his worst brutalities—as in Halabja, where Iraq attacked Kurds with poison gas in 1988. At the time, the murderer Saddam was more dangerous than he is today.

As for a U.S. attack against Iraq, no one, including Donald Rumsfeld, can realistically guess the possible costs and consequences. Radical Islamist extremists surely hope that an attack on Iraq will kill many people and destroy much of the country, providing recruits for terrorist actions.

They presumably also welcome the "Bush doctrine" that proclaims the right of attack against potential threats, which are virtually limitless. The president has announced: "There's no telling how many wars it will take to secure freedom in the homeland." That's true.

Threats are everywhere, even at home. The prescription for endless war poses a far greater danger to Americans than perceived enemies do, for reasons the terrorist organizations understand very well.

Twenty years ago, the former head of Israeli military intelligence Yehoshaphat Harkabi, also a leading Arabist, made a point that still holds true. "To offer an honorable solution to the Palestinians respecting their right to self-determination: that is the solution of the problem of terrorism," he said. "When the swamp disappears, there will be no more mosquitoes."

At the time, Israel enjoyed the virtual immunity from retaliation within the occupied territories that lasted until very recently. But Harkabi's warning was apt, and the lesson applies more generally.

Well before September 11 it was understood that with modern technology, the rich and powerful will lose their near monopoly of the means of violence and can expect to suffer atrocities on home soil.

If we insist on creating more swamps, there will be more mosquitoes, with awesome capacity for destruction.

If we devote our resources to draining the swamps, addressing the roots of the "campaigns of hatred," we can not only reduce the threats we face but also live up to ideals that we profess and that are not beyond reach if we choose to take them seriously.

Noam Chomsky is professor of linguistics at the Massachusetts Institute of Technology and author of *Hegemony or Survival: America's Quest for Global Dominance (The American Empire Project)*, published by Metropolitan Books in 2003.

[Thank you, Noam Chomsky, for your kind words and support for this book when it was in the proposal stages. As I worked on *Nurturing the Peacemakers in Our Students*, I struggled through the harsh realities of what children in war experience. I could barely read their narratives. At the same time, my admiration for you grew. You have spent most of your life speaking out. You continue to do so with the 2006 publication of your book titled *Failed States: The Abuse of Power and the Assault on Democracy*. Perhaps, my book will encourage students and teachers to become activists, too.]

Works Cited

Introduction

Everding, G. 1995. "Study Finds Inner-City Teens Influenced by Real-Life Violence." http://record.wustl.edu/archive/1995/08-24-95/7807.html (08 Sept. 2003).

Greene, M.B. 1996. "Youth and Violence: Trends, Principles, and Programmatic Interventions." In Apfel, R.J. & B. Simon, eds. *Minefields in Their Hearts: The Mental Health of Children in War and Communal Violence*. New Haven, CT: Yale University Press.

Kinzie, J.D. & W.H. Sack. 1991. "Severely Traumatized Cambodian Children: Research Findings and Clinical Implications." In F.L. Ahern, Jr. & J.L. Athey, eds., *Refugee Children: Theory, Research and Services*. Baltimore, MD: John Hopkins University Press.

Marans, S. & D.J. Cohen. 1993. "Children and Inner-City Violence: Strategies for Intervention." In Leavitt, L.A., & N.A. Fox, eds. *The Psychological Effects of War and Violence on Children*. Hillsdale, NJ: Lawrence Erlbaum Associates.

Mollica, R.F., Poole, C., Son, L., Murray, C.C., & S. Tor. 1997. "Effects of War Trauma on Cambodian Refugee Adolescents' Functional Health and Mental Health Status." *Journal of the American Academy of Child and Adolescent Psychiatry* 36(8), 1098–1106.

Pilger, John. April 20, 2003. "The Unthinkable Is Becoming Normal." *The Independent*. UK.

Richters, J.S. & P. Martinez. 1993. "Children as Victims of and Witnesses to Violence in a Washington, D.C. Neighborhood." In Leavitt, L.A., & N.A. Fox, eds. *The Psychological Effects of War and Violence on Children*. Hillsdale, NJ: Lawrence Erlbaum Associates.

Sack, W.H., C. Him, & D. Dickason. 1999. "Twelve Year Follow-up Study of Khmer Youths Who Suffered Massive War Trauma as Children." *Journal of the American Academy of Child and Adolescent Psychiatry* 38(9), 1073–1179.

Sheley, J.F. & J.D. Wright. 1993. "Gun Acquisition and Possession in Selected Juvenile Samples." Washington, D.C.: U.S. Department of Justice.

Swope, Sam. 2005. "The Occidental Tourist." *Teacher Magazine*.

UNICEF. 2003. "Child Protection: Armed Conflict." www.unicef.org/protection/index_armedconflict.html (11 Aug. 2003).

Chapter 1

Center for Research on Learning and Teaching. 2003. "Guidance for UM Instructors Leading Class Discussion on the Tragedy of September 11, 2001." www.crlt.umich.edu/publinks/tragedydiscussion.html (20 July 2003).

Constitutional Rights Foundation. 2003. "Response to War: How Do You Feel? What Do You Think?" http://crfusa.org/Iraqwar_html/iraqwar_feelthink.html (11 Aug. 2003).

Ting-Toomey, S. 1994. "Managing Intercultural Conflicts Effectively." In Samovar, L.A. & R.E. Porter, eds., *Intercultural Communication: A Reader.* Belmont, CA: Wadsworth Publishing Company.

Chapter 2

Elbow, Peter. 1973. "Appendix Essay. The Doubting Game and the Believing Game: An Analysis of the Intellectual Process." In *Writing Without Teachers.* Oxford: Oxford University Press.

———. 1986. "Methodological Doubting and Believing: Contraries in Inquiry." In *Embracing Contraries: Explorations in Learning and Teaching.* Oxford: Oxford University Press.

———. 2005. "Bringing the Rhetoric of Assent and the Believing Game Together— and into the Classroom." *College English* 67(4), 388–99.

Graff, Gerald. 2003. *Clueless in Academe: How Schooling Obscures the Life of the Mind.* New Haven: Yale.

Lippman, Walter. 1939. "The Indispensable Opposition." *Atlantic Monthly,* August 1939. It's notable that this essay is canonized in many editions of *The Norton Reader* (e.g., in the 6th edition, pages 850–55).

Mill, John Stuart. 1951. *On Liberty.* London: Dent.

Rogers, Carl. 1961. "Communication: Its Blocking and Its Facilitation." *On Becoming a Person.* New York: Houghton Mifflin.

Tannen, Deborah. 1998. *The Argument Culture: Moving from Debate to Dialogue.* New York: Random House.

Chapter 3

Burke, Jim. 2003. "Write a Reflective Essay." From Chapter 51 (pp. 272–277) in *Writing Reminders: Tools, Tips, and Techniques.* Portsmouth, NH: Heinemann.

Costa, Arthur, & Bena Kallick. 2000. *Habits of Mind.* Alexandria, VA: Association for Supervision and Curriculum Development.

Hillocks, G. 1995. *Teaching Writing as Reflective Practice.* New York: Columbia University, Teacher's College Press.

Trupe, Alice L. 2001. "Effective Writing Text: Reflective Writing." http://bridge water.edu/~atrupe/Eng101/Text/Reflection.htm (2 Feb. 2005).

Chapter 4

Bruun, Christine. 2004. "The Importance of Empathy." International Network on Personal Meaning at www.meaning.ca/articles04/bruun-empathy.htm (23 March 2004).

Casagrande, June. 1998. "Burbank Poet to Appear at Holocaust Center," 11 Feb. *The Burbank Leader.* A10.

Fisch, Robert O. 1994. *Light from the Yellow Star: A Lesson of Love from the Holocaust.* Minneapolis: Frederick Weisman Art Museum of the University of Minnesota.

Fischl, Peter L. 1994. "To the Little Polish Boy Standing with His Arms Up." Los Angeles: Archives of Simon Wiesenthal Center.

Gorrell, Nancy. 1997. "Teaching the Holocaust: Light from the Yellow Star Leads the Way." *English Journal* 86: 50–55.

Hollander, John. 1995. *The Gazer's Spirit: Poems Speaking to Silent Works of Art*. Chicago: University of Chicago Press.

Karski, Jan. 1997. "Foreword." In Del Calzo, N., ed. *The Triumphant Spirit: Portraits and Stories of Holocaust Survivors . . . Their Messages of Hope and Compassion*. Denver: Triumphant Spirit Publishing.

New Jersey Commission on Holocaust Education. 1994. "The Betrayal of Mankind."

Roy, Arundhati. 1999. "Word from the Ghetto," *Newsweek* 8 March: 47.

———. 2003. *War Talk*. Cambridge, MA: South End Press.

Chapter 6
International Campaign to Ban Landmines. October 23, 2003. "Responding to Landmines: A Modern Tragedy and Its Solutions." Diana, Princess of Wales. June 12 1997. Keynote address for a one-day seminar co-hosted by Landmine Survivors Network and the Mines Advisory Group. www.landminesurvivors.org/stories_feature.php?id=38 (11 July 2004).

Mitrovic, Zdravko. 2004. "How I Live with Mines." *Survive the Peace*. 1999–2006, www.redcross.ca/article.asp?id=001987&tid=011 (5 April 2004).

Chapter 7
BBC World Service. 2004. "Children of Conflict." www.bbc.co.uk/worldservice/people/features/childrensrights/childrenofconflict/soldtxt.shtml#03 (23 Dec. 2004).

Brett, R. & M. McCallin. 1998. *Children, the Invisible Soldiers*. Stockholm, Sweden: Rädda Barnen.

Brett, R. & I. Specht. 2004. *Young Soldiers: Why They Choose to Fight*. Boulder, CO: Lynne Rienner Publishers.

Coalition to Stop the Use of Child Soldiers. 2003. "Child Soldiers Use 2003: A Briefing for the 4th U.N. Security Council Open Debate on Children and Armed Conflict." http://library.amnesty.it/cs/childsoldiers.nsf/Document/CHILD%20SOLDIERS%201379%20REPORT%20(2002)?OpenDocument (27 Dec. 2004).

Deen, Thalif. 2005. "UN Report on Child Soldiers Ignores Worst Offenders." Common Dreams News Center. www.commondreams.org/headlines02/1107-05.htm (12 Feb. 2005).

DuBrin, Doug. 2004. "Lesson: Children at War." www.pbs.org/newshour/extra/teachers/lessonplans/world/childsoldiers_12-22.html (28 Dec. 2004).

Dusauchoit, Tine, MD. 2003. "Enough Is Enough: Why Sexual Violence Demands a Humanitarian Response." www.doctorswithoutborders.org/publications/ar/i2003/sexualviolence.shtml (23 Dec. 2004).

ePals Classroom Exchange. 2004. "Child Soldiers." www.epals.com/waraffectedchildren/chap2/.

Farrell, Michael B. 2005. "Children Make Deadly Soldiers in the World's Rebel Groups: Poverty and AIDS Provide Thousands of Young Recruits." *Christian Science Monitor,* January 18.

Human Rights Watch. 2004a. "Stop the Use of Child Soldiers!" http://hrw.org/cam paigns/crp/index.htm (6 Dec. 2004).

———. 2004b. "The Voices of Child Soldiers!" www.humanrightswatch.org /campaigns/crp/voices.htm (17 Dec. 2004).

———. 2004c. "The Burma Army." http://hrw.org/reports/2002/burma/Burma0902 -04.htm#P862_215566 (25 Dec. 2004).

———. 2004d. "Child Soldiers Global Report 2004." www.childsoldiers.org /document_get.php?id=944 (15 Feb. 2006).

Machel, Graça. 1996. *Impact of Armed Conflict on Children.* New York: UNICEF.

Radio Nederland Wereldomroep. 1998. "Stories." www2.rnw.nl/rnw/en/features /humanrights/storiesliberia.html (22 Dec. 2004).

Save the Children. 2003. "Ban the Use of Child Soldiers." www.savethechildren .org.uk/globalview/soldiers.html [now a defunct link] (20 May 2004).

UNICEF. 2003. *Adult Wars, Child Soldiers: Voices of Children Involved in Armed Conflict in the East Asia and Pacific Region.* New York: UNICEF.

Zelinski, Liz. 2005. "Singer Shocks and Awes in Child Soldier Lecture." www.the whitonline.com/media/paper291/news/2005/11/17/News/Singer.Shocks .And.Awes.In.Child.Soldier.Lecture-1108494.shtml?norewrite&source domain=www.thewhitonline.com (18 Nov. 2005).

Chapter 8

British Refugee Council. 1998. *Refugees: A Resource Book for Primary Schools.* London, England: British Refugee Council.

Burger, L., & D.L. Rahm. 1996. *United Nations High Commissioner for Refugees: Making a Difference in Our World.* Minneapolis, MN: Lerner Publications Company.

Catholic Charities of Green Bay. 2002. "Refugee Myths." www.gbdioc.org/pg/RIS.tpl (25 Nov. 2004).

Cheal, Beryl. 2001. "Helping Adults Help Children: Refugees and Immigrants Have Different Experiences." www.disastertraining.org/Articles/refugees.html.

Cutts, M. et al. 2000. *The State of the World's Refugees 2000.* Oxford, England: UNHCR.

Global Express. 2004. "Activity on Refugees for Primary and Secondary Classrooms." http://atschool.eduweb.co.uk/rmext05/glo/ref.html (20 Nov. 2004).

Lamb, Christina. 2001. "They Call This Slaughterhouse." *Sunday Telegraph.* December 9.

Machel, Graça. 1996. "Impact of Armed Conflict on Children. Report of the Expert of the Secretary-General, Ms. Graça Machel, Submitted Pursuant to General Assembly Resolution 48/157." gopher://gopher.un.org/00/ga/docs/51/plenary /A51=306.EN (11 Aug. 2003).

Mayell, Hillary. 2004. "For Refugee Children, 'Home' Is a Changing Concept." *National Geographic News.* http://news.nationalgeo graphic.com/news/2004 /03/0309_040309_angelinajolieposter.html#main (28 Oct. 2004).

Perry, Alex. 2001. "Lying to Refugees." Time.com. www.time.com/nation/article10, 8599,185636,00.html.

Piper, M. 2002. *The Middle of Everywhere*. New York: Harcourt, Inc.

Porter, Keith. 2003. "Dangerous Escapes." www.warchildren.org/print/print_danger ous_escapes.html (20 Nov. 2004).

Sanghar, Nadil. 2004. "Ask Actress Angelina Jolie." BBC News. http://news.bbc.co.uk /2/hi/talking_point/3584021.stm (11 Oct. 2005).

Save the Children. 2002. "The RAP: Refugee Activity Packet." Save the Children United Kingdom.

Steele, Jonathan. 2001. "Bombing Brings Flood of Refugees. Camps Set Up as Thousands Flee US Attacks," *The Guardian*. November 21, 2001.

UNHCR. 2000. *Refugee Children: Escape from Persecution and War*. Geneva, Switzerland: UNHCR.

———. 2003. *Refugees in Numbers*. Geneva, Switzerland: UNHCR.

———. 2004. "2003 Global Refugee Trends." Geneva, Switzerland: UNHCR.

USA for UNHCR. 2004. "Where are the Refugees?" www.unrefugees.org/usaforunhcr /dynamic.cfm?ID=65 (10 Nov. 2004).

U.S. Committee for Refugees and Immigrants. 2005. *World Refugee Survey 2005*. Washington, D.C.

Weber, Chris. 1986. *Treasures 2: Stories & Art by Students in Oregon*. Portland, Oregon: Oregon Students Writing & Art Foundation (OSWAF).

———. 1994. *Treasures 3: Stories & Art by Students in Japan & Oregon*. Portland, Oregon: Oregon Students Writing & Art Foundation (OSWAF).

Wilkinson, R. 2003. "Seeking Protection's Holy Grail." *Refugees* 3(132), 2.

Chapter 9

American College of Physicians. 1982. "Heath Policy Committee." *Annals of Internal Medicine* 97: 447. www.3ammagazine.com/magazine/issue_5/articles/nuclear _war_medical_effects.html (19 July 2005).

Arkin, William M. 2002. "Secret Plans Outline the Unthinkable: A Secret Policy Review of the Nation's Nuclear Policy Puts Forth Chilling New Contingencies for Nuclear War." wwwlatimes.com/news/opinion/la-op-arkinmar10.story (19 July 2005).

Arkin, William & Robert Norris. 2005. "NRDC Nuclear Notebook: U.S. Forces." *Bulletin of Atomic Scientists* 61(01), 73–75.

The Associated Press. 2005. "Most Americans Say No Nation Should Have Nuclear Weapons." www.KOTV.com/main/home/storiesPrint.asp?id=80564&type=t (2 April 2005).

Borger, Julian. 2005. "US nuclear warhead plan under fire." *Guardian Limited*. April 9, 2005. www.guardian.co.uk/usa/story/0,12271,1455607,00.html#article_con tinue (19 July 2005).

Brinkley, Joel & William J. Broad. 2004. "U.S. Lags in Recovering Fuel Suitable for Nuclear Arms." *The New York Times*, March 7, 2004. www.nytimes.com/2004/03 /07/international/worldspecial2/07NUKE.html (18 July 2005).

Bunn, Matthew, Anthony Wier & John Holdren. 2003. "Nuclear Threat Initiative and the Project on Managing the Atom." *Controlling Nuclear Warheads and Materials*. Boston: MA: Harvard University.

Easterbrook, Gregg. 2003. "American Power Moves Beyond the Mere Super." *New York Times* online edition. http://www.nytimes.com/2003/04/27/weekinreview/27EAST.html?ex=1111381200&en=e0656071f04fe2e6&ei=5070 (18 March 2005).

Friends Committee on National Legislation. 2002. "At the Crossroads: Disarmament or Re-Nuclearization." Washington: D.C.

Goodman, Amy & John Goodman. 2004. "Hiroshima Cover-up: How the War Department's Timesman Won a Pulitzer." www.common dreams.org/views04/0810-01.htm (1 Aug. 2005).

Joint Project of Association of World Citizens and Friends of the Earth Anti-Nuclear Weapons Campaign. 2005. "Take Nuclear Weapons off Alert Status: A Plea by Nobel Laureates, Parliamentarians, the Europarliament, and NGOs around the World." www.wagingpeace.org/articles/2005/04/00_take-nuclearweapons-off-alert-status.htm (18 July 2005).

King Jr., Martin Luther. 1964. "Address in Acceptance of Nobel Peace Prize." Oslo, Norway, December 10, 1964.

Lester, Will. 2005. "Poll: No Nation Should Have Nuke Weapons." http://abcnews.go.com/US/print?id=626541 (3 April 2005).

Moore, Carol. 2004. "Is Nuclear World War Inevitable? or How Easily Accidents or Terrorists Can Start a World Nuclear War." http://www.carolmoore.net/nuclearwar/#Accidental (18 July 2005).

Phillips, Alan F., M.D. 1998. "20 Mishaps that Might Have Started Accidental Nuclear War." www.wagingpeace.org/articles/1998/01/00_phillips_20-mishaps.htm (18 July 2005).

———. 2001. "The Immediate Effect: Medical Problems after Nuclear War." www.3ammagazine.com/magazine/issue_5/articles/nuclear_war_medical_effects.html (19 July 2005).

Pincus, Walter. 2005. "Pentagon Revises Nuclear Strike Plan Strategy Includes Pre-emptive Use Against Banned Weapons." Washington post.com at www.washingtonpost.com/wpdyn/content/article/2005/09/10/AR2005091001053_pf.html (20 Feb. 2006).

Rachel's Environment & Health News. 2004. "Fiery Hell on Earth, Part 1." http://rachel.org/bulletin/index.cfm?St=4 (18 July 2005).

Rotblat, Sir Joseph. 2004. "The Nuclear Policy of the Bush Administration." *Los Angeles Times.* www.wagingpeace.org/articles/2004/09/00_rotblat_nuclear-policy-bush-administration_print.htm (7 July 2005).

Schell, Jonathan. 1982. *The Fate of the Earth.* New York: Knopf.

———. 2002. "Letter from Ground Zero: Manhattan." *The Nation* April 1, 2002. www.thenation.com/doc.mhtml?i=20020401&s=schell (20 July 2005).

Steinberg, Jeffrey. 2003. "U.S. Pre-emptive Nuclear Strike Plan: It Keeps Getting Scarier and Scarier." *Executive Intelligence Review*, March 7, 2003. www.larouchepub.com/pr/2003/030224nukefirst.html (19 July 2005).

Taylor, Andrew. July 1, 2005. "Senate OKs Continued Study of Nuclear Arms." *The Washington Post*, www.washingtonpost.com/wp-dyn/content/article/2005/07/01/AR20050701000048_pf.html (19 July 2005).

Union of Concerned Scientists. 2005. "U.S. Nuclear Weapons Policy: Dangerous and Counterproductive." *Global Security*. www.ucsusa.org/globalsecurity/nuclear_weapons/page.cfmpgeID=1520 (19 July 2005).

Weber, Chris. 1994. *Treasures 3: Stories & Art by Students in Japan & Oregon*. Portland, Oregon: Oregon Students Writing & Art Foundation (OSWAF).

Chapter 10

Bowie, Geoff. 2003. "Media Statement: The European, Canadian, Scandanavian (etc.) MAVM." www.mnsi.net/~pwatkins/european.htm (5 March 2005).

Diemand, Mariellen. 2003. "Media & Iraq: War Coverage Analysis." Media Education Foundation. www.mediaed.org/news/articles/mediairaq (6 March 2005).

Fisk, Robert. "Amid Allied Jubilation, A Child Lies in Agony, Clothes Soaked in Blood." April 8, 2003. *Independent* Online Edition. http://news.independent.co.uk/world/middle_east/story.jsp?story=395117 (9 April 2003).

Rendall, S., & T. Broughel. 2003. "Amplifying Officials, Squelching Dissent: FAIR Study Finds Democracy Poorly Served by War Coverage." www.fair.org/extra/0305/warstudy.html (10 June 2003).

Reynolds, Dwight F. 2003. "Which War Are You Watching?" Veterans for Peace. www.veteransforpeace.org/Which_war_are_you_watching_050703.htm (5 March 2005).

Rosen, Michael. 2005. "From Iraq." *Socialist Worker Online*. www.socialistworker.co.uk/article.php4?article_id=6964 (25 July 2005).

Whitehurst, Dr. Teresa. 2005. "Why Go to College, When You Can Be Cannon Fodder? Do You Know What Your Kids Are Watching on 'Educational' TV at School?" *Information Clearing House*, www.informationclearinghouse.info/article8125.html (28 Feb. 2005).

Zinn, Howard. 2003. "My Country: The World." TomPaine.com (28 Sep. 2005).

Chapter 12

Roy, Arundhati. 2001. "The Algebra of Infinite Justice." *Guardian Unlimited*, September 29, 2001. www.robert-fisk.com/arundhati_sept29_2001.htm.

Shiva, Vandana. 2001. "Solidarity Against All Forms of Terrorism." www.zmag.org/shivacalam.htm (18 Sep. 2001).

Chapter 13

Jackson, Peter. 2002. *Lord of the Rings: The Two Towers*. New Line Home Entertainment.

Chapter 16

Engel, Janice. 1994. *Jackson Browne: Going Home*. Mojo Productions.